# THE CULTING OF AMERICA

# RON RHODES

**HARVEST HOUSE PUBLISHERS**
Eugene, Oregon 97402

**THE CULTING OF AMERICA**

Copyright © 1994 by Harvest House Publishers
Eugene, Oregon 97402

Library of Congress Cataloging-in-Publication Data

Rhodes, Ron.
        The culting of America / Ron Rhodes.
            p.   cm.
        ISBN 1-56507-186-7
            1. Cults—United States—Controversial literature.    2. Christian sects—
United States—Controversial literature.    3. United States—Religion—1960—
I. Title.
        BL2525.R48       1994                                              94-6868
        239'.9—dc20                                                       CIP

**Printed in the United States of America.**

94   95   96   97   98   99   00   —   10   9   8   7   6   5   4   3   2   1

*To Paul, Gary, Pat, Marsha,*
*Brett, Mark, and Rick*

*With Thanks*

First and foremost I want to thank my wife, Kerri, not only for her support but also for her many suggestions that have made this a better book. My children David and Kylie also deserve special recognition. They're the greatest!

I want to express appreciation to Bob Hawkins, Jr. and Eileen Mason at Harvest House Publishers for their faith in this project. Also at Harvest House I want to acknowledge Steve Miller, my editor. Thanks, Steve, for your hard work on this book.

Thanks also go to Hank Hanegraaff and the entire staff of the Christian Research Institute (CRI). What a talented and committed group of individuals God has gathered at CRI!

I especially want to express gratitude to the countless people across the United States and Canada who have committed to regularly praying for our work at CRI. Without such prayers, there is no way we could carry on the work we do. Annie Belle Carothers—a prayer warrior if I ever knew one—deserves special mention.

Finally, to CRI's many volunteers—may God bless you richly for the time and effort you have donated to the cause of Christ at CRI.

# Contents

With Thanks

The Approaching Darkness

## Part 1:
### Crumbling Foundations

## Part 2:
### Penetrating Mainstream America

# Part 3:
## *Enticing Mainstream America*

# Part 4:
## *Redeeming America*

# The Approaching Darkness

*In due course the United States will "embosom all the religious sects and denominations in Christendom."* [1]

—Congregationalist preacher
Ezra Stiles (1783)

Take an imaginary journey with me. The year is 1725. The location is the port at Boston (a favorite among the early Puritans), where you've just arrived by boat from Europe. The circumstances: You, along with many other immigrants and settlers from different parts of the world, want to start a new life in America. You've heard that America is the land of the free, the land of unlimited opportunity, the land where your dreams can come true.

You're on your way to the Carolinas to meet family and friends who have traveled on ahead of you. Because transportation is slow (no jets, trains, or automobiles), you know you have quite a journey ahead of you. You therefore resolve to take your time and enjoy the rich scenery along the way.

The journey begins. You set out with great excitement and anticipation. As you travel, you meet many fellow pilgrims. And you have the opportunity to spend time with many people who have already settled in some city between Boston and the Carolinas. You find this to be an incredibly enriching experience.

One observation you make as you inch your way step by step toward your destination is the seemingly boundless religious diversity of the people of America. *Many of these folks really have a strong belief in God,* you think to yourself, *but they have such widely differing views regarding how He should be worshiped.* This is not at all the way it was back home.

Reflecting on all this as you travel, it suddenly dawns on you why there is such religious diversity in this new land of opportunity. People from all across Europe—and, to a lesser extent, Asia and Africa—have been immigrating to America for years, bringing all their diverse religious traditions with them. *America is a vast religious melting pot,* you surmise.

While en route to the Carolinas, you encounter all kinds of "believers," many of them from faraway parts of the world. You encounter a variety of Congregationalists, Baptists of several types, Presbyterians, and Quakers; Dutch, German, and French Reformed believers; Swedish, Finnish, and

German Lutherans; Mennonites and radical pietists; Anglicans; Roman Catholics; an occasional Jewish congregation; as well as a vast number of unchurched people.[2]

You finally arrive in the Carolinas. And though your journey is finished, you know that the journeys of many others have just begun. The massive immigration of people from around the world to America continues. This means the diversity of religions continues to grow as well. With each passing year, the variety increases. The melting pot continues to expand.[3]

Many years pass. You've lived a long, rich life. In your old age you reflect on how the freedom of the American way of life—in religion and everything else—has been the most precious thing in the world to you.

Then, in the year when the nation's independence is officially recognized (1783), you hear a sermon by the famous Congregationalist preacher, Ezra Stiles. This sermon—titled "The United States Elevated to Glory and Honor"—prophesied that in due course the nation would "embosom all the religious sects and denominations in Christendom," allowing religious freedom to them all.[4] Stiles's prophecy, you reflect, is bound to be fulfilled. After all, the great tide of immigration into the United States continues . . . and continues . . . and continues.[5]

The above story is fiction, but Ezra Stiles's sermon is historical fact. And since Stiles's time, the United States has indeed come to "embosom all the religious sects and denominations in Christendom." Ours truly is a religiously diverse and pluralistic society. And underlying America's religious history is one fundamental concept: *freedom.*

Every American is guaranteed the free exercise of religion. This is one of the things that makes America so great. The First Amendment, ratified in 1791, affirmed that "Congress shall make no law respecting an establishment of religion or prohibiting the free exercise thereof."[6]

In keeping with this, James Madison, who was the fourth president of the United States (1809–17), wrote, "The religion . . . of every man must be left to the conviction and conscience of every man. . . . We maintain, therefore, that in matters of religion no man's right is [to be] abridged by the institution of civil society."[7] Such religious freedom is cherished by every American.

When Ezra Stiles preached his famous sermon in 1783, little did he know that eventually the United States would embosom not just all the religious sects and denominations of Christendom, but a vast kingdom of the cults as well.[8] Today, the cults have reached an epidemic level in the United States.

This book's title—*The Culting of America*—is very descriptive of its contents. We will focus on the explosive penetration and influence of the cults in America. More specifically, we will focus on *how* and *why* America has shifted from being a predominantly Christian land to becoming a stronghold—a haven of darkness—for the kingdom of the cults.

Let me hasten to emphasize, however, that *The Culting of America* is not just about "exposing darkness." It's also about Christians "lighting a candle" in the midst of the darkness. Jesus has called each of us as Christians to be salt and light in our world (Matthew 5:13-16). One purpose of this book is to help you see just how important it is that each of us *be* that salt and light in our society.

# Part 1

## *Crumbling Foundations*

# 1

# Cult Explosion
# U.S.A.

*This is the most crucial decade in history. Designer, à la carte religion flourishes as traditional Christianity is undermined by counterfeits.*[1]

—Pollster George Gallup
on religion in America

**P**RIOR TO 1850, cultists were practically unheard of in America. Today there are tens of millions of Americans involved in the cults and the occult. A significant and ever-increasing portion of our population is intimately involved in the culting of America.[2]

Current statistics reveal some rather disturbing trends for those who hold biblical Christianity dear to their hearts.[3] For example:

- Most Americans reject the notion of absolute truth.

- A growing proportion of Americans—now up to one-third of the population—do not believe in the God of the Bible, but have other notions of who (or what) God is or means.

- Most Americans believe it does not matter what god you pray to because the deities of the world religions are ultimately the *same* deity, yet shrouded in different names and attributes by humankind.

- Nearly two out of three American adults contend that the choice of one religious faith over another is irrelevant because all faiths teach the same basic lessons about life.

- A minority of Americans have a personal relationship with Jesus Christ.

- Americans are nearly evenly divided regarding whether or not Christ was perfect; almost half of all Americans believe Jesus made mistakes while He was on earth.

Obviously, for Bible-believing Christians, the above statistics do not paint a pretty picture of the religious state of America. And present trends indicate that our condition will continue to get worse—*much* worse—in coming years. No wonder one observer said, "The times smell of sunset."[4]

|| *This downward spiral shows* ||
|| *no signs of abating.* ||

America's demise has been described in sobering terms in recent years. Chuck Colson, in his book *Against the Night,* laments that "encroaching darkness casts long shadows across every institution in our land."[5] Carl F. Henry speaks of the twilight of Western culture.[6] Malcolm Muggeridge has predicted the end of Christendom.[7] Even secular publications sound the alarm: *Newsweek* magazine declares "the American century . . . over," and *Time* points to the "moral malaise overhanging American life."[8]

This downward spiral shows no signs of abating. The cults continue to grow at an explosive, geometric pace in the United States. Make no mistake about it—the cultic challenger is within the gates, and his grip is firm. Discerning Christians scan the dark horizon with great concern. Difficult days lie ahead.

### The Mormons:
### Wealthy, Aggressive,
### and Growing Fast

The Mormon church, also known as the Church of Jesus Christ of Latter-day Saints, is unquestionably one of the largest and most influential cults in the United States. Contrary to biblical Christianity, the Mormons

- deny the scriptural doctrine of the Trinity and the deity of Christ;

- believe in more than one God (they believe there are _many_);

- believe that God the Father is a literal exalted man with a physical body of flesh and bones;

- believe that men can become gods ("As man is, God once was; as God is, man may become");

- believe that Jesus was born into the world out of the physical, sexual union between God the Father and the Virgin Mary;

- believe that salvation is attained by works and not by grace.[9]

Without a doubt, the Mormon church is one of the wealthiest cults in the world. It takes in an estimated $4.7 billion per year, controls at least 100 companies or businesses (including a $300-million-a-year media conglomerate), and has an investment portfolio in excess of $1 billion.[10] That's a lot of money for a cult to control.

According to an eight-month investigation conducted by the _Arizona Republic_ newspaper, the Mormon church's annual income would place it about 110th on the Fortune 500 list of industrial corporations. It would rank among companies such as Gillette and Chiquita Brands International.[11]

The _Arizona Republic_ also reports that the Mormon church's business subsidiaries "generate an additional $4 billion per year in sales, which, if counted in the total, would make [it] an $8 billion-a-year corporation, comparable with Union Carbide and Borden Products."[12] As well, the Mormon church is "one of the nation's largest private landowners, with holdings in all 50 states."[13]

Such wealth is a key factor in the steady growth of the church. Indeed, the Mormons spend roughly $550 million per year on their worldwide missionary efforts.[14] This breaks down to over $10 million spent each week on their missionary program.

The Mormons are making extremely effective use of the media. Mormon radio and television outlets reach more than 2.3 million adults per day.[15] And, according to Mormon Elder Russell M. Ballard, baptisms by Mormon missionaries have "increased by 7 percent in the U.S. and missionary productivity by 16 percent in [Mormon] missions through radio and television."[16] Ballard estimates the total audience reached by Mormon media to be an astounding 357.4 million people in a single year.[17]

In 1950 there were only one million Mormons in the United States.[18] Today there are over four million. In terms of worldwide growth, it is estimated that the Mormon church is growing at a rate of 1,500 new members per day.[19]

The Barna Group of Glendale, California, polled adults in the United States, asking: "What is your impression of the Mormon church? Is it very favorable, somewhat favorable, somewhat unfavorable, or very unfavorable?" Six percent responded "very favorable," and 21 percent (almost one-fourth of all adults in the United States) responded "somewhat favorable."[20] The poll also indicated that among those claiming to be born-again Christians, some five percent responded "very favorable" and 18 percent responded "favorable" when asked about their impression of the Mormon church.[21] For a cult to be viewed in such a positive light by so many people—including professing Christians—is alarming indeed.

## Jehovah's Witnesses:
## Over One Billion Man-Hours
## of Proselytizing Per Year

The Jehovah's Witnesses are another fast-growing cult in the United States, due almost entirely to relentless proselytizing by members of the cult. Contrary to biblical Christianity, the Jehovah's Witnesses

- believe that Jesus was created as an angelic being by the Father millions of years ago;

- believe that Jesus is "a god" but not God Almighty like the Father;

- believe that the Holy Spirit is neither a person nor God but is rather God's "active force";

- believe that the "satanic" doctrine of the Trinity is rooted in paganism;

- believe that there is no conscious existence of the soul after death;

- believe that there is no fiery hell for the unsaved;

- believe that the "spiritual" second coming of Christ took place in 1914.

Incredibly, almost 4.5 million Jehovah's Witnesses are presently devoting more than one billion man-hours each year spreading these false doctrines around the world.[22] By comparison, in 1940 there were only 95,327 Jehovah's Witnesses in the world. These numbers indicate _dramatic_ growth, and the momentum is gaining with every passing day.

Especially disconcerting is the phenomenal growth of the "peak" (active, baptized) Jehovah's Witnesses within the boundaries of the United States. In 1940, there were 58,009 "peak" members in this country. This figure jumped to 108,144 by 1950; 205,900 by 1960; 416,789 by 1970; 565,309 by 1980; 850,120 by 1990; 892,551 by 1991; and is now approaching one million.[23]

It is also noteworthy that each year almost two million people in the United States attend Watchtower memorial conventions. These are people who, though not actively involved Witnesses like those mentioned above, are nevertheless sympathetic supporters of the movement.[24]

Unfortunately, most Christians are not equipped to respond doctrinally when Jehovah's Witnesses show up on the doorstep.[25] The average Jehovah's Witness can make a doctrinal pretzel out of the average Christian in about 30 seconds. This is the primary reason I wrote _Reasoning from the Scriptures with the Jehovah's Witnesses_ (Harvest House, 1993).

## The New Age Movement:
## Cosmic Cancer
## Eroding the West

The New Age movement has been called "the fastest growing alternative belief system in the country."[26] But it's really more of a fast-growing spiritual cancer. Just as an aggressive cancer relentlessly eats away at the human body, so does the rapidly growing New Age movement eat away at the West, eroding its spiritual foundations.

In my book _The New Age Movement_ (Zondervan, 1994), I point out that because the movement is so broad in nature, strictly speaking it cannot be categorized as a single cult.[27] Rather, the New Age movement is an "umbrella" term that encompasses various individuals and organizations who share a common vision of a new age of enlightenment and harmony as well as a common worldview (common way of viewing or interpreting all of reality). This broad definition allows for both _unity_ and _diversity_ within the New Age movement.

In terms of _diversity,_ the New Age movement includes a wide spectrum of individuals such as goddess worshipers, reincarnationists, channelers, gurus, astrologers, human-potential advocates, UFOnauts, holistic-health professionals, ecologists, political activists, educationists, and much more. New Agers have many and varied interests.

In terms of *unity*, New Agers are united by their particular worldview, which is *monistic* ("all is one") and *pantheistic* ("all is God"). This common worldview enables New Agers to cooperate and network together with a view toward accomplishing their common ends despite their distinctive interests within the movement.

Without going into greater detail, New Agers are typically

- *eclectic* (they draw from many and varied sources of "truth");

- *syncretistic* (they do not render exclusive devotion to any one teacher or teaching);

- *interested in various forms of occultism* (such as channeling or spiritism, out-of-body experiences, astrology, and psychic phenomena);

- *transformational* (emphasizing both personal and planetary transformation);

- *ecologically oriented* (they are a part of what is called the "green" movement);

- *utopian-minded* (they are desirous of a "new age"—often described as involving a one-world government, global socialism, and a New Age religion).

(My book *The New Age Movement* provides more details on the above characteristics.)[28]

## How Many New Agers Are There?

Because the New Age movement is so diverse and encompasses such a wide variety of people with distinctive interests, it is difficult to ascertain precisely how many New Agers there are in this country. However, religious polls are highly revealing of just how thoroughly different aspects of this movement have penetrated American society. For example:

- A Gallup poll in 1978 indicated that ten million Americans were involved in Eastern mysticism at that time. This number has steadily escalated in the past 15 years.[29]

- About 67 percent of American adults claim to have had a psychic experience such as extrasensory perception.[30]

- A 1993 Gallup poll indicated that about 43 percent of teens believe in extrasensory perception.[31]

- About 21 percent of teens believe in clairvoyance (the "seeing" of physical objects "at a distance").[32]

- Twenty-four percent of American adults believe in precognition— the psychic ability to predict the future.[33]

- One out of three American adults believe that fortune-tellers can actually foresee the future.[34]

- Approximately 30 million Americans (one in four) believe in reincarnation.[35]

- One in four American adults believe that people's horoscopes "can affect the course of their future."[36]

- 25 percent of Americans believe in a nonpersonal energy or life force which they roughly equate with God.[37]

- A survey by Northern Illinois University suggests that over half of all Americans believe extraterrestrials have visited planet earth (a belief common among New Agers).[38]

- In a 1993 article in the _Los Angeles Times_, New Ager Marilyn Ferguson said that "sociologists at UC Santa Barbara . . . estimate that as many as 12 million Americans could be considered active participants [in the New Age movement], and another 30 million are avidly interested. If all these people were brought together in a church-like organization, it would be the third-largest religious denomination in America."[39]

Ferguson also notes that an article in _American Demographics_ defines New Agers as a well-educated, upscale group: "More than 90% of the subscribers to _New Age_ magazine are college graduates, compared to less than half the general population. They are three times likelier than others to travel abroad and four times more likely to be active in politics or community affairs. The demographers conclude that these individuals 'are hungry for something mainstream society has not given them.' "[40]

## New Age Spiritism

"Spiritism" may be defined as the practice of attempting communication with departed humans or extrahuman intelligences (extraterrestrials, for example) through the agency of a human medium with the intent of receiving paranormal (*beyond* normal) information.[41]

Today, spiritism has been renamed "channeling." Jane Roberts, who died in 1983, channeled an entity named "Seth." Roberts was largely responsible for the current rise of interest in channeling. Her books on Seth have attracted virtually millions of readers.

Recent polls indicate that some 14 percent of Americans endorse the work of spirit mediums or channelers.[42] Moreover, some 42 percent of American adults presently believe they have been in personal contact with someone who has died. Just ten years earlier, only 27 percent made this claim.[43]

## Defining "God" in the New Age

According to *The Barna Report 1992-93*, millions of Americans presently worship false gods: "Ten percent of the [American] public believe that 'God is the total realization of personal, human potential.' Another 6% claim that 'God represents a state of higher consciousness that a person may reach.' "[44] As well, "smaller proportions of the public ascribe to the following definitions of God: 'everyone is God' (2%); 'there are many gods, each with different power and authority' (2%). One percent said 'there is no such thing as God.' Another 6% did not know how to describe God."[45]

> *Millions of Christians espouse*
> *New Age beliefs without*
> *realizing what they are doing.*

Alarmingly, George Barna (who heads the Barna Group, a polling organization) tells us that in 1993 seven percent of people claiming to be born-again Christians assumed a nonorthodox view of God. "Most of these adults claimed that God is the full realization of human potential (5%); 2% described Him as a state of higher consciousness that we can reach."[46] Three out of ten Catholics and three out of ten Methodists rejected the orthodox Christian view of God in favor of the New Age definition.[47]

In view of the above, it is clear that New Age prophets and gurus—many of whom are in the top echelons of the media industry—are making a substantial impact on Americans. Barna thus warns: "Make no mistake about it: the appeal of New Age ideas and practices is continuing to grow. Millions of Christians espouse New Age beliefs without realizing what they are doing. Many leaders in the church are poorly informed and unaware of this subtle threat to Christian orthodoxy."[48]

## The East Goes West:
## The Influx of Hinduism

Not only are the "American-based" cults exploding in popularity; world religions such as Hinduism have anchored deeply into American soil as well. Hinduism has infiltrated the United States primarily through the New Age movement. Many New Age ideas about man, God, salvation, and the world are rooted in Hinduism.

There is a distinction we must make, however. Hinduism, strictly speaking, is world- and self-_denying_. Because the spiritual and earthly realms are viewed as being in conflict, Hinduism emphasizes the need to _renounce_ earthly things. New Age critic Elliot Miller observes that in Hinduism "the world is _maya_ (illusion), and is considered a formidable obstacle to eternal bliss. In the enlightened state, all is seen as God. Events in the world (being illusory) have no ultimate importance."[49] This is why Hinduism is world-denying.

By contrast, New Age spirituality is life- and world-_affirming_. New Agers value other people, worldly pleasures, culture, and the entire universe.[50] We might say, then, that millions of Americans in the New Age movement hold to a Westernized form of Hinduism specifically adapted to American tastes.[51]

But besides the hybrid form of Hinduism present in the New Age movement, the unadulterated Eastern form of Hinduism is also practiced by many in the United States. Indeed, there are now over 500,000 Hindus in the United States—and that number is steadily growing.[52] As well, former _Los Angeles Times_ religion editor Russell Chandler informs us that "there are more than forty Hindu temples and 500 Hindu religious organizations in the United States."[53]

The magazine _Hinduism Today_ ran an article on the "growing missionary spirit in Hinduism."[54] Among other things, the article notes that "missionaries" of both yoga and Transcendental Meditation (both of which are based on Hinduism) will be extremely active throughout the rest of the 1990s in bringing people into Hinduism's fold.[55]

## The Invasion of Islam

Islam is a monotheistic religion founded by Muhammad in the seventh century A.D. Members of this world religion are called Muslims, and they base most of their beliefs on the Koran, their sacred book.

Among the central themes of Islam are 1) belief in one God (Allah), 2) belief in Muhammad as God's prophet, and 3) belief in a universal day of judgment to come. In addition to Muhammad being God's prophet, Allah is also alleged to have sent 27 other prophets—including Moses and Jesus.

Recent statistics indicate that Islam is growing at a phenomenal pace in the United States:

- According to magazines like *Time* and *Newsweek*, there are now over four million Muslims in North America.[56] Some estimates place the figure much higher—in the seven- to eight-million range.

- In the Los Angeles area alone there are between 250,000 and 300,000 Muslims, and 50 Islamic centers.[57]

- Recent polls indicate there are now more Muslims in the United States than Episcopalians.[58]

- Similarly, recent polls indicate there are now more Muslims than Methodists in the United States.[59]

- Some observers claim there are now more Muslims than Jews in North America, "which would make Islam the second-largest religion in the United States and Canada."[60] More conservative estimates indicate that while this may not be true *yet*, Islam will certainly numerically surpass Judaism in the next few years.[61]

- Likewise, it is projected that within the next decade or so, there will be more Muslims in the United States than Presbyterians.[62]

- Muslims have built over 1,100 mosques in the United States. "Almost every state has at least one, and a recent [1993] study indicated that about 80 percent had been founded within the last 12 years."[63]

- Russell Chandler notes that "Saudi Arabia and other Muslim countries are spending tens of millions of dollars in community development and other projects in America in order to help Muslim communities expand."[64]

- A 1993 _New York Times_ article reports that "Muslims have strong hopes of exercising real influence on American policies toward Islamic movements and populations overseas, and on shaping the social environment at home."[65]

- Gutbi E. Ahmed, the director of the Moslem World League, is reported as saying, "We are at a new stage in which we cease to be a religion on the margins, but [are] a religion of American people related to American life."[66]

- Likewise, Professor Yvonne Y. Haddad, an expert in Islamic studies at the University of Massachusetts, said that "Islam is an American religion."[67] Haddad "sees Islam taking on an American flavor, and at the same time influencing the nation's culture."[68]

- Haddad says that "many thousands of American citizens face Mecca and pray to Allah five times a day, and some girls in public schools are wearing head covers in traditional Islamic fashion. There are tens of thousands of children for whom religious teaching is not catechism or lessons in Hebrew, but an introduction to the Five Pillars of Islam and the Arabic language."[69]

- In the same vein, Dr. Maher Mohammed Hathout, an Egyptian-born cardiologist and the chairman of the Islamic Center of Southern California, said, "We feel proud of our American Islamic identity. . . . We want to be part of the mosaic. We don't consider ourselves to belong to the Middle East or to South Asia. Our roots are there but our present and our future are here."[70]

## Americans and Truth

With so much doctrinal confusion being dispensed in this country, it is little wonder that Americans now predominantly deny that there is such a thing as absolute truth. Recent polls indicate that two-thirds of adults (66 percent) agree that there is no such thing as absolute truth. "This perspective has relatively consistent levels of support across all subgroups. Even a majority of born again Christians (53%) concur with the sentiment. Unexpectedly, among the people groups most ardently supportive of this viewpoint are mainline Protestants (73%)."[71]

This view of truth relates to how many Americans view religion. Since there is no absolute truth, then obviously there is no absolutely true religion to the exclusion of all others.

In fact, many people in the United States claim to see truth in *all* the religions, and believe that God has manifest Himself in them all. The polls indicate that four out of every ten American adults strongly concur that when Christians, Jews, Buddhists, and others pray to their god, all of them are actually praying *to the same god,* but simply use different names for that deity. Only one out of every six American adults strongly disagree with this view.[72]

Astonishingly, the polls also indicate that larger proportions of born-again Christians and people who attend evangelical churches concur with this sentiment than reject it.[73] The lack of discernment among born-again Christians is appalling.

## Baby Boomers and Their Return to Religion

The term "baby boomer" generally refers to an adult born in the span of time between the end of World War II to the early or mid 1960s. Presently a whopping 44 percent of American adults fall into this age bracket.[74]

Wade Clark Roof, a sociologist at the University of California at Santa Barbara, recently (1993) conducted a massive survey of baby boomers. His findings were highly revealing—and highly disturbing.

### The Religious Tastes of Baby Boomers

Roof found that some 95 percent of baby boomers grew up with parents who were religious. However, two-thirds of them dropped out of the church or synagogue in their teens.[75] Today, though many baby boomers have returned to religion, their beliefs largely reflect a New Age worldview. For example:

- Sixty percent of baby boomers say "it is better to explore the teachings of various religions than to stick with a particular faith."[76]

- Twenty-eight percent of baby boomers believe in reincarnation and 14 percent practice Eastern meditation.[77]

- Seventy percent of baby boomers believe in psychic powers.[78]

> *Eighty percent of baby boomers*
> *say you can be a good Christian*
> *without attending church.*

One of the more interesting discoveries in Roof's research is the growth of what he calls "believers but not belongers." As reported in _Time_ magazine, "Americans who leave religious institutions do not necessarily abandon religious faith. Even most dropouts say they believe in God."[79] But these boomers don't necessarily feel the need to attend church. In fact, eighty percent of baby boomers say you can be a good Christian without attending church.[80]

**Religious but Not Orthodox**

Roof's survey also uncovered the fact that even though many boomers are returning to religion, "the God of their understanding is not necessarily the personal, all-powerful, and all-knowing deity of orthodoxy. Nor is the Jesus affirmed by boomers necessarily the Son of God and unique Savior of humanity."[81] In fact, many boomers hold to unorthodox views of God and Jesus.

For example, _Newsweek_ magazine reported that "the quintessential boomer church may well be the Unitarian Universalist Association [UUA], which emphasizes, says UUA president William Schulz, 'that each individual is the ultimate source of authority.' Never very large, the UUA now has 200,000 members and is enjoying its largest growth spurt in 20 years."[82]

Many boomers are seeking a religion or a church that specifically meets human felt needs. _Time_ notes that while increasing numbers of baby boomers are turning religious again, "many are traveling from church to church or faith to faith, sampling creeds, shopping for a custom-made God."[83]

Many Christian churches are seeking to lure these boomers into their congregations. Unfortunately, in the process, a number of them end up compromising Christian doctrine. _Time_ reports that "a growing choir of critics contends that in doing whatever it takes to lure those fickle customers, churches are at risk of losing their heritage—and their souls."[84]

## The Culting of America

Though there are many other cultic groups, movements, and world religions we could examine, the above sampling is sufficient to illustrate how thoroughly the cults have penetrated mainstream America.

Of course, there are no skull-and-crossbones POISON warning labels stamped on the cults—labels like those found on bottles containing deadly elements. Tragically, though, innumerable people in the United States are drinking down spiritual cyanide by the megadose and are completely oblivious to the fact that they are bringing about their own doom.

As we examine the contemporary religious scene, it is clear that the cults have taken advantage of the great American heritage of freedom of speech and religion to spread their poisonous doctrines. The result? The culting of America.

Are you as alarmed as I am at the statistics cited above? I hope so. I think you can see that the cults in America are—to borrow a phrase from the military—*a clear and present danger.*

But how did matters get this way in the United States? *Why* are we witnessing such a ferocious explosion of the cults in this country? Throughout the rest of this book, we will address specific issues that will help answer those questions.

It is my hope and prayer that *The Culting of America* will serve as a wake-up call for the church. It's time to get about the business of contending for the faith once for all delivered to the saints (Jude 3).

# 2

# Christianity Astray: America's Churches on the Skids

*We do not want a church that will move with the world. We want a church that will move the world.*[1]

—C.K. Chesterton
(1874-1936)

*The culture-forming energies of Christianity depend upon the church's ability to resist the temptation to become completely identified with, or absorbed into, the culture.*[2]

—Christopher Dawson

THE WINDS OF CHANGE are rapidly escalating toward hurricane force on the religious landscape in America today, and the implications should send chills down the spine of every concerned Christian. The reality is, however, that many Christians are indifferent—not only regarding the counterfeit religions sweeping across our land, but also regarding the church.

As the ominous dark clouds continue to gather on the horizon, many Christians go merrily about their way, utterly oblivious to the danger that lies all about them. And the one institution that could give them shelter in the midst of the gathering storm—the church, of which Christ is the Head—is either ignored or assigned a low priority by many.

Sad to say, a contributing factor to the flourishing of counterfeit religions in America is what many perceive to be an impotent and lifeless Christian church. It is with this in mind that one Christian observer has suggested: "It will do very little good for the Church to confront the cults unless we simultaneously confront our own participation in the conditions which have produced them. The ultimate spiritual counterfeit is . . . a Christianity which is culturally co-opted, socially irrelevant, and spiritually dead."[3]

## Indifference Toward the Church

British evangelist and Bible teacher John Blanchard said that "the one reaction the Christian church ought never to produce in the community is indifference."[4] Today, however, there are not only communities that are indifferent to the church, but Christians as well are largely disinterested in the church.

Pollster George Barna has reported that one out of four born-again Christians does *not* have a strong desire to be part of a church.[5] He adds, "Almost half of the adults associated with mainline Protestant churches, and more than half of all Catholics, do *not* have a strong desire to be an integral part of the church in the future."[6]

The polls indicate that a massive realignment of the way people think is presently taking place all across America. What was formerly considered "necessary" by many is now being placed in the category of "optional." Among items now in transition from the necessary to the optional are church attendance, worship, prayer, and Bible reading.[7] This shift in thinking spells *disaster* for the church.

Recent polls indicate that there is widespread confusion among Americans regarding whether church attendance is a biblical mandate.[8] Indeed, 47 percent of the people interviewed said the Bible does not command church attendance. These people say it is a "man-made requirement."[9] (Hebrews 10:25, however, instructs us not to forsake "our own assembling together" [NASB]. *See* also Ephesians 2:19; 1 Thessalonians 5:10,11; and 1 Peter 3:8.)

In keeping with the above findings, only 78 percent of the evangelicals that were polled said they attended a church worship service in the past week; 52 percent said they attended a Sunday-school class; and 50 percent said they had volunteered their time for a church.[10]

All outward indications show that Sunday school in the typical American church is in particularly big trouble today. In his book *Racing Toward 2001*, Russell Chandler laments: "Sunday school attendance is on the skids. . . . In the major old-guard Protestant churches, Sunday school enrollments are plummeting even faster than overall membership. . . . Between 1970 and 1990, church-school participation in the mainline denominations decreased an average of 55 percent."[11]

Chandler quotes Dorothy Bass, a Chicago Theological Seminary professor, who says this decline in Sunday-school attendance is due to a failure "to transmit the meaning and excitement of Christianity from one generation to another, one person to another."[12] I think Bass is entirely correct. Many Christians today are simply not excited about their faith, and unexcited parents are passing this lack of interest on to their children. Ecclesiastical boredom is plaguing the modern American church on a massive level.

This lack of interest in the church has profound implications, for apart from the church there is simply no way the individual Christian will receive the kind of spiritual blessing and nurturing that God intends for His children. Throughout church history, it has never been an acceptable option *not* to be involved in the local church.

- John Wesley, the founder of Methodism, said, "There is nothing more unchristian than a solitary Christian."[13]

- C.S. Lewis commented, "The New Testament does not envisage solitary religion; some kind of regular assembly for worship and instruction is everywhere taken for granted in the Epistles. So we must be regular practicing members of the church."[14]

- Billy Graham said, "Church-goers are like coals in a fire. When they cling together, they keep the flame aglow; when they separate, they die out."[15]

Yes, the church has problems that must be dealt with (more on this shortly). But Christians must realign their priorities and commit to keeping the church in the *necessary* category, not the *optional*. Anything less than this is patently unbiblical.

## The Ministry: A Crisis Profession

A recent Gallup poll showed that less than ten percent of Americans are "deeply committed Christians."[16] And only six to ten percent of Americans fall into the category Gallup describes as having "high spiritual faith."[17]

Gallup's findings are confirmed by *The Barna Report 1992-93:* "The evidence of an intense pursuit of faith is thin. There is no indication of an increase in church attendance, Sunday School attendance, participation in small groups, or involvement in other church-related activities."[18]

As one might expect from the congregational crisis evidenced above, the "ministry" itself may well be described as a crisis profession in modern America. Management consultant Peter Drucker said that ministers compose the "most frustrated profession" in the country.[19] Russell Chandler said that "by many estimates, the 1990s will be a time of continued confusion for the clergy. . . . The incidence of clergy stress and burnout is high, and the average career length for ministers is steadily decreasing."[20]

Things are not well with the modern American church.

## Cultists: Former Church Attenders

Statistically speaking, a significant percentage of cultists formerly attended a Christian church.[21] Dr. Paul R. Martin is the director of the Wellspring Retreat and Resource Center, which has as its mission to help former cultists overcome the harmful effects of their experience. It is highly revealing that of the cultists Martin has personally worked with at Wellspring, some 25 percent formerly attended evangelical or fundamentalist churches, and over 40 percent had backgrounds in the large, more liberal Protestant denominations.[22] Chris Elkins, a former Unification Church "Moonie," agrees, noting that "in most cults, a majority of the members left a mainline, denominational church."[23]

This fact has led cult watcher Ruth Tucker to conclude that "the increase in cult membership is a direct result of a failure on the part of the church."[24] Cult expert J.K. Van Baalen likewise says the cults are "the unpaid bills of the church."[25]

> *It is a common myth that unbelievers join cults and believers don't.*

Of course, this raises the thorny question as to whether church-attenders who have been deceived and joined a cult were just *professing* Christians or were genuine, *born-again* Christians. Though many such individuals were undoubtedly just professing Christians, Paul Martin is firmly convinced that many were genuinely born again. Indeed, as reported in the *Christian Research Journal*, Martin says it is a common *myth* that while normal unbelievers may get involved with cults, born-again believers will not.[26]

Martin is not alone in this viewpoint. Dr. Harold Bussell expressed this same view in his book *Unholy Devotion: Why Cults Lure Christians*. In this book, Bussell points out that the reason some Christians join up with a cult is because they are ill-equipped and unable to distinguish cultic belief from what they learned as Christians.[27]

Is there biblical support for the idea that believers can be deceived by cultic doctrine and led astray? I believe there is. Ezekiel 34:1-7, for example, indicates that God's sheep can be abused and led astray by wicked shepherds.[28] There are New Testament passages that make this same point:

- Jesus warned His followers: _"Watch out_ for false prophets. They come to you in sheep's clothing, but inwardly they are ferocious wolves" (Matthew 7:15,16, emphasis added). Why would Jesus warn His followers to "watch out" if there was no possibility that they could be deceived?

- Jesus also warned His followers: "Watch out that no one deceives you. For many will come in my name, claiming, 'I am the Christ,' and will _deceive many_. . . . many false prophets will appear and _deceive many people"_ (Matthew 24:4,11, emphasis added). Again, why would Jesus warn His followers of such deception if it were not possible that they be deceived and end up believing a lie?

- In 2 Corinthians 11:2,3 the apostle Paul warned Christians, "I am jealous for you with a godly jealousy. I promised you to one husband, to Christ, so that I might present you as a pure virgin to him. But I am afraid that just as Eve was deceived by the serpent's cunning, _your minds may somehow be led astray_ from your sincere and pure devotion to Christ" (emphasis added). Paul clearly saw the possibility that Christians could be deceived and led astray by false doctrine.

- In Acts 20:28-30 the elders of the Ephesian church were warned: _"Keep watch_ over yourselves and all the flock of which the Holy Spirit has made you overseers. Be shepherds of the church of God, which he bought with his own blood. I know that after I leave, savage wolves will come in among you and _will not spare the flock._ Even from your own number men will arise and distort the truth in order to draw away disciples after them" (emphasis added).

It seems clear, in view of such passages, that Christians can indeed be deceived and led astray. Those who are ungrounded in biblical truth are especially vulnerable.

As important as doctrinal grounding is, however, it is not the only consideration when it comes to people leaving a church to join a cult. According to what I've been able to discover—based on personal research and speaking with cultists and ex-cultists—many of these individuals dropped out of what they perceived to be an impotent, lifeless church and joined up with a group (cult) which to them seemed to be full of life and offer real answers to today's problems.[29] What a condemning indictment this is against the Christian church!

## How American Churches Fail

The widespread failure of churches in America is multifaceted. The available evidence points to a broad failure to 1) make a real moral difference in the lives of church members; 2) provide a sense of belonging among members; 3) meet people's deepest needs; and 4) make Bible doctrine a high priority. Judge the following facts for yourself.

### The Failure to Make a Real Moral Difference

A study conducted by the Roper organization tested the behavior of born-again Christians before and after their conversion experiences. The shocking result: Conversion made little difference in terms of moral behavior.[30] This study suggests that genuine discipleship and training is simply not occurring at the local church level. *Lives are not being changed in the church.*

In an interview with Chuck Colson conducted at the Christian Research Institute (CRI), Colson said, "A Gallup poll found that there was no difference in the ethical behavior of people who go to church and people who *don't* go to church. And so, one has to conclude—painful though it is—that over the past decade in American life, churches have made *very little* difference in the lives of people. As a matter of fact, polls taken among pastors show that pastors themselves acknowledge that they aren't doing the job they're supposed to do."[31]

> *Today, there is little moral difference between people inside and outside the church.*

Many people today seem to take a consumerist approach to church attendance. In this same interview, Colson lamented, "We live in a consumerist
culture. People go to church to get a spiritual fix. They pick the church they
think will make them *feel* the best, or that's closest to them, or that has a
schedule that best conforms with their plans for going to brunch on Sunday
morning. People are going to church for all the wrong reasons."[32]

Colson's point is well taken. It would seem today that many people take a
"social club" attitude toward church participation. They seek a lively institution that allows them to foster convivial relationships but avoids influencing how they live and behave.[33] The result: There is little moral difference
between people inside and outside the church.

Related to all this, evangelist Dwight L. Moody once said, "Depend
upon it, as long as the church is living so much like the world, we cannot
expect our children to be brought into the fold."[34] Could it be that one reason
so many of our young people are joining up with cults and counterfeit religions today is that they are disillusioned with the moral fiber of their
parents' church?

### The Failure to Provide a Sense of Belonging

Cult researcher J. Gordon Melton is right when he says that "large impersonal churches on the corner don't give most people a sense of belonging."[35]
But it is not just the large churches that have this problem; smaller churches
have failed in this regard as well.

After many years of research, cult expert Orville Swenson has concluded, "Many people unfortunately have failed to find a warm, friendly
atmosphere in churches they have visited during their search for truth, and
then have eventually found it in the company of cultists. Some church bodies
are internally plagued with cliques, small exclusive groups of people who
tolerate no penetration of their inner circle by an 'outsider,' leaving such
without either acceptance or fellowship with those who ought to welcome
and help him."[36]

By contrast, the cults typically provide a genuine sense of belonging to
members. People are welcomed and made to feel a "part of the family."
(We'll see more on the "family feel" of the cults in chapter 4.) Until the
Christian church deals with this problem, the cults will continue to suck
people right out of church pews and into their folds.

### The Failure to Meet People's Needs

People today are seeking answers to life's most perplexing questions: Who am I? Where did I come from? What is life all about? Why am I here? Where am I going when this life on earth is over? When answers to these basic questions are not provided by church leaders, people turn elsewhere for answers.[37]

Perhaps one of the most tragic failures of the church is the failure to meet the deepest needs of its members. This should never, ever happen. But in reality, the church is failing on a massive level in this regard.

As a result, many today view the church in a less-than-enthusiastic light. A recent report indicates that of the four major Christian denominations whose images were evaluated via polls, *none* of them were seen as "very favorable" by even a third of America's population.[38]

Polls also indicate that only about one-quarter of all American adults (28 percent) believe that the churches in their area are relevant to the way people live today.[39] To put it another way, about three-quarters of American adults *do not* believe the modern church has relevance to the way they live.

It is especially disheartening to learn that only nine percent of non-Christian adults believe that Protestant churches are "very sensitive" to their needs.[40] One Christian observer said that "in a world in which Christians are called to be the change agents influencing the lives of people who do not know Jesus Christ personally, little can be more heart-piercing than to learn that our target audience does not perceive us to be in touch with their needs."[41]

One fact that should be of concern to all of us as Christians is that, according to the polls, Christians think they are doing better in meeting the needs of unbelievers than unbelievers think they are doing. In other words, while only nine percent of non-Christians believe Protestant churches are "very sensitive" to their needs, some 26 percent of Christians claim that churches meet this challenge sufficiently.[42]

What do all these percentages mean? In a capsule, when the majority of people in this country say that Christian churches are out of touch with (and unresponsive to) their needs, this spells *trouble* on a catastrophic level for the church.

To be sure, the church's failure in this area has been a contributing factor in the culting of America. How so? you ask. Sociologist and cult authority Ron Enroth explains that "people join cults because they hope such groups will fulfill very real, perceived needs. These needs are generated in large part by the changing and confusing society that is America today, and reflect a spiritual vacuum in what many believe is rapidly becoming a post-Christian era."[43]

People with emotional problems are particularly vulnerable to the cults. I think Robert and Gretchen Passantino are right when they say that "a person does not usually join a cult because he has done an exhaustive analysis of world religions and has decided that a particular cult presents the best theology available. Instead, a person generally joins a cult because he has problems that he is having trouble solving, and the cult promises to solve these problems. Often these problems are emotional."[44]

The cults seem to attract a disproportionate number of young adults whose lives lack direction and purpose. Such people seem to thrive on external authority to provide a framework for their lives in this often-confusing world. Enroth says that "in new religious groups these youths find their needs are met—simple, black-and-white answers; a group structure to help them overcome their insecurity and loneliness; and leaders who manifest absolute conviction and certainty."[45]

Now, here's the challenge: Statistical research _proves_ that one of the keys to an effective church ministry is to understand and effectively meet people's felt needs.[46] Churches that focus on meeting people's needs—providing realistic, practical solutions to life's many problems—are among the fastest growing in this country. If the culting of America is going to be met head-on and turned back, churches that genuinely meet needs will have to become the _norm_ and not the _exception_ in this country.

## The Failure to Make Doctrine a High Priority

Many cult experts have noted that one factor giving rise to the cult explosion in the United States is that churches have failed to make Bible doctrine and Bible knowledge a high priority. Walter Martin once said that the rise of the cults is "directly proportional to the fluctuating emphasis which the Christian church has placed on the teaching of biblical doctrine to Christian laymen. To be sure, a few pastors, teachers, and evangelists defend adequately their beliefs, but most of them—and most of the average Christian laymen—are hard put to confront and refute a well-trained cultist of almost any variety."[47]

Let me give an example. Typically, in their door-to-door witnessing, the Jehovah's Witnesses point to isolated passages in the New Testament that "prove beyond any doubt" that Jesus is lesser than the Father and hence is not God Almighty. For example, they point to John 14:28, where Jesus says, "the Father is greater than I." They cite Jesus' words to Mary in John 20:17: "I am returning to my Father and your Father, to my God and your God." They quote 1 Corinthians 11:3, which says that "the head of Christ is God." They point to 1 Corinthians 15:28, where the apostle Paul says that Jesus "will be made subject to him who put everything under him, so that God may be all in all." They cite John 3:16, where Jesus is called God's "only begotten Son" (NASB). They quote Colossians 1:15, which says that Jesus is "the firstborn over all creation." They point to Revelation 3:14, which says that Jesus is the *beginning* of God's creation (NASB).

How would *you* stand up against this barrage of proof texts from a Jehovah's Witness? Could you adequately explain these passages within the orthodox framework of Christ's absolute deity? If not, you are in good company. As Walter Martin used to put it, the average Jehovah's Witness can make a doctrinal pretzel out of the average Christian in about 30 seconds.

There are many indications of the low priority placed on Bible doctrine in the local church. For example, it is a *fact* that many church pulpits today are avoiding much discussion of sin. Indeed, Kenneth Woodward, religion writer for *Newsweek* magazine, says that some clergy have simply "airbrushed sin out of their language. Having substituted therapy for spiritual discernment, they appeal to the nurturing God who helps his (or her) people cope. Heaven by this creed is never having to say no to yourself, and God is never having to say you're sorry."[48]

This low priority on Bible doctrine is also evident in the unbiblical views held by many Christians. A 1993 report indicates that one out of ten people who claim to be born again in America believe that sin is an outdated concept. Though this percentage is less than that of non-Christians (25 percent), it nevertheless represents a significant number of Christians who hold to an unorthodox view of sin.[49] This reminds me of the book penned by Karl Menninger, *What Ever Became of Sin?*[50]

Regarding salvation, this same report indicates that four out of ten American adults believe that leading a good life wholly apart from a relationship with Christ can earn them a place in heaven.[51] What is of particular concern is the statistical finding that three out of ten "born-again" Christians agreed that good people go to heaven regardless of whether they have a personal relationship with Christ.[52] To break the figures down more precisely, the view that "good behavior gets you to heaven" is held by 65 percent of Catholics, 51 percent of Methodists, 35 percent of Lutherans, and 26 percent of Baptists.[53] *How can those who claim to be Christians be so far off-base when it comes to the fundamental doctrines of sin and salvation?*

> **Doctrine is practical! In fact, nothing is more practical than doctrine.**

The best available data suggests that Christians today are less than enthused about Bible doctrine and are far more interested in "practical" issues—such as how to bring up kids, how to have a good marriage, how to survive financially in the 1990s, and how to retire early. They are not interested in theology for its own sake. They are interested in "practical answers to tough questions about the meaning of life, the best strategies for achieving success in life, and how to experience the best that God has to offer on earth."[54]

Certainly churches must strive to provide practical solutions to life's challenges. But as long as the church continues to make doctrine a low priority, America's religious soil will remain richly fertilized for the continued growth of cultic weeds. People must come to realize, as John MacArthur does, that "the distinction between doctrinal and practical truth is artificial; doctrine is practical! In fact, nothing is _more_ practical than sound doctrine.[55] Indeed, "no believer can apply truth he doesn't know. Those who don't understand what the Bible really says about marriage, divorce, family, child raising, discipline, money, debt, work, service to Christ, eternal rewards, helping the poor, caring for widows, respecting government, and other teachings won't be able to apply it."[56]

The apostle Paul makes reference to "God's household, which is the church of the living God, _the pillar and foundation of the truth_" (1 Timothy 3:15, emphasis added). If the church fails to set forth and defend doctrinal truth, it fails to fulfill its God-appointed role.

## The Church: A Place of Equipping

If the church is to succeed in standing against the culting of America, then it must rectify the problems noted above. That is, the church _must_ make a real moral difference in the lives of its members; the church _must_ provide a sense of belonging; the church _must_ genuinely meet people's needs; and the church _must_ make doctrine a high priority.

In conjunction with all this, the church must return to its primary role as a place of equipping. In the interview with Chuck Colson conducted at the Christian Research Institute, Colson emphasized:

> If you read Ephesians 4, the job of the pastor is to equip the saints so that when the saints come together in their congregations—for worship, for the study of the Word, for the celebration of the sacraments, for discipline and accountability—they are being _discipled_ by that pastor and equipped for works of service in the world. And by being

equipped they can be the light and the salt that influences the world. This is the *whole* purpose of the church. The task of the church is to be a *place of equipping.*[57]

Colson illustrates the importance of equipping with a story from his past:

I compare it to my experience in the Marines. I was a lieutenant in the Marines during the Korean War. And that was a very dangerous time. Fifty percent of the Marine lieutenants being commissioned then were coming back in pine boxes. And so, when I went to basic training, let me tell you, I became "equipped" for eighteen hours a day—going over that obstacle course, disassembling my rifle, assembling it blindfolded, engaging in night maneuvers, going under barbed wire, learning to survive live artillery shells, and memorizing the Marine handbook. Why? Because I was going into combat, and I was going to have fifty lives in my hands.[58]

"Should we be any less serious about the equipping and disciplining of the church?" Colson asks. *"No!* We're in spiritual combat—cosmic combat for the heart and soul of humankind. We ought to treat it just as seriously as I treated preparing to be a Marine lieutenant in the Korean War."[59]

Abraham Kuyper once said, "When principles that run against your deepest convictions begin to win the day, then battle is your calling, and peace has become sin; you must, at the price of dearest peace, lay your convictions bare before friend and enemy, with all the fire of your faith."[60]

The question you must answer, then, is, Will you be an equipped soldier, ready and prepared for Christian service? Or, will you become a battle casualty in the midst of the onslaught of the cults?

# 3

# Truth Decay: The Bible's Disuse, Misuse, and Abuse

---

*The source of all our troubles is in not knowing the Scriptures.*[1]

—Chrysostom (A.D. 347-407)

*We owe to Scripture the same reverence which we owe to God.*[2]

—John Calvin (A.D. 1509-1567)

*There is no substitute for reading the Bible; it throws a great deal of light on the commentaries!*

—Anonymous

MANY YEARS AGO I visited a Sunday-school class at a particular church with my friend Kerri, who today is Kerri Rhodes—my wife. It was a class for young singles. We had been invited by a mutual friend.

As it turned out, the director of education at the church (a theological "liberal") was teaching the class. I don't remember everything that happened that day, but one incident that stands out in my mind is the verbal exchange I had with the director.

He taught that Christianity is one of many religions that lead to God. Just as spokes on a wheel all lead to the same hub, so also do the different religions lead to the same God, we were told. All the leaders of the various world religions were said to teach the same ultimate truth. *(Somebody pinch me,* I thought to myself. *Am I really in a "Christian" church?)*

I raised my hand. Kerri knew what was coming. When the director acknowledged me, I launched into my defense: "Jesus said in John 14:6 that 'I am the way and the truth and the life. No one comes to the Father *except through me.*' And Peter said in Acts 4:12 that 'salvation is found in *no one else*, for there is *no other name* under heaven given to men by which we must be saved.' Furthermore, 1 Timothy 2:5 tells us that 'there is one God and *one mediator* between God and men, the man Christ Jesus.' If there is *one mediator* between God and man—Jesus Christ—that rules out others like Muhammad, Buddha, and Krishna, right?"

After I said these words you could have heard a pin drop in that room. There was a look of sheer shock on the faces of the other young singles in that class. How dare someone challenge the director of education! And especially how dare someone (a mere visitor) challenge the director by quoting verses from the Bible!

A few moments later (it seemed like an eternity), the director looked at me and said, "Ron, I really feel sorry for you going through life so narrow-minded." Every eye in the place was focused on me. How would I respond?

I almost quoted Jesus' words from the Sermon on the Mount: "Enter through the narrow gate. For wide is the gate and broad is the road that leads to destruction, and many enter through it. But small is the gate and narrow the road that leads to life, and only a few find it" (Matthew 7:13,14). However, I decided I had sufficiently made my point and no further quotes from Scripture were necessary (to Kerri's relief).

In the one-hour duration of that Sunday-school class, I witnessed the Bible's disuse, misuse, and abuse. What a travesty! The Bible's disuse was clearly evident in that the other young singles in the class hadn't the foggiest idea what Scripture really had to say about the uniqueness of Jesus Christ and Christianity. The Bible's misuse and abuse was evident in that the director twisted Scripture by focusing exclusively on verses speaking of God's love and avoiding other texts such as the ones I mentioned.

Such a mishandling of Scripture is one of the underlying causes of what I call "truth decay" in Western society. Just as a mishandling of teeth results in tooth decay, so a mishandling of Scripture results in truth decay. And, as we will see in a moment, this truth decay has made it all the easier for religious counterfeits to flourish on American soil.

## Christians and Their Disuse of the Bible

Many Christians today do not read the Bible. In fact, statistics show that among born-again Christians who attend church on a regular basis, more than one-third (35 percent) do not read the Bible.[3] Let's put this statistic into the context of a typical local church. In a church of 500 adult members, all of which attend regularly, about 175 are not Bible readers. In a megachurch with 5,000 adult members, some 1,750 are not Bible readers. The bottom line: A huge percentage of Christians who attend church are biblically illiterate and spiritually malnourished from lack of Bible reading.

Another poll asked people the question, "During the past month did you 'read part of the Bible other than while you were at church?'" Some 47 percent of Protestants and 69 percent of Catholics answered _no_.[4]

These dismal statistics cause me to think back to what Mortimer J. Adler said in his modern classic, _How to Read a Book_. Adler observed that the one time people read for all they are worth is when they are in love and are reading a love letter:

> They read every word three ways. They read between the lines and in the margins. They read the whole in terms of the parts, and each part in terms of the whole. They grow sensitive to context and ambiguity, to insinuation and implication. They perceive the color of words, the order of phrases, and the weight of sentences. They may even take the punctuation into account. Then, if never before or after, they read carefully and in depth.[5]

This is the way believers _should_ read the "love letter" that the Eternal Lover of our souls has given to us—the Bible—so that we may better know Him and His purposes. But alas, such believers are rare indeed. Could it be that this disuse of the Bible among Christians is indicative of a lack of a passionate love for the Savior?

### Fast-Food Society, Fast-Food Bibles

Ours is a fast-food society. Speed and convenience are prime considerations for people in the United States of America. People want it _now_ and they want it _easy_.

One can even detect a fast-food mentality in the reading habits of American Christians. For example, we can now read _The One-Minute Bible_.[6] In this single volume we have "the heart of the Bible arranged into 366 one-minute readings." This is "a daily Bible-reading program at which anyone can succeed."[7]

Another "fast-food" Bible is appropriately called *Kwik-scan*. As reported in *Newsweek* magazine, this version of the Bible highlights the essential passages in boldface and requires no more than 30 half-hour sittings to read from Genesis to Revelation.[8]

One must ask, Is it possible to become biblically and doctrinally literate by daily engaging in one-minute readings of the Bible, which add up to a whopping one-year total of a little over six hours worth of reading? There is nothing wrong with using a one-minute Bible for a quick devotion here and there. But if this is done at the expense of more detailed Bible reading and study, it is woefully insufficient.

In an interview, popular theologian R.C. Sproul illustrated the importance of a time commitment to Bible study with an analogy from his personal life: "I have a friend who wants to learn how to play the piano. So I gave him a book of instructions that I put together over the years containing fifteen lessons. I sat down with him and said, 'Now, if you will master these fifteen lessons, you're going to be off and running in your desire to play the piano.'"

Sproul then instructed his friend, "These are the basics. These are the fundamentals. You're going to have to spend time mastering these things if you're going to learn how to play the piano."

"Now," Sproul said, "my friend can gain great strides if he practices religiously for fifteen minutes a day. He'll definitely make some progress. But to understand the whole scope of music, he's never going to be an accomplished musician on fifteen minutes a day. No one's ever done that. Likewise, you can't be accomplished in your understanding of the riches of the things of God in five, or ten, or fifteen minutes a day."[9] The fast-food variety of Bible reading simply will not cut it if your goal is biblical literacy.

### Signs of Biblical Illiteracy in America

The biblical illiteracy in America has reached epidemic levels—a fact that is more than adequately proved by a brief look at the polls:

> • Recently the American public was asked, "Does the Bible say God helps those who help themselves?"[10] *Over half* of all Americans agreed that the Bible teaches this—even though the Bible nowhere makes such a statement (and, in fact, indicates that God helps *the helpless*). Many of the remaining Americans indicated that they didn't know whether the idea came from the Bible or not. Either way,

this points to an alarming deficiency in Bible knowledge in the average American.[11]

- A 1993 poll indicated that most Americans cannot name the four Gospels in the New Testament.[12]

- Another 1993 poll indicated that a majority of Americans cannot name even half of the Ten Commandments.[13]

- Still another poll—one conducted by the Gallup organization—found that only about half of all Americans could identify who delivered the most famous sermon in history—the Sermon on the Mount. (It was Jesus.)[14] This is an amazing statistic when it is realized that a high percentage of those polled *were Christians*.[15]

- As of 1993, some 44 percent of American adults believe that Jesus was imperfect and made mistakes while on earth.[16] What is particularly revealing about this poll is that a majority of the people who made this claim also believe the Bible is accurate in all it teaches.[17] (Keep in mind that the Bible teaches Jesus was *perfect* and made *no* mistakes.)

Conclusion: The biblical illiteracy of this nation is truly abysmal. And worse, the religious profile that emerges of the typical American Christian—at least in terms of Bible knowledge—is nothing less than frightening.

## Out with Doctrine, In with Practical Answers

In the previous chapter I noted that churchgoing Christians today seem to be more interested in practical answers to problems they encounter in daily life than they are in Bible doctrine. People want their needs met. They want wisdom on attaining their life goals. They want practical advice on marriage and the family, raising children, finances, and all the other matters that affect real people in modern America.

Tragically, people who make doctrine a low priority don't realize how self-defeating they are. The fact is, Bible doctrine enables us to develop a realistic worldview, without which we are doomed to ineffectual living (Romans 12:1,2; 2 Timothy 4:3,4). Moreover, right doctrine can protect us from false beliefs that can lead to destructive behavior (1 Timothy 4:1-6; 2 Timothy 2:18; Titus 1:11). Hence, those who are interested in practical Christianity *ought* to be making doctrinal Christianity a high priority, not minimizing it.

## Biblical Illiteracy and Cultic Involvement

Tragically, some church attenders have ended up in the cults because they were not given the biblical-discernment skills that should have been given them in the church. Such people end up in cults because they are unable to distinguish cultic belief and practice from what they learned in the Christian church.[18]

|| *The consequences of biblical* ||
|| *illiteracy can be deadly.* ||

There are many real-life examples I could give to illustrate this, but one that stands out in my mind relates to David Koresh and the Branch Davidian cult that met a fiery end in Waco, Texas. I recall reading in a news publication that two of the girls who had joined the cult and died in the flaming inferno formerly attended a Christian church and had even attended a Christian school together. If these girls had become biblically literate enough (in their former church) to detect the Scripture-twisting antics of David Koresh, perhaps they would be alive today. The consequences of biblical illiteracy can be deadly.

## Cultic Misuse and Abuse of the Bible

If Christians in America are guilty of *dis*using the Bible, then to a much greater extent cultists are guilty of *mis*using and *ab*using the Bible. This misuse and abuse takes many forms.

When dealing with cults, one must keep in mind that they are always built *not* upon what the Bible teaches but upon what the founders or leaders of the respective cults *say* the Bible teaches.[19] James Sire, in his book *Scripture Twisting: 20 Ways the Cults Misread the Bible* (InterVarsity Press, 1980), documents the many techniques cult leaders use in constructing their cultic theology.

Related to this, Walter Martin once observed that the average cult owes its very existence to the fact that it has "utilized the terminology of Christianity, has borrowed liberally from the Bible, almost always out of context, and sprinkled its format with evangelical clichés and terms wherever possible or advantageous."[20] By using such a strategy, many cults have successfully deceived people into thinking that their group is actually "Christian."

## Scripture Twisting: Finding "Hidden Meanings" in the Bible

Many cult leaders seek hidden, secret, or inner spiritual meanings of Bible verses—especially in the teachings of Jesus. Christian Science founder Mary Baker Eddy, for example, said that "the one important interpretation of Scripture is the spiritual."[21]

Madam Blavatsky, the founder of Theosophy (a metaphysical cult and forerunner of the New Age movement), taught likewise, saying, "The greatest teachers of divinity agree that nearly all ancient books [including the Bible] were written symbolically and in a language intelligible only to the initiated."[22] In other words, the Bible is not to be interpreted literally but each statement in it is believed to have a symbolic meaning. Statements in Scripture are not literal statements of truth but "symbols of deeper truths" that one must "mystically uncover" from the text.

Let's look at a few representative examples of how cultists have twisted Scripture by using this type of methodology.

_Did Jesus teach that all people are God?_ John 8:58 quotes Jesus as saying to some hostile Jews, "I tell you the truth . . . before Abraham was born, I am!" Christians have always understood these words of Jesus to be a unique claim to undiminished deity (_see_ Exodus 3:14).

Mark and Elizabeth Clare Prophet, however, interpret these words with a New Age twist, exalting _all_ human beings to the level of God. When Jesus uttered these words, the Prophets tell us, He did so "in the full awareness that the 'I AM' of him had always been the Christ [a kind of cosmic divine spirit]. And he also knew that the permanent part of each one of you was and is that same Christ. Yes, one Universal Christ . . . but many sons and daughters of God embodying and personifying that One."[23]

The Prophets assert: "Certainly the flesh-and-blood Jesus did not exist before his birth in Bethlehem. . . . Jesus knows his True Self to be the Light-emanation of this Christ [or cosmic divine spirit] that always was, is, and ever shall be. And he wants you to know that your Real Self is also that selfsame Light."[24]

The Prophets tell us that "Jesus' I AM Presence looks just like yours. This is the common denominator. This is the coequality of the sons and daughters of God. He created you equal in the sense that he gave you an I AM Presence—he gave you a Divine Self."[25] They conclude that "the Christ is within every man. He's a spark in some and a burning brand in others."[26]

_Did Jesus teach followers that they were to help others recognize their godhood?_ In Matthew 5:13 Jesus instructs His followers, "You are the salt of the earth. But if the salt loses its saltiness, how can it be made salty again? It is no longer good for anything, except to be thrown out and trampled by men." Evangelical Christians have always understood these words to mean that Christians are to have a preservational effect on the world by influencing it for Christ.

New Ager David Spangler, however, interprets Matthew 5:13 in a more man-exalting way. Spangler tells us that "what is seeking to emerge [in our present day] is a body of people who are nourishers and who are quite literally what Jesus called 'the salt of the Earth' . . . accepting their divinity without becoming inflated by it, and acting within the sphere of their influence to draw that same divinity out of others."[27] In other words, when Jesus refers to human beings as "the salt of the earth," He has in mind enlightened individuals who not only recognize *their own* divinity, but who also help *others* recognize theirs.

*Did Jesus prophesy the coming of Baha'u'llah?* Jesus said in John 16:12,13, "I have much more to say to you, more than you can now bear. But when he, the Spirit of truth, comes, he will guide you into all truth. He will not speak on his own; he will speak only what he hears, and he will tell you what is yet to come."

Members of the Baha'i Faith (who believe in the spiritual union of humankind) cite this verse to support their contention that each age needs updated revelation from God. In this understanding, Jesus was one among many prophets who communicated revelation from God specifically for His age. However, the greatest of the prophets (we are told) is Baha'u'llah, who came on the scene in the nineteenth century. And John 16:12,13 is said to be a prophecy of him. Baha'u'llah is interpreted to be the "Spirit of truth" who has come to guide us into all truth.[28]

Of course, a simple look at the broader context of John 14–16 shows how absurd this interpretation is. First, Jesus clearly identifies the Spirit of truth as being the Holy Spirit (John 14:16,17,26). And Jesus said almost 2,000 years ago that His promise of the Holy Spirit would be fulfilled "in a few days" (Acts 1:5), not in the nineteenth century. Indeed, the fulfillment came in Acts 2 on the day of Pentecost.[29] Moreover, Jesus said one function of the Holy Spirit would be to make known *Jesus'* teaching, not replace it with the teaching of another prophet (John 16:14).[30] And finally, Jesus said the Holy Spirit will "be with you forever" (John 14:16). Baha'u'llah lived a mere 75 years and died in 1892.[31] This hardly constitutes "forever."

## Scripture Twisting in the Word-Faith Movement

The Word-Faith teachers in America are notorious for twisting Scripture in the worst sorts of ways to come up with their heretical doctrines. In his book *Christianity in Crisis*, Hank Hanegraaff notes that the Faith teachers are masters of attributing "mystical meanings to biblical passages, thereby spawning doctrinal monstrosities."[32] Let's look at a few examples.

_Is God a "faith being"?_ Hebrews 11:3 reads, "Through faith we understand that the worlds were framed by the word of God, so that things which are seen were not made of things which do appear" (KJV). Faith teachers say this means that God, _by means of His own faith_, created the world. Hence, God is a faith being.[33] And Christians can allegedly have this same God-kind of faith to accomplish miracles today.[34]

As the context clearly reveals, however, all Hebrews 11:3 is really saying is that human beings, by faith, _understand_ that God created the world. God didn't exercise faith in order to create the world. Rather, He created the world by His sovereign power (Genesis 1–2; John 1:3; Colossians 1:16), and _our understanding_ of this fact rests upon faith.

_Is man a "little god"?_ In Genesis 1:26 God said, "Let us make man in our image, in our likeness, and let them rule over the fish of the sea and the birds of the air, over the livestock, over all the earth, and over all the creatures that move along the ground."

Faith teacher Jerry Savelle suggests that the Hebrew word for "likeness" in this verse literally means "an exact duplication in kind."[35] This verse is twisted out of context to support the Word-Faith doctrine that man is a "little god."

Kenneth Hagin says that man "was created on terms of equality with God, and he could stand in God's presence without any consciousness of inferiority. . . . God has made us as much like Himself as possible. . . . He made us the same class of being that He is Himself."[36]

Contrary to Savelle and Hagin, however, all Genesis 1:26 is teaching is that man was created in God's image or likeness in the sense that he is a finite reflection of God in his _rational_ nature (Colossians 3:10), his _moral_ nature (Ephesians 4:24), and his _dominion_ over creation (Genesis 1:27,28). In the same way that the moon reflects the brilliant light of the sun, so finite man (as created in God's image) is a reflection of God _in these aspects_. Genesis 1:26 has nothing to do with human beings becoming God or being in God's class.

If it were true (hypothetically) that human beings are "little gods," then we would expect them to display qualities similar to those known to be true of God. This seems only logical. However, when we compare the attributes of humankind with those of God, we find more than ample testimony for the truth of Paul's statement in Romans 3:23 that human beings "fall short of the glory of God." Consider the following:

- God is all-knowing (Isaiah 40:13,14), but man is limited in knowledge (Job 38:4);

- God is all-powerful (Genesis 18:14), but man is weak (Hebrews 4:15);

- God is everywhere-present (Psalm 139:7-12), but man is confined to a single space at any given time (John 1:50);

- God is holy (1 John 1:5), but even man's "righteous" deeds are as filthy garments before God (Isaiah 64:6);

- God is eternal (Psalm 90:2), but man was created at a point in time (Genesis 1:1,26,27);

- God is truth (John 14:6), but man's heart is deceitful above all else (Jeremiah 17:9);

- God is characterized by justice (Acts 17:31), but man is lawless (1 John 3:4; *see* also Romans 3:23);

- God is love (Ephesians 2:4,5), but man is plagued with numerous vices like jealousy and strife (1 Corinthians 3:3).

If man is a god, one could never tell it by his attributes!

## The Path to Understanding Scripture

The word "method" comes from the Greek word *methodos*, which literally means "a way or path of transit." Methodology in Bible study is therefore concerned with "the proper path to be taken in order to arrive at Scriptural truth."[37] This clearly implies that *improper* paths can be taken. The Bible interpretations of cultists and Word-Faith teachers are illustrations of such errant paths.

> *Do your best to present yourself*
> *to God as one*
> *approved ... who correctly*
> *handles the word of truth*
> (2 Timothy 2:15).

Of course, proper methodology is essential to many fields of endeavor. A heart surgeon does not perform open-heart surgery without following proper, objective methodology. (Would you trust a heart surgeon to operate on you if he told you that he intended to discard objective methodology and instead opt for a *subjective* approach—cutting you where he *feels* like cutting you?)

Improper methodology in interpreting Scripture is not new. Even in New Testament times, the apostle Peter warned that there were teachings in the inspired writings of Paul "which ignorant and unstable people *distort*, as they do the other Scriptures, to their own destruction" (2 Peter 3:16, emphasis added). This verse also tells us that mishandling the Word of God can be very dangerous. Indeed, mishandling the Bible is a "path" to destruction.

Contrary to the practices of some false teachers in Corinth, the apostle Paul assured his readers that he faithfully handled the Word of God: "We do not use deception, *nor do we distort the word of God.* On the contrary, *by setting forth the truth plainly* we commend ourselves to every man's conscience in the sight of God" (2 Corinthians 4:2, emphasis added). Paul admonished young Timothy to follow his example: "Do your best to present yourself to God as one approved, a workman who does not need to be ashamed and who *correctly handles the word of truth*" (2 Timothy 2:15, emphasis added).

## Seeking the Author's Intended Meaning

Instead of superimposing a meaning on the biblical text, the objective interpreter seeks to discover the author's intended meaning (the only *true* meaning). One must recognize that what a passage means is fixed by the author and is not subject to alteration by readers. Meaning is *determined* by the author; it is *discovered* by readers.[38]

Our goal must be *exegesis* (drawing the meaning out of the text) and not *eisogesis* (superimposing a meaning onto the text). By using eisogesis instead of exegesis, a Marxist interpreter could, for example, so skew the meaning of the U.S. Constitution that it would come out reading like a socialistic document.[39] Cultists and Word-Faith teachers have done the same type of thing with the holy Scriptures. They have so skewed the meaning of the biblical text that it comes out saying something entirely different than what was intended by the author.

In his book *Searching the Scriptures*, H.E. Dana says that "a given biblical passage was written by a real living author, whose purpose was to convey a definite idea, and that the passage consequently has one primary meaning, and that meaning likely lies on the surface instead of being hidden in the depths of Scripture, as is frequently proposed."[40] Dana thus affirmed that "interpretation is the effort of one mind to follow the thought processes of another mind by means of symbols which we call language."[41]

Only by objective methodology can we bridge the gap between our minds and the minds of the biblical writers. Indeed, our method of interpreting Scripture is valid or invalid to the extent that it really unfolds the meaning a statement had for the author and the first hearers or readers.

## The Importance of Context

In seeking the biblical author's intended meaning, it is critical to interpret Bible verses *in context*. Every word in the Bible is part of a verse, every verse is part of a paragraph, every paragraph is part of a book, and every book is part of the whole of Scripture.

No verse of Scripture can be divorced from the verses around it. Interpreting a verse apart from its context is like trying to analyze a Rembrandt painting by looking at only a single square inch of the painting, or like trying to analyze Handel's "Messiah" by listening to a few short notes. The context is absolutely critical to properly interpreting Bible verses.

In interpreting Scripture, there is both an immediate context and a broader context. The immediate context of a verse is the paragraph (or paragraphs) of the biblical book in question. The immediate context should *always* be consulted in interpreting Bible verses.

The broader context is the whole of Scripture. As Bernard Ramm has noted, "the entire Holy Scripture is the context and guide for understanding the particular passages of Scripture."[42] We must keep in mind that the interpretation of a specific passage must not contradict the total teaching of Scripture on a point. Individual verses do not exist as isolated fragments, but as parts of a whole. The exposition of these verses, therefore, must involve exhibiting them in right relation both to the whole and to each other. *Scripture interprets Scripture.* As J.I. Packer puts it, "if we would understand the parts, our wisest course is to get to know the whole."[43]

## The Importance of Historical Considerations

Historical considerations are especially vital in properly interpreting the Word of God. The Christian faith is based on historical fact. Indeed, Christianity rests on the foundation of the historical Jesus whose earthly life represents God's full and objective self-communication to humankind (John 1:18).[44]

Jesus was _seen_ and _heard_ by human beings as God's ultimate revelation (1 John 1:1-3). This is why He could forcefully claim, "If you really knew me, you would know my Father as well" (John 14:7).

The apostle Paul, when speaking with the religious men of Athens, affirmed that the reality of the future judgment of all humanity rests on the objective, historical evidence for the resurrection of Jesus (Acts 17:16-31). This evidence is recorded for us in the New Testament Gospels—documents that are based on eyewitness testimony and written very close in time to the events on which they report. Based on how people respond to God's objective, historical revelation contained in Scripture, they will spend eternity in a real heaven or a real hell.

## Dependence on the Holy Spirit

Scripture tells us that we are to rely on the Holy Spirit's illumination to gain insights into the meaning and application of God's Word (John 16:12-15; 1 Corinthians 2:9-14). The Holy Spirit, as the "Spirit of truth" (John 16:13), guides us so that "we may understand what God has freely given us" (1 Corinthians 2:12). This is quite logical: Full comprehension of the _Word of God_ is impossible without prayerful dependence on the _Spirit of God_, for He who _inspired_ the Word (2 Peter 1:21) is also its supreme _interpreter_.

It is beyond the scope of this chapter to provide a full discussion of the Holy Spirit's ministry of illumination. Other good sources are available for this.[45] However, I do want to emphasize that this aspect of the Holy Spirit's ministry operates within the sphere of man's rational capacity, which God Himself gave man (_see_ Genesis 2–3). James Sire comments that "illumination comes to the 'minds' of God's people—not to some nonrational faculty like our 'emotions' or our 'feelings.' To know God's revelation means to use our minds. This makes knowledge something we can share with others, something we can talk about. God's Word is in words with ordinary rational content."[46]

Related to this, theologian Roy Zuck reminds us that the ministry of the Holy Spirit in interpretation does not mean interpreters can ignore common sense and logic. Since the Holy Spirit is "the Spirit of truth" (John 14:17; 15:26; 16:13), He does not teach concepts that fail to meet the tests of truth. In other words, "the Holy Spirit does not guide into interpretations that contradict each other or fail to have logical, internal consistency."[47]

> *Satan is a crafty*
> *misinterpreter of*
> *God's Word.*

It must also be kept in mind that the function of the Holy Spirit is not to communicate to the minds of people any doctrine or meaning of Scripture that is not *contained already in Scripture itself*. The Holy Spirit makes men "wise *up to* what is written, not beyond it."[48] Indeed, "the function of the Spirit is not to communicate *new* truth or to instruct in *matters unknown*, but to illuminate what is revealed *in* Scripture."[49]

One further point bears mentioning. Though some cultists claim to depend on their own "inner illumination," they are utterly blind to the possibility that the *un*holy spirit—Satan, the father of lies—may be behind their "illumination." From the account of Jesus' temptation in the wilderness, we learn that Satan is a crafty misinterpreter of God's Word. Indeed, in his attempt to bring about Christ's downfall, he quoted two passages out of context (Matthew 4:1-11). Christ responded by quoting the Word of God *in* context, thus defeating Satan's purposes. However, though Satan lost in this encounter with Jesus, he is still promoting the misinterpretation of Scripture through the cults.

## Correctly Handling the Word of Truth

Jesus said His words lead to eternal life (John 6:63). But for us to receive eternal life through His words, they must be taken as He *intended* them to be taken. A cultic reinterpretation of Scripture that yields *another Jesus* and *another gospel* (2 Corinthians 11:3,4; Galatians 1:6-9) will yield only eternal death (Revelation 20:11-15).

As Christians we must not forget that as long as the disuse, misuse, and abuse of the Bible continues in America, so will the culting of America continue. One way we can shine as lights in our world (Matthew 5:16) is to set a consistent example before others of what it means to correctly handle the word of truth (2 Timothy 2:15). By so doing, others may come to imitate us in this regard. And as others learn to imitate us in correctly handling Scripture, so they too can be used of God to set an example before still others.

The process begins with one person—you!

# 4

# Broken Children in Broken Families

*Parents have little time for children, and a great vacuum
has developed, and into that vacuum is going to move some
kind of ideology.[1]*

—Billy Graham

IN 1991 DR. ARMAND Nicholi, a respected professor at the Harvard
Medical School and a staff physician at Massachusetts General Hospital,
gave a presentation entitled, "What Do We Know About Successful Families?" In it he said, "Why talk about family? We all fall short and the talk
only makes us uncomfortable. The answer is simple. Our family experience
is the most significant experience of our lives. No human interaction has
greater impact on our lives than our family experience."[2]

In this presentation, Nicholi spoke of how the breakdown of the family
contributes significantly to the major problems confronting our society
today. "Research data make unmistakably clear a strong relationship between broken families and the drug epidemic, the increase in out-of-wedlock
pregnancies, the rise in violent crime, and the unprecedented epidemic of
suicide among children and adolescents."[3]

In view of this, Nicholi suggests that we need a radical change in our
thinking about the family. "We need a society where people have the freedom to be whatever they choose—but if they choose to have children, then
those children *must* be given the highest priority."[4]

I think Dr. Nicholi is entirely correct in saying we need a radical change
in our thinking about the family. The statistics I've been able to compile

regarding the family unit in America are highly disturbing, as we will see in a moment. And if present trends continue, matters are going to get worse— much worse—throughout the rest of the nineties.[5]

My goal in this chapter will be to show the relationship between broken families and the culting of America. First, however, we need to take a look at the sweeping changes presently taking place in the family unit in America.

## A Shift in Family Roles

It used to be that the father went to work to support the family and the mother stayed home to care for the children. In fact, 40 years ago over half of all American families were this way.[6] Now only about ten percent of families are this way.[7]

In America today a typical family involves a father and mother who *both* work—indeed, *must* work—in order to make ends meet financially. And in many cases, father and mother must work *more* than 40 hours a week to survive financially. Obviously, this means little time is left for the children.[8]

## A Shifting Household Structure

The structure of the American family is shifting. Fewer and fewer households in the United States are made up of married couples. In 1970, some 71 percent of American adults were part of a married-couple family. The same arrangement dropped to just 55 percent by 1991.[9] This trend will likely continue in the next decade. In fact, some demographers are confidently predicting that a majority of American adults will be single by the time the year 2001 rolls around.[10]

In keeping with these statistics, there are presently some 14 million single-parent families in America. This amounts to one out of every seven families in the nation, representing an increase of 36 percent since 1970. Moreover, the Census Bureau estimates that more than six out of every ten children born to Americans in the mid-nineties will live in a single-parent home before they reach the age eighteen.[11]

## The Nouveau Family

Families were once defined in terms of a married couple with children. But many today find this definition far too restrictive and old-fashioned.

Coming into prominence today is what has been called the nouveau family, which can be defined as "two or more people who care about each other. The individuals need not be related by marriage or other legal bonds, nor even be living together. What must be true of them, instead, is that they demonstrate, either tangibly or intangibly, a significant degree of mutual care or concern."[12]

Though many in our day are drawn to this concept of the family, I believe it has frightening implications for American society. Among other things, the nouveau family lacks the important element of _permanence_. As one critic put it, "at any time, as soon as one of the people involved in the 'family' feels that he or she is either not adequately being cared for or feels drawn to other individuals, the definition of that person's family instantly changes."[13] Alarmingly, some research indicates that this type of scenario is actually attractive to some adults.[14]

What such people fail to recognize, however, is that without the element of permanence, the family can no longer truly be a haven of stability, security, and dependability. And people—especially children—_need_ stability, security, and dependability in order to be emotionally well-adjusted.

## The "Quality Time" Myth

Regardless of one's concept of the family (traditional or nouveau), most Americans—a whopping nine out of ten adults—say they do not view _quantity_ of time spent with family members being as important as the _quality_ of the time spent.[15] What kind of "quantity" of time are we talking about? Russell Chandler reports that "some statistics indicate that many teenagers spend an average of less than thirty minutes a week in a 'meaningful relationship' with their mothers and fifteen minutes a week with their fathers."[16] Such statistics are appalling.

|| _Children spell the word_ ||
|| _"love" t-i-m-e._ ||

One family counselor said, "Kids need intimate interaction with their parents. Ten minutes of superficial conversation around the dinner table won't do it."[17] Another counselor commented, "If our parents devoted the same amount of time to their children as they do some of their hobbies and shopping, today's kids would be transformed in a generation."[18]

Specialists agree that if a meaningful relationship is to develop between persons—especially between parents and children—there must be a commitment of time. Intimacy *demands* time. Indeed, someone said that children spell the word "love" t-i-m-e. Until Americans recognize the fallacy of "quality time," the likelihood of creating a truly healthy home environment for children seems minimal.[19]

## The Impact of Child Care and "Substitute Parents"

According to recent statistics, almost a third of all preschoolers are cared for in their homes by someone other than their mothers (by fathers, relatives, babysitters, nannies, and the like). Another one-fourth of preschoolers are cared for in day-care centers or nursery schools.[20]

It is not yet entirely clear what impact this type of home situation will have on children in the long run. The fear is that many of these children are not receiving the same level of loving support, intimacy, and psychological nurturing they would have otherwise received had their mothers been home caring for them.

Issues that family specialists are concerned about include the following:

- When a child is passed from one caretaker to another, what kind of emotional bonding does that child experience (or *not* experience)?

- How can values be passed on from parent to child when the dominant influences in a child's life are paid caretakers, television, and Nintendo games?

- Since children model behavior from their parents, what kind of parents will the children themselves be when they grow to adulthood?[21]

Alarmingly, a poll taken among American adults reveals that some 32 percent believe that even when a child is enrolled in a *good* child-care facility, the experience can leave "long-term, negative effects on the child."[22] But many parents feel they have little choice about putting their kids in such facilities because they require two incomes to survive financially. Single parents obviously have even less choice. Millions of Americans feel they are trapped by financial demands that do not necessarily reflect their personal preferences.[23]

## Sexual Sin and the American Family

God created humans as sexual beings. But God intended sexual activity to be confined to the marriage relationship. Unfortunately, as is true with so many other things, many people have taken that which God intended for good and have perverted its use. The result: *sexual enslavement.*

Sexual sin has long plagued America. But today, sexual perversion and enslavement have reached epidemic levels. Consider the following statistics:

- Some 28 percent of men in 1993 admitted to inappropriate sexual behavior.[24] (The key word here is "admitted." The percentage may actually be higher.)

- Presently, nine out of ten born-again Christians say they are faithful to God regarding His command against adultery.[25] This means, however, that one out of ten Christians admit to having failed in this area. (That adds up to a lot of people in a church of 1,000 members.)

- Only five percent of 15-year-olds were sexually active in 1970; today, it is close to one-third. Moreover, two decades ago just under half of all 19-year-olds were sexually active; today, a whopping nine out of ten are sexually active.[26]

- About three out of every ten high-school seniors have had four or more sexual partners.[27]

- Each year more than one million teens become pregnant. Four out of five of them are unmarried, and 30,000 of them are under the age of 15.[28]

- Statistics reveal that cohabitation (living together without marriage) increased by 740 percent between 1970 and 1989. If we narrow the field to adults age 18 to 25, cohabitation skyrocketed by 1,892 percent from 1987 to 1989—almost a twentyfold increase in just three years.[29]

- Statistics reveal that almost half of all adults under the age of 30 will live out of wedlock with someone prior to getting married. Not unexpectedly, the divorce rate among such individuals is higher than that of the general public.[30]

- In 1990 about one in fifteen children were born to people living out of wedlock.[31] This represents a fairly significant number of children being raised by people who are not committed to each other by solemn marriage vows. Should they "fall out of love" with each other, a clean and easy split takes place. What do such "convenient" splits do to children? They cause emotional shipwreck!

What an incredible state of affairs! The family unit in America is deteriorating before our very eyes, and so little is being done to save it.

The statistics above paint a truly sobering picture. Stable family life in America has seemingly become the exception, not the rule. And the projections for the year 2000 are even worse. The family in America is in serious trouble.

The question that remains to be answered is, What does all this have to do with the culting of America? It is to this issue that we now turn our full attention.

## Broken Families and the Culting of America

### Disillusionment with Parental Values

Reformer Martin Luther once said that "family life is a school for character."[32] By this he meant that young people gain their values and indeed their moral character from their parents. But things are not as they once were. Though we cannot make a blanket statement that is true of all families, it is true that *many* families in modern America have proved to be a dismal failure in being a "school for character."

Today it would seem that many young people have become disillusioned with the values held by their parents. In a discussion of the ingredients that contribute to cultic growth and advancement, Walter Martin explained it this way:

> Beginning with the "rock 'n' roll" era of the early fifties, the youth of America have become increasingly disillusioned with their parents' values and unwilling to submit to those values. Because of a newly dominant feeling that the self is the ultimate judge of what is right and wrong, young people have reexamined all the values passed down to them from the adult population. In their examination of these traditional values, the youth have lacked an objective ethical standard and have therefore found no reason to keep those values. Thus, many of our

youth today are valueless; truth and morality have become completely subjective.[33]

Instead of deriving values from their parents, many youth today are constructing their own values via, for example, New Age public education programs like Values Clarification. The idea in this particular program is that values are not to be imposed from *without* (such as from Scripture or from parents) but must be subjectively discovered from *within*. The underlying assumption is that there are no absolute truths or values.[34] "Whatever works for you" is considered right.

Because of this rejection of traditional values that are based on the absolute Word of God, young people feel they are free to believe what they want. This fertile soil of relativism is one in which the weed of cultism can grow at an unhindered pace.

## Lack of Direction Among Young People

Many young people today—perhaps as a result of diminished parental involvement—seem to have a pervasive lack of direction in their lives. Though this in itself does not necessarily cause one to want to join a cult, I believe it at least makes one more vulnerable or susceptible to the lure of the cults.

> *People look to cults in search of a genuine sense of identity.*

Many young people who lack direction latch on to authority figures around whom they can govern their lives. Such people seem to thrive on external authority figures to provide structure to their aimlessness in life. In his book *The Lure of the Cults*, sociologist Ron Enroth notes that "in new religious groups these youths find their needs are met—simple, black-and-white answers; a group structure to help them overcome their insecurity and loneliness; and leaders who manifest absolute conviction and certainty."[35]

As well, people look to cults in search of a genuine sense of identity. They seek a place where each individual member plays an important role and is given recognition—a place where he is known and is assured that he is needed. What a tragedy that many young people fail to find this sense of identity in their own families.

## Cults as Surrogate Families

Experts have long noted that some cults provide the sense of belonging to a family that is lacking in many biological families. Indeed, as Enroth notes, many of the new cults and religious movements actually function as surrogate families for their members.[36] Cult leaders are sometimes spoken of as "spiritual parents" or "parents in the Lord."[37]

Such cults virtually replace biological families for some members and meet all the needs that the biological families failed to meet. A Unification publication boasts, "More than ever we are a Family, serving each other as daughters and sons, brothers and sisters, mothers and fathers under Our True Parents [Rev. Moon and his wife]."[38]

It is not without significance that many cult members address the leaders of their cult in parental terms.[39] For example, New Ager Elizabeth Clare Prophet, who heads the Church Universal and Triumphant, is affectionately known among her followers as "Guru Ma."[40] David "Moses" Berg, founder of the Children of God, is often called "Father David" by cult members.[41] Likewise, Reverend Moon is often called "Father Moon" by members of the Unification Church.[42]

In keeping with this, some cults even use the word "family" in their name.[43] For example, the Children of God have long been known as the "Family of Love." More recently, the Children of God are simply calling themselves "The Family."

Related to all this, Paul Martin in his recent book entitled *Cult-Proofing Your Kids* suggests that early childhood experiences can contribute to the emotional needs that one exhibits as an adult. "The unmet emotional needs of a child from a broken, cold, or abusive home may make a cult seem more attractive. 'Here,' the person may reason, 'is the love, the warmth, and the security that I never had as a child.' He or she may think, 'I've found my true family.' The person enmeshed in the cult may often in fact start to call the leaders of the group 'Mom' and 'Dad.' "[44]

## Vulnerability Following a Personal Crisis

In evaluating the data of this chapter, we must be careful to note that just because a person comes from a broken home *does not* mean that he will necessarily join a cult. Though a number of cult members do in fact come from disturbed or dysfunctional homes, there are also many people from such homes who do not end up in cults. There are also cases in which young people from seemingly normal families end up in cults. What, then, should we make of all this?

A key factor in answering this question would seem to be that recruitment into a cult is much more likely to occur in association with a severe crisis in a young person's life. The fact is, many young people who join cults are in the midst of experiencing a personal crisis at the time they join. Ron Enroth notes, "Studies show that many young people who join cults are experiencing some form of personal crisis when first approached. They are down on their luck, depressed, confused, and lacking a sense of direction. Research involving 237 members of the Unification Church, for example, revealed that nearly two-thirds of the respondents had serious emotional or drug-related problems prior to joining the Moonies."[45]

Paul Martin likewise warns, "Research shows that young people are more vulnerable to cultic affiliation during or immediately after suffering a severe crisis."[46] Martin notes that "some of these crises are the death of a relative or close friend; a broken romance or a divorce in the family; job loss or inability to find employment; poor grades or failure in school; excessive amounts of business-related travel for one or both parents; illness, whether of self or of a close friend or relative; transition from high school to college; or criminal victimization, including burglary, rape, or mugging."[47]

## Cult-Proofing Your Kids

It stands to reason that a young person who comes from a disturbed or dysfunctional home and encounters a severe crisis will be much more susceptible to a cult than one who is from a healthy home. Why? Simply because he or she is unlikely to find loving support and sympathy from other family members when a crisis hits. A young person in a healthy home, by contrast, will have a much higher level of emotional support and psychological nurturing during times of trouble.

Paul Martin thus suggests that healthy families may be able to do two things to cult-proof their kids that a more problem-ridden family could not: "First, a healthier family fosters better communication and is far more likely to know about their child's severe stress and crisis, and they would be talking to that child about it. (Because of the pattern of noncommunication within the family structure, dysfunctional families may have less chance of even knowing about the crisis.)"[48]

Second, Martin says, "healthier families are not only more aware of a family member's crisis, but they have also discussed it and provided a sense of comfort and support. Healthier families are also more eager to seek outside professional help to aid their loved one to resolve the personal crisis more completely."[49] These kinds of factors, Martin believes, help insulate children from cultic involvement.

## Taking Preventive Steps

A young successful attorney once said, "The greatest gift I ever received was a gift I got one Christmas when my dad gave me a small box. Inside was a note saying, 'Son, this year I will give you 365 hours, an hour every day after dinner. It's yours. We'll talk about what you want to talk about, we'll go where you want to go, play what you want to play. It will be your hour!'"

"My dad not only kept his promise," he said, "but every year he renewed it—and it's the greatest gift I ever had in my life. I am the result of his time."[50]

Parent-child intimacy—a living reality to this father and son—is the heart-cry of children everywhere. Family therapists tell us that those who enjoy such a relationship with their parents are, in general, emotionally and psychologically healthy children. To be deprived of such intimacy can cause great stress to a child.

In this type of intimate family, communication is always open and the parents actually *listen* to their children.[51] Kids in such families know they can always talk to their parents about anything. And the environment in such families is one of affirmation and acceptance—*not mere toleration*.[52]

Furthermore, such families are characterized by mutual love and support.[53] This kind of care and concern is especially important when a youngster is going through a time of crisis—such as a failure at school or a broken romance. Let us be clear on this: Children *must* be made to feel secure in their family environment and *must* be made to feel that they can come to their parents for any need.[54]

> *Every Christian parent ought to make a habit of regularly meditating on God's instructions on the family.*

As parents, we have the potential to be *powerfully good* or *powerfully bad* influences on our children. The way we can be a powerfully good influence is to govern our family relationships not according to the fluctuating, relativistic values of society, but according to the clear teachings of Scripture.

Every Christian parent ought to make a habit of regularly meditating on God's instructions on the family. I have found the following passages to be particularly helpful: Genesis 1–2; Deuteronomy 6:1-9; Proverbs 3:11,12;

6:20-23; 13:24; 22:6,15; 29:15; Matthew 15:21-28; 18:1-10; 19:1-15; 1 Corinthians 7; Ephesians 5:22-29; 6:1-9; 1 Thessalonians 2:7-12; and 1 Timothy 5:3-16.

If you don't think your family is what it should be, there's no better time to start on the road to better days than today. Excellent materials are available to help show you the way![55]

# 5

# America's
# Shifting Sands

*Encroaching darkness casts long shadows across every institution in our land.*[1]

—Charles Colson

I'LL NEVER FORGET THE first time I experienced an earthquake in Southern California. The ground started moving beneath my feet. Everything was in motion. I heard creaking sounds all around me as my sturdy house swayed back and forth. The lamp hanging from the ceiling by a chain swayed to and fro. The water in the cat's bowl splashed over the side.

Then it was over. It lasted only about seven seconds. But seven seconds is an awfully long time when everything around you is moving.

My wife, Kerri, and I immediately turned on the television, only to discover that the earthquake we had just experienced was actually rather mild. It registered about a 4 on the Richter scale. *But if that was mild,* I thought to myself, *I'd sure hate to go through a big earthquake.*

Later that evening, we learned from television news reports that no one had been hurt in the earthquake, and there was no substantial damage to houses or businesses in the area. But, as usual, the newscasters used this opportunity to remind viewers that though this earthquake was mild, the "Big One" was coming in the next 30 years or so, and people had better be prepared for it.

You see, in a powerful earthquake, the ground not only moves violently, but it can do so for as long as a minute or more. In such an earthquake, the damage can be catastrophic. Foundations of houses and buildings can be severely damaged or destroyed. Sturdy structures can crumble to the ground like a house of cards.

For the last three decades or so, America has been experiencing a powerful earthquake—that is, a *worldview* earthquake. What is a "worldview"? A worldview may be simply defined as a way of viewing or interpreting the world around us. It is an interpretive framework through which we endeavor to make sense out of the data of life and the world.[2] In the last 30 years, the way Americans look at and interpret the world has changed dramatically The worldview "sands" have been shifting beneath our very feet.

How have things shifted in our society? And how have these shifts contributed to the culting of America? To find out, we will now focus our attention on four critical issues: the rise and fall of secular humanism; the explosive growth of religious pluralism (in which numerous distinct religions coexist and prosper in our nation); the invasion of Eastern religions into the West; and the onslaught of moral relativism.

## The Rise and Fall of Secular Humanism

Around 500 B.C. a philosopher by the name of Protagoras said that "man is the measure of all things."[3] His era marked the first wave of secular humanism.

Almost two millennia later, a second wave emerged in the fourteenth-century Renaissance. Without going into detail, Renaissance humanists sought to study "humane" literature as opposed to strictly sacred literature. In the early years of the Renaissance, God was not necessarily excluded from the picture, but the focus was clearly on man and his strides toward advancement.

With the passing of time, God was progressively deemphasized to the point where He was no longer viewed as being intimately involved with His creatures. Deism—which affirmed belief in God but said He was detached from the affairs of His creation—became the prominent worldview in the seventeenth and eighteenth centuries.

Eventually, the deistic worldview gave way to naturalism. This perspective completely dismissed God from the picture and denied anything that had to do with the supernatural. Naturalism attempted to explain all phenomena by means of strictly natural categories.

Over the course of time, human reason and scientific innovation became the final authority for life and thought, replacing God's revelation. This emphasis on human thinking and scientific development is a prominent aspect of the secular humanism of our day.

## What Secular Humanists Believe

_There is no supernatural._ As stated in _Humanist Manifesto II_ (signed by such luminaries as author Isaac Asimov, psychologist B.F. Skinner, and ethicist Joseph Fletcher), "We find insufficient evidence for belief in the existence of a supernatural; it is either meaningless or irrelevant to the question of the survival and fulfillment of the human race. As nontheists, we begin with humans not God, nature not deity."[4]

_There is no God._ In his book, _What Is Secular Humanism?_ Dr. James Hitchcock states, "Groups like the American Humanist Association are not humanists just in the sense that they have an interest in the humanities or that they value man over nature. . . . In their self-definition, God does not exist. . . . They promote a way of life that systematically excludes God and all religion in the traditional sense. Man, for better or worse, is on his own in the universe. He marks the highest point to which nature has yet evolved, and he must rely entirely on his own resources."[5]

Isaac Asimov, one of the most prolific authors and science writers of all time, is bluntly honest regarding his disbelief in God: "Emotionally I am an atheist. I don't have the evidence to _prove_ that God doesn't exist, but I so strongly suspect he doesn't that I don't want to waste my time."[6]

Likewise, scientist Carl Sagan asserted at the beginning of his "Cosmos" television series on PBS, "The Cosmos is all that is or ever was or ever will be."[7] In other words, there is no deity with whom we need concern ourselves.

_There is no creator._ Isaac Asimov tells us that the "universe can be explained by evidence obtained from the universe alone . . . no supernatural agency need be called upon."[8] The typical explanation of man's origin is the theory of evolution.

Frederick Edwords, in an article published in _The Humanist_ magazine, explains man's origin this way:

> Human beings are neither entirely unique from other forms of life nor are they the final product of some planned scheme of development. . . . All life forms are constructed from the same basic elements, the same sorts of atoms, as are nonliving substances. . . . Humans are the current result of a long series of natural evolutionary changes, but not the only result or the final one. Continuous change can be expected to affect ourselves, other life forms, and the cosmos as a whole. There appears to be no ultimate beginning or end to this process.[9]

Humanists have even produced children's books that argue against any role for a Creator-God. Most children today are aware of the Berenstain Bears books. In one of these books, Papa Bear explains to his son, "Nature is you, nature is me. It's all that is or was or ever will be."[10] This sounds amazingly similar to the famous words of Carl Sagan: "The Cosmos is all that is or ever was or ever will be."[11]

Humanist Chris Brockman wrote a children's book entitled, *What About Gods?* In it we read, "We no longer need gods to explain how things happen. By careful thinking, measuring, and testing we have discovered many of the real causes of things, and we're discovering more all the time. We call this thinking."[12]

*There is no divine purpose for humanity.* The *Humanist Manifesto II* asserts, "We can discover no divine purpose or providence for the human species. While there is much that we do not know, humans are responsible for what we are or will become. No deity will save us; we must save ourselves."[13] In other words, we are all alone in this great big universe, with no ultimate purpose or destiny.

> ||  *Can you see how depressing*
> *the universe is from a*
> *humanistic worldview?*  ||

*There is no afterlife.* In his book *Forbidden Fruit: The Ethics of Humanism*, humanist leader Paul Kurtz said that "the theist's world is only a dream world; it is a feeble escape into a future that will never come."[14] Kurtz also stated: "Promises of immortal salvation or fear of eternal damnation are both illusory and harmful. They distract humans from present concerns, from self-actualization, and from rectifying social injustices. . . . There is no credible evidence that life survives the death of the body. We continue to exist in our progeny and in the way that our lives have influenced others in our culture."[15]

## The Failure of Secular Humanism

Whether humanists admit it or not, their philosophy robs humankind of ultimate purpose, meaning, and value. *How could* there be purpose, meaning, and value when human beings are viewed simply as products of chance evolutionary forces? Secular humanism all too easily leads to *nihilism*—the belief that everything is meaningless and absurd.[16] Can you see how depressing the universe is from a humanistic worldview?

Since its emergence, secular humanism has not been able to satisfactorily answer the foundational questions of life, such as, Who am I? Where did I come from? What is life all about? Why am I here? Where am I going when life is done on earth? This has brought about a strong sense of foreboding and dread for many people, causing a desire for change.

For many years secular humanism focused so much on the all-sufficiency of humanity that God was left entirely out of the picture. As a result of this, man lacked a sense of the *transcendent*—something he yearned for in the deepest part of his being. Indeed, the inadequacy of secular humanism has made man crave for something more—something divine, something sacred. As Mircea Eliade put it, secular man "killed a God in whom he could not believe but whose absence he could not bear."[17]

Men of words have often noted man's intrinsic need for the transcendent. Allan Bloom, for example, finds evidence for a longing for the transcendent on our university campuses today.[18] Charles Colson, in his book *Kingdoms in Conflict*, declares that human beings "desperately long to know the Power beyond us and discover a transcendent purpose for living."[19] Anglican theologian John Stott proclaims that "without transcendence, the person shrivels. . . . Ecclesiastes demonstrates the meaninglessness of a life that is imprisoned within time and space."[20]

To be sure, secular humanism is still alive and well in Western culture. Yet there are multitudes who have reacted against the meaninglessness and futility of this worldview. Victims of humanism are seeking fulfillment and meaning, and *do not know where to find it.*

All that these poor people know is that secular humanism is an unlivable worldview. As Douglas Groothuis puts it, while secular humanism "appeals to humanity's quest for autonomy and crowns 'man the measure of all things,' we find ourselves the lords of nothing—nothing but a meaningless universe with no direction, destiny, or purpose."[21]

## Secular Humanism and the Culting of America

It is a fact that when people lack a sense of fulfillment and meaning—when they feel despair in the deepest part of their being—it is much easier for a cult leader to victimize them, promising a solution to the emptiness they feel inside. As Orville Swenson has aptly noted, "the prevailing feeling of despair that permeates American society fosters the climate in which a leader with 'charisma' can bring some sense of hope, no matter how false it may be."[22]

Cult expert Ron Enroth agrees, and even fingers the Christian church as failing to satisfy the spiritual hunger that so many Americans have: "People today are spiritually starving. Western society is now almost totally secularized—little satisfaction for spiritual hunger can be found in its institutions. Even the Christian church, in many cases, has lost sight of the meat and drink of God's Word. The result is that many who 'hunger and thirst for righteousness' remain unfilled, craving food but not knowing where to find it."[23] Tragically, many have turned to one or another of the many cults in America to find fulfillment.

One of the most significant reactions against secular humanism in America is the emergence of what may be called "cosmic humanism" in the New Age movement.[24] How does it differ from secular humanism? Douglas Groothuis explains it this way: "Whereas the old humanism says we are 'naked apes'—the product of chance evolution—the new cosmic humanism sees us as gods in disguise."[25]

Groothuis explains that in the New Age movement, "man is not only the measure of all things, he is the metaphysical master; we . . . thus have access to unlimited potential."[26] In other words, the cosmic humanism of the New Age movement says man is his own god and can create his own reality. I am convinced this is one reason for the popularity of the New Age movement in America. Man craved for something more and he found it: He discovered he was God.

## The Explosive Growth of Religious Pluralism

America has always been fertile soil for the growth of new religions. Historian Sydney Ahlstrom says that "American civilization from the beginning and in each passing century has been continuously marked by extraordinary religious fertility, and continues to exhibit this propensity to the present day."[27]

Since the 1960s, there has been a virtual explosion of religious pluralism in this country. This explosion has led one observer to comment, "More than ever ours is a pluralistic society in which Christianity is no longer a consensus but just another option in a whole cafeteria of religious choices."[28] Cults and religions that *used* to be a minority in America are now seeking mainstream status and are proliferating at a geometric pace.

A *Christianity Today* report tells us that "the concept of 'Christendom' has given way to 'the Pluralist Society.' There are now more Muslims than Methodists in the U.S., and it is estimated that within three years there will be more Muslims than Jews in the U.S. We can no longer imagine that we live in a Christian country in which the Christian faith is the only real option."[29]

## The Erosion of Christianity's Credibility

One of the big problems with the growth of pluralism is that when so many religions and cults proliferate all at once, it has the effect of diminishing the legitimacy of any one of those religious belief systems. Indeed, "the sheer bulk of belief-options serves to erode the credibility of any one option."[30]

One observer has commented that millions of Americans are presently "less than impressed by Christianity because it is indistinguishable from other faiths to which they have exposure. The Christians they meet act no different from other people. The churches they pass on the way to work have little presence in the community and appear to do little apart from their Sunday morning rituals. The teachings of the faith seem like the same do-gooders code they hear from other religious entities."[31]

Christianity, then, is viewed by many Americans as simply *one of many* acceptable options. Other choices include Islam, Hinduism, Mormonism, Christian Science, and the Jehovah's Witnesses. As columnist Pat Buchanan noted, "Americans of left and right no longer share the same religion, the same values, the same codes of morality; we only inhabit the same piece of land."[32]

## The 1993 Parliament of the World Religions

Related to the phenomenal growth of religious pluralism in America is the 1993 Parliament of the World Religions, which met in Chicago. This Parliament involved a "meeting of the minds" of religious leaders of virtually every imaginable faith (about 250 religious traditions) from every corner of the globe. Besides Christians, there were Buddhists, Hindus, Muslims, Jains, Sikhs, Confucianists, Taoists, Zoroastrians, Baha'is, Theosophists, Rastafarians, witches, goddess worshipers, and many others in attendance.

The Parliament marked the centennial of the 1893 World's Parliament of Religions—a landmark in American religious history. Though this 1893 Parliament was predominately Christian, it nevertheless introduced Eastern religions like Hinduism, Buddhism, and Baha'i to a wide public, aiding their growth on these shores. Following the Parliament, various Hindu missionary outposts were established on American soil.

The 1893 Parliament also marked the beginning of the interfaith movement, with its formal pursuit of dialogue and cooperation among the world's religions.[33] Today the interfaith movement is flourishing, as evidenced by the 6,500 people who attended the 1993 Parliament.

Two of my colleagues at the Christian Research Institute—Hank Hanegraaff and Elliot Miller—attended the 1993 Parliament. Upon returning, Miller wrote a special report on the historic event for the *Christian Research Journal*. I'd like to share a few of his findings.

Miller says the leaders of the 1993 Parliament had hoped to reach an agreement on a "universal declaration of human values," and perhaps even lay the groundwork for a future organization akin to a United Nations of Religions.[34] He cites Asad Hussain, the president of the American Islamic College in Chicago and a trustee of the Parliament, as saying, "I'm very much in favor of a United Nations of Religions. . . . We are going . . . for a religious renaissance that will give real hope and happiness to the people of the world."[35]

In his report Miller addressed the question, Was there a New Age agenda underlying the Parliament's ostensible purpose of furthering interreligious dialogue? "I suspected beforehand that this was the case, after noting that many prominent New Agers were involved at different levels with the organization of the event. As the week unfolded I became increasingly convinced: the occasion of the first Parliament's centennial was being exploited by the present Parliament's organizers, who wished to gather the world's religious leaders and then win them over to their own cause."[36]

The first plenary address, "Interfaith Understanding," was delivered by former United Nations assistant secretary-general Robert Müller, a popular New Age political figure. His message was vintage New Age: "There is one sign after the other, wherever you look, that we are on the eve of a New Age which will be a spiritual age. There is no doubt about it."[37]

As reported by Miller, Robert Müller indicated that the heart of humankind's crisis is a spiritual anarchy and spiritual impotence.[38] In Müller's thinking, "there are no compelling convictions to unite us. Since none of the ideologies presently controlling our societies can bring about an integration of the various spiritual traditions, 'men everywhere are searching for a new universalism.' "[39]

Müller says this search coincides with the fact that human beings "are entering an age of universalism. Wherever you turn, one speaks about global education, global information, global communications—every profession on Earth now is acquiring a global dimension. The whole humanity is becoming interdependent, is becoming one."[40]

Without going into all the specifics of Müller's message,[41] he suggested that as the heads of state are working toward formulating a new *political* world order, it is being brought to their attention that a new *spiritual* world order is needed as well. Müller thus urged that a permanent institution be created toward this end:

> What is needed is a place where you have a good number of people ... work together on a daily basis. This is the miracle I have seen in [the] United Nations. ... And when you do this in the religions—if you create an international secretariat, or a permanent parliament, or a world spiritual agency—if you do this, everything will change. ... This is, in my opinion, the most important single result that could come out of this parliament—at least to have a recommendation that a preparatory committee should be established to come up with a proposal of a world spiritual institution which could then be approved by another parliament in a few years from now. And I would very much like to have this done by 1995—the fiftieth anniversary of the UN—so that this would be the great spiritual contribution as we go towards the year 2000.[42]

With speeches like this, I can see why Elliot Miller believes there was a New Age agenda underlying this 1993 Parliament. Other addresses delivered at the Parliament set forth similar New Age ideas (there were 12 plenary sessions and almost 800 symposiums, lectures, workshops, exhibits, and the like).[43] There can be no doubt that the Parliament served to further diminish Christianity's place in the vast smorgasbord of religions in the United States.

## Do All Religions Teach the Same Truth?

There are many today who view all the various religions as essentially teaching the same "core" truth. This is a prevalent view within the New Age movement. New Ager Julia Spangler explains that "we honor the truth and beauty of all the world religions, believing each to have a seed of God, a kernel of the spirit that unites us."[44] Her husband David agrees, noting that "no human path can contain all of God's possibilities and truths."[45]

In keeping with this, the New Age movement views Jesus as one of many religious teachers. Others that are claimed to be in His league include Buddha, Krishna, Muhammad, Zoroaster, Orpheus, and Hermes. The Bible can therefore make no claim to be God's *only* revelation to humankind.

Jesus Himself is said to have taught that all the various world religions worship the same God using different names. According to Levi Dowling's (occultic) *Aquarian Gospel of Jesus the Christ*, Jesus allegedly said, "The nations of the earth see God from different points of view, and so he does not seem the same to everyone. . . . You Brahmans call him Parabrahm; in Egypt he is Thoth; and Zeus is his name in Greece; Jehovah is his Hebrew name."[46]

> *Forty percent agree that when Christians, Jews, Buddhists, and others pray, they are praying to the same god but using different names.*

What is the "core" truth that all the various religions teach? According to New Agers, *all is one* (monism), *all is God* (pantheism), and *man is God*.[47] These ideas are said to be at the heart of every religion.

## Confusion Even Among Christians

It is disheartening to recognize that many Americans are so biblically illiterate that they fail to see the distinctiveness of the God of Christianity. Pollster George Barna surveyed the American public in 1993 and his findings are highly revealing: "About four out of every ten adults strongly concur that when Christians, Jews, Buddhists, and others pray to their god, all of those individuals are actually praying to the same god, but simply use different names for that deity."[48]

Barna also found that "larger proportions of born again Christians and people who attend evangelical churches *concur* with this sentiment than reject it."[49] The mindset of those who agree with this idea seems to be this: "The important thing is not which religion you buy into, but that you accept the fact that there is a spiritual dimension to life, and you immerse yourself in it somehow. Muhammad, Buddha, Jesus Christ, they all teach the same things; they all stand for a higher plane of personal development and sensitivity."[50] What a sad reflection this is of the church's inability to doctrinally equip its people.

As I point out in *The New Age Movement* (Zondervan, 1994), a simple look at what the various leaders of the world religions teach about God settles once and for all the myth that when people of varying faiths pray, they are praying to the same God with different names for that deity.[51] Consider the following:

- *Jesus Christ* taught that there is one and only one personal God who is triune in nature (Mark 12:29; John 4:24; 5:18,19).

- *Muhammad* taught that there is only one God, but that God cannot have a son.

- *Buddha* taught that the concept of God was essentially irrelevant.

- *Confucius* was polytheistic (he believed in many gods).

- *Krishna* believed in a combination of polytheism (belief in many gods) and pantheism (all is God).

- *Zoroaster* believed in religious dualism—that is, he believed there is both a good god and a bad god.

*How can it be said that people in these faiths are praying to the same God when their respective leaders set forth such utterly contradictory and diametrically opposing concepts of God?*

It would seem that many Christians in our country are unaware that Jesus was very exclusivistic in His truth claims—indicating that what He said took precedence over all others. Jesus said He is uniquely and exclusively *man's only means* of coming into a relationship with God. He asserted, "I am the way and the truth and the life. No one comes to the Father except through me" (John 14:6). Jesus' exclusivity caused Him to warn, "Watch out that no one deceives you. For many will come in my name, claiming, 'I am the Christ,' and will deceive many. . . . if anyone says to you, 'Look, here is the Christ!' or, 'There he is!' do not believe it" (Matthew 24:4,5,23).

As well, Jesus' apostles made exclusive truth claims about Jesus. A bold Peter said that "there is salvation in no one else; for there is no other name under heaven that has been given among men, by which we must be saved" (Acts 4:12 NASB). Paul affirmed that "there is one God, and *one mediator* also between God and men, the man Christ Jesus" (1 Timothy 2:5 NASB, emphasis added).

*How urgently we need a return to biblical literacy in the church!*

## The East Invades the West

Related to the growth of religious pluralism in this country is the Eastern invasion of the West. Popular Christian writer Os Guinness once said, "The East is still the East, but the West is no longer the West. Western answers no longer seem to fit the questions. With Christian culture disintegrating and humanism failing to provide an alternative, many are searching the ancient East."[52] Guinness is absolutely correct in this observation.

As long ago as 1978 a Gallup poll indicated that ten million Americans were involved in some form of Eastern mysticism.[53] Since then the number of Americans involved in Eastern mysticism has skyrocketed. But how did things get this way in America? We look to the 1960s for the answer.

### The Counterculture of the 1960s

The counterculture of a generation ago played a key role in the explosive growth of Eastern religions in the West. Among the key elements that found support in the counterculture were Transcendental Meditation and Zen Buddhism.

One of the most influential gurus to arrive on the scene in the mid-1960s was Maharishi Mahesh Yogi, who taught his followers all about Transcendental Meditation (TM). Partially responsible for Maharishi's rise to fame was the fact that his early disciples included the Beatles, one of the most popular rock groups of all time. This gave TM more than a little media attention in America.

Over a million Americans have now been initiated into TM. Indeed, one observer said that "what McDonald's has done for the hamburger, Transcendental Meditation has done for Eastern mysticism."[54] Transcendental Meditation has succeeded in making Eastern mysticism acceptable, fashionable, and desirable to the American public.

Then there is Zen Buddhism. Cult expert Ron Enroth notes that with its emphasis on inner experience and the achieving of a detached tranquillity, "Zen Buddhism has been one of the most pervasive influences on the American counterculture and, in turn, on the larger youth culture. Thirty years ago in the United States one might have thought that a *guru* was an exotic animal. Today, because of Zen and other Eastern disciplines, it is practically a household word."[55]

Of course, there were other Eastern gurus who left their mark in the 1960s and beyond. These include Yogi Bhajan (who founded the Healthy, Happy, Holy Organization), Swami Muktananda (a guru who transmitted his powers by the touch of a peacock feather), and Guru Maharaj Ji (the "Lord of the universe" who headed up the Divine Light Mission).[56]

These and other gurus contributed to bringing the East to the West—especially in terms of the Eastern doctrines of monism (all is one) and pantheism (all is God). These doctrines not only helped set aside the idea of a personal Creator-God (as taught in Christianity), but also contributed greatly to the growth of moral relativism in America. (Obviously, since all is one and all is God, the distinction between good and evil is blurred, if not obliterated. Hence moral relativism!)

## America's Openness to the East

James Sire, author of _The Universe Next Door_, believes that the openness to Eastern ideas among the Western youth of the 1960s was largely a reaction against traditional Western values. These values include high technology, reason and rationalism, materialism, economics, and the like.[57]

Is there no other way besides the traditional way of the West? "Indeed, there is," Sire says, "a very different way. With its antirationalism, its syncretism, its quietism, its lack of technology, its uncomplicated lifestyle, and its radically different religious framework, the East is extremely attractive."[58] Many Americans have concluded that the East, "that quiet land of meditating gurus and simple life, has the answer to our longing for meaning and significance."[59]

> _American soil is now saturated_
> _with Eastern ideas._

Sire says Westerners are _still_ trekking East. "And so long as the East holds out promise—promise of peace, of meaning, of significance—people are likely to respond. What will they receive? Not just an Eastern Band-Aid for a Western scratch but a whole new world view and lifestyle."[60]

As a result of the Eastern explosion, American soil is now saturated with Eastern ideas. Though Americans may be less fascinated with the world of Eastern gurus, the _teachings_ of these gurus remain with us. Douglas Groothuis is right when he says, "The age of exotic, Eastern 'guruism' may be waning, but the gurus' teachings are not. What was once on the esoteric periphery has moved into the spotlight. Much of what used to be underground is seeping—if not rushing—into the mainstream, as a plethora of New Age teachers, practices, and events contend for our souls."[61]

## The Onslaught of Moral Relativism

A recent poll indicates that a whopping 66 percent of Americans believe there is no such thing as absolute truth. This is disturbing in itself. What's especially appalling, however, is that a majority of "born-again" Christians (53 percent) and "adults associated with evangelical churches" (also 53 percent) agree that there is no such thing as absolute truth. According to this poll, "among the people groups most ardently supportive of this viewpoint are mainline Protestants (73%)."[62]

For such a large portion of the Christian community to dismiss absolute truth is truly an eye-opening statement about the low spiritual condition of the Christian church today.[63] (Keep in mind, Christianity *rests* on a foundation of absolute truth—1 Kings 17:24; Psalm 19:7,8; John 1:17; 8:44; 14:17; 17:17; 2 Corinthians 6:7; Ephesians 4:15; 6:14; 2 Timothy 2:15; 1 John 3:19; 3 John 4,8.)

### Moral Relativism in the New Age Movement

The New Age movement has given moral relativism its greatest boost in modern times. According to Elliot Miller, New Agers believe "it is the height of presumption to think that one knows the key truth for all people. On the other hand, it is the apex of love to 'allow' others to have their own 'truth.' 'Thou shalt not interfere with another's reality' might be called the First Commandment of New Age revelation."[64]

*All is God, all is one, all is relative.* The New Age doctrines of pantheism (all is God) and monism (all is one) relate very closely to the issue of moral relativism. Obviously, if pantheism is true, then this means that man himself is God. And if man is God, then man is a *law unto himself* and need not obey the laws of any deity external to himself.[65]

Also, if it is true that all is one (monism), then the distinction between good and evil disappears. Swami Vivekananda accordingly said, "Good and evil are one and the same."[66] Likewise, Shirley MacLaine in her book *Dancing in the Light* relates what an entity named "Higher Self" allegedly said to her: "Until mankind realizes that there is, in truth, no good and there is, in truth, no evil, there will be no peace."[67] In other words, all is relative!

_Values Clarification._ New Age moral relativism has entered the public schools through what is known as Values Clarification, which we briefly touched on earlier in this book. Viewing human beings as intrinsically good, Values Clarification is a New Age ethical system that denies the moral absolutes of the Word of God. Each student is encouraged to come up with his or her own moral values. Such values are considered to be "neutral" (ultimately neither good nor bad). Values are determined on a strictly subjective basis.

In the book _Values Clarification_, Sidney B. Simon, Leland W. Howe, and Howard Kirschenbaum say that the goal of Values Clarification "is to involve students in practical experiences, making them aware of their own feelings, their own ideas, their own beliefs, so that the choices and decisions they make are conscious and deliberate, based on their own value systems."[68]

I am reminded of a song by a Christian recording artist I heard recently on the radio. I don't know who the artist was (forgive me, whoever you are), but the song made an excellent point. It began by portraying a teacher instructing her students in the fine art of Values Clarification. The students were to come up with their own values. By the end of the song, the students have lifted the teacher up on their shoulders and are headed for the window where they are about to toss her out, against her will. _That_ is the value determination the students made. And since Values Clarification says there are no _absolute_ values, who is to say the students were wrong?

## Moral Relativism and the Culting of America

Clearly, if all truth is relative, then one person's "truth" is just as good as another person's "truth." This ultimately means that any religion and cult's "truth" is as good as Christianity's truth.

As a result of the widespread influence of moral relativism in America, Christian thinker Carl F. Henry commented that the West has lost its moral compass.[69] There is no way to tell which way is north and which way is south when it comes to right and wrong. The result? _America is engulfed in a sea of moral confusion!_

> _We will either be strong in the power of the Lord's might, or we will become casualties._

As we accelerate down the road where moral relativity takes us, there is no absolute truth, "no center stripe down the highway of life."[70] There are many casualties on this highway. Indeed, as Russell Chandler puts it, "The loss of objective authority and a transcendent morality has infected our national ethical foundations with a sickness nigh unto death."[71]

As Christians, we are called to point out to the world that absolute morals are grounded in the absolutely moral God of the Bible. Scripture tells us, "Be perfect, therefore, *as your heavenly Father* is perfect" (Matthew 5:48; cf. 1 Peter 1:15,16). Moral law flows from the *moral Lawgiver* of the universe—God. And He stands against the moral relativist whose behavior is based on "whatever is right in his own eyes" (Deuteronomy 12:8; cf. Judges 17:6; 21:25; Proverbs 21:2).

## A Foundational Truth

I think you can see what I mean when I say we have been experiencing a powerful worldview earthquake in America. And just as physical earthquakes alter the appearance of the landscape, so this worldview earthquake has altered America's *religious* landscape—almost beyond recognition.

Because earthquakes are common in Southern California, houses are structurally designed and built to withstand the shaking and swaying that is characteristic of earthquakes. Let us learn a lesson here. As Christians, we must make sure our *spiritual* foundation is built such that assaults on our worldview—assaults from religious pluralism, moral relativism, and the like—will not cause our spiritual lives to crumble (*see* the words of Jesus in Matthew 7:24-27).

We will either be strong in the power of the Lord's might (Ephesians 6:10), or we will become casualties.

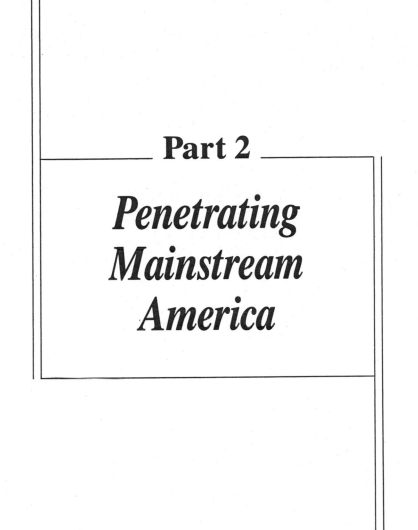

# Part 2

# *Penetrating Mainstream America*

# 6

# Mainstreaming: Cultic Agenda for the 1990s

*History teaches that today's "cults" may become tomorrow's mainstream religions.*[1]

—James M. Dunn

IN THE 1830s the Frenchman Alexis de Tocqueville, having visited America, wrote a remarkable account of American life and manners. The religious atmosphere in America, he said, was the first distinction that strikes a visitor from abroad. He concluded that "there is no country in the world where the Christian religion retains a greater influence over the souls of men than in America."[2]

During the nineteenth century, cultic challengers to Christianity were on the fringes of society—on the outer periphery of the religious landscape. But that has changed in a big way in modern America.

To be sure, Christianity still reigns supreme in this country in terms of sheer numbers. Nevertheless, unlike before, Christianity is now just one among many items in a vast and ever-growing smorgasbord of religious options in America. And cultic groups that used to be on the outer edges of society are today moving into the mainstream—ever seeking to increase their reach and influence.

One of the difficulties I found in writing this chapter was choosing which cults to address. The fact is, there are *many* cults that are presently vying for mainstream status on American soil. Indeed, there are far more cults to discuss than there is room to write about them in a single chapter. I will therefore limit my attention to three representative cultic groups that are presently—and aggressively—seeking to penetrate mainstream America—the New Age movement, Mormonism, and the Unification Church.

## The New Age Movement:
## Penetrating Mainstream America

The New Age movement undoubtedly represents one of the greatest challenges ever to face Christians in America. Current statistics reveal just how thoroughly this fast-moving, tidal wave-like movement has engulfed Western society. For example:

- Tens of millions of Americans are involved in some form of Eastern mysticism.[3]

- Some 67 percent of American adults claim to have had a psychic experience such as extrasensory perception.[4]

- Approximately 30 million Americans believe in reincarnation.[5]

- Some 25 percent of Americans believe in a nonpersonal energy or life force which they roughly equate with God (a common New Age view).[6]

- Forty-three percent of teens believe in extrasensory perception. And 21 percent of teens believe in clairvoyance (the "seeing" of physical objects "at a distance").[7]

Moreover, according to a Gallup poll, only seven percent of Americans *deny* believing in any of a list of 18 paranormal experiences—such as UFOs, astrology, extrasensory perception, telepathy (mental communication through mystical means), clairvoyance, telekinesis (the ability to move physical objects by mystical powers), reincarnation, psychic healing, contact with the dead, witchcraft, and channeling. Almost 50 percent of the people polled said they believe in five or more of these items, and fully 75 percent said they'd had a personal experience in at least one of the categories.[8]

### New Age Astrology

Astrologers believe that man's evolution goes through progressive cycles corresponding to the signs of the zodiac. Each of these cycles allegedly lasts from 2,000 to 2,400 years.

New Agers say we are now moving from the Piscean Age (the age of intellectual man) into the Aquarian Age (the age of spiritual man). The New Age itself is often referred to as the Aquarian Age or the Age of Aquarius.[9]

Current statistics indicate a high level of interest in astrology among Americans. For example:

- In 1987 Northern Illinois University conducted a survey which found that 67 percent of American adults read astrology columns.[10]

- Over 80 percent of all newspapers in the United States carry horoscope columns.[11]

- Astrology is presently the subject of over 100 magazines.[12]

- Estimates of the number of astrologers range as high as 10,000 full-time and 175,000 part-time.[13]

- According to a 1993 poll, some 14 percent of the American public believe "horoscopes and astrology usually provide an accurate prediction of the future."[14]

- Alarmingly, 14 percent of Protestant Christians and 14 percent of Catholic Christians agreed that "horoscopes and astrology usually provide an accurate prediction of the future."[15]

Of course, horoscope columns have been popular in America for years. But one event that gave astrology a strong boost toward the mainstream in 1988 was the revelation that Nancy Reagan, the wife of President Reagan, had consulted an astrologer on a regular basis during the Reagan White House years. Though this happened some time back, it is important to make note of it simply because it served to give an air of respectability to astrology on a worldwide level.

News of Nancy Reagan's involvement with astrology first surfaced in 1988 when Donald Regan, President Reagan's chief of staff for two years, disclosed in his book _For the Record_ that astrology exercised an inordinately powerful influence in the Reagan White House. Some time later, Joan Quigley—Nancy Reagan's astrologer, who operated out of San Francisco—published a book entitled _"What Does Joan Say?" My Seven Years as White House Astrologer to Nancy and Ronald Reagan_, debuting with a first printing of 175,000 copies.[16] In this book Quigley documents her consultations with Nancy Reagan.

Nancy Reagan also wrote a book entitled _My Turn_, which remained on _The New York Times_ bestseller list for 14 consecutive weeks. In this book,

Mrs. Reagan devotes ten pages to Joan Quigley. "I want to state one thing again and unequivocally," she writes. "Joan's recommendations had nothing to do with policy or politics—ever. Her advice was confined to timing—to Ronnie's schedule and to what days were good or bad, especially with regard to his out-of-town trips."[17]

Mrs. Reagan reportedly paid Quigley $3,000 to $5,000 per month for her services. "You learn something from living in the White House," Mrs. Reagan explains in her book, "and I didn't think an astrologer should be sent checks signed by the First Lady. And so I asked a friend back in California [Betsy Bloomingdale] to pay Joan, and I reimbursed her each month."[18]

Lloyd Shearer, who wrote a *Parade* magazine article on Nancy Reagan's use of astrology, phoned Quigley to ask her how important a role she played as White House astrologer. Quigley claimed that "for seven years, she had selected the times for his [Reagan's] press conferences, most of his important speeches, his State of the Union addresses, [and] many of the takeoffs and landings of Air Force One. 'I delayed President Reagan's first cancer operation from July 10, 1985, to July 13,' she said, 'and I chose the time for Nancy's mastectomy.' "[19]

I bring all this up not to personally attack the former president and first lady, but simply to highlight the role this episode played in astrology's continuing emergence into the mainstream of America. Ponder for a moment: Can you think of anything that would give astrology a higher degree of respectability than the revelation that it played a significant role in the lives of the president of the United States and his wife?

Now, I must point out that astrology (including reading horoscopes) is strictly off-limits for the Christian. Astrology can be traced back to the religious practices of ancient Mesopotamia, Assyria, and Egypt. It is a form of divination—an attempt to seek counsel or knowledge by occultic means—that was popular among the people of these nations.[20]

It should come as no surprise to the Christian that astrology is a practice that is flatly condemned by God in Scripture. In Isaiah 47, for example, we find a strong denunciation of astrologers and their craft. Verse 15 explicitly states that "each of them goes on *in his error*" (emphasis added), and "there is not one that can save you." The book of Daniel confirms that astrologers lack true discernment, and that the only source of accurate revelation is God Almighty (Daniel 2:2,10,27,28).

## New Age Meditation in Mainstream America

A *Los Angeles Times* article entitled "Meditation Wins U.S. Converts" proclaimed, "East increasingly meets mainstream West these days as meditation and other relaxation techniques—often with roots deep in Eastern philosophies—gain acceptance and credence among Americans ranging from true spiritual seekers to yuppie Type-A's just trying to relax."[21] Meditation is definitely "in" today!

Eastern meditation typically employs techniques such as concentrating on objects, exercising "controlled" breathing, and uttering mantras (holy words) with a view to emptying the mind of all distractions. This supposedly enables a person to reach an altered state of consciousness—a state of supreme harmony with himself and the universe.

Eastern meditation "really fits the American mentality well," says William Roll, who teaches a course on meditation at West Georgia College. "It fits what the scientific world tells us."[22] (Scientific instrumentation allegedly shows that meditation lowers blood pressure and has other positive physiological effects.)

"I think part of what enabled meditation to go from the 'guru image'— you know, people who went to India and things—to mainstream was the use of machines and scientific research" to confirm its efficacy, says Diane Dreher, a professor at Santa Clara University in California and author of _The Tao of Peace_.[23] "Americans seem to be able to deal with things when they can use technology, when they can see it objectively."[24]

Meditation is even practiced at—of all places—the Pentagon in Washington, D.C. In fact, the Pentagon Meditation Club meets weekly in the Pentagon chapel to meditate for peace. Members of the group call it the SDI—the Spiritual Defense Initiative.[25]

Related to the popularity of meditation, Shirley MacLaine's 1989 book _Going Within: A Guide for Inner Transformation_ rocketed to the number-one position on the _New York Times_ and _Publishers Weekly_ nonfiction bestseller lists. An accompanying video, "Shirley MacLaine's Inner Workout," was popular as well.[26] MacLaine's book and video served to introduce virtually millions of Americans to Eastern meditation. Interestingly, the person who helped market the MacLaine video was former congresswoman Bella Abzug, who said she was never able to meditate until she took one of MacLaine's classes in 1987.[27]

_The Rise of Transcendental Meditation._ You may recall in the previous chapter the critic who said, "What McDonald's has done for the hamburger, Transcendental Meditation has done for Eastern mysticism." This same critic went on to say that "Transcendental Meditation has made Eastern mysticism acceptable, fashionable, and desirable to the public by saturating the American consciousness."[28] Consider:

- Transcendental Meditation (TM) is now in virtually every major city in this country.

- TM is taught in 200 centers across America.[29]

- About one million people in the United States practice TM regularly.[30]

- About 6,000 doctors practice TM or recommend it to their patients.[31]

Many people have found applications for TM beyond personal relaxation. Indeed, Maharishi Mahesh Yogi (TM's founder) and his followers fight crime by TM. According to a report in *The Washington Times*, several hundred lawyers, doctors, and executives regularly gather twice daily to meditate for a reduction in crime.[32]

*The Washington Times* said "the secret weapon being used to effectuate that transformation [toward reducing crime] is the Super Radiance Effect, also known as the Maharishi Effect. Basically, it means good vibrations emitted collectively [by those meditating] are greater than the sum of their parts."[33]

Maharishi has an even loftier goal in mind. His pet project is his "world-peace proposal." In the coming decade he wants to gather 7,000 people in one location to perform his advanced Sidhi meditation technique on a steady basis. "Seven thousand people represents the square root of 1 percent of the world's population. According to some cosmic precept, that is the threshold of participation necessary for the Maharishi Effect to have its full, global impact."[34]

Small-scale group meditations, Maharishi claims, have already produced a trickle of "positivity." He takes a measure of responsibility, for example, for the thawing of East-West relations in recent years.[35]

Plans for the expansion of TM in the future include:

- One hundred schools to teach a classical Indian music said to promote peace. Four schools are already involved—in Fairfield, Iowa; Los Angeles, California; Washington, D.C.; and Fairfield, Connecticut.[36]

- Fifty "Maharishi Cities of Immortals"—cities that are free of crime, pollution, noise, and stress. Contracts have allegedly been signed with developers in Austin, Texas; Hartford, Connecticut; San Diego and Los Angeles, California; Washington, D.C.; and Fairfield, Iowa.[37]

*The Rise of Yoga.* Yoga is another form of Eastern (New Age) meditation that has penetrated mainstream America. Yoga is a spiritual discipline by which the practitioner seeks to condition the self at all levels—physical, psychical, and spiritual. The ultimate goal is a state of well-being, the loss of self-identity, and absorption into union with "the Absolute."

*Newsweek* magazine reported that "yoga classes are in demand at urban health clubs across the country, and longstanding yoga studios in New York, Chicago, and California report sharp rises in attendance in the past year [1992]."[38] The magazine also noted that "such high-profile practitioners of the 6,000-year-old art as Kareem Abdul-Jabbar and Raquel Welch (whose exercise videos are yoga-heavy) have only brought it more attention."[39] Not surprisingly, the magazine reported that the Berkeley-based *Yoga Journal* has nearly doubled its circulation over the past five years.[40]

> *New Age meditation involves mysticism and emptying the mind. Christian meditation calls us to look upward to God to fill our minds with wisdom.*

*Biblical meditation.* Of course, as Christians we must be careful not to write off *all* meditation simply because it is practiced (in an unbiblical way) by New Agers. Unlike New Age meditation, biblical meditation doesn't involve mysticism or emptying the mind. Rather, biblical meditation involves objective contemplation and deep reflection on God's Word (Joshua 1:8) as well as His Person and faithfulness (Psalm 119; cf. 19:14; 48:9; 77:12; 104:34; 143:5).

Christian meditation calls us to look *upward to God* so that our minds may be filled with godly wisdom and insight and so that our hearts may be filled with comfort, happiness, and joy. To echo the opening words of the psalmist, "Blessed is the man . . . [whose] delight is in the law of the LORD, and on his law he meditates day and night" (Psalm 1:1,2).

## The Growing Popularity of the Goddess

New Age spirituality involves a revival of paganism—called *neo*paganism. Neopagans reject Western distinctives such as organized religion, male-dominated society (including patriarchal, male-exalting religion that is evidenced by such phrases as "God *the Father*"), and man's abuse of the world of nature. Instead, neopagans share a feminist perspective and seek to reharmonize themselves with the *mother goddess*.[41]

Well-known goddess-worshiper Miriam Starhawk elaborates: "Mother Goddess is reawakening and we can begin to recover our primal birthright, the sheer intoxicating joy of being alive. We can open our eyes and see that there is nothing to be saved from . . . no God outside the world to be feared and obeyed."[42] According to Starhawk, "the Goddess . . . is the world. Manifest in each of us, she can be known by every individual, in all her magnificent diversity."[43] Goddess worshipers often speak of kindling the "goddess within" (that is, inner divinity).

Some 500,000 women in the United States are alleged to be involved in the goddess-worship movement, and the movement is growing rapidly.[44] *Time* magazine reports that "most participants are women who seek a deity other than God the Father, and a faith less patriarchal than the Judeo-Christian tradition seems to offer."[45] Goddess worship represents a "female-centered focus for spiritual expression."[46]

Diana Hayes, a professor of theology at Georgetown University, says that "within Christianity, theology and spirituality have been male-oriented, male-dominated, because they are the ones articulating it. But we all are affected by who we are, where we came from, our life experience, our relationship with God. So the challenge has been to get this realization out in the open and to have the men who dominate theological circles realize that they cannot speak for the rest of the human race. Women do not think or act the way men do. Therefore our spirituality will not be the same as men's."[47]

Goddess-oriented books are presently among the most popular at New Age bookstores. Moreover, representatives of major book distributors such as Waldenbooks and B. Dalton say neopagan/goddess books are very strong sellers in their stores.[48] The future looks truly bright for neopaganism and goddess worship in America.

## Mormonism: From the Fringes to the Mainstream

Since its founding in 1830, the Mormon church has steadily moved away from the fringes and into the mainstream of American religion. This is largely due to a conscious effort by the church to present a strong image of respectability to the public.[49]

There are presently over four million Mormons in the United States. This represents impressive growth, for in 1950 there were only one million

Mormons.[50] In terms of worldwide growth, it is estimated that the Mormon church is growing at the rate of 1,500 new members per day.[51]

Without a doubt, the Mormon church is one of the wealthiest churches in the world. Such wealth is a key factor in the steady growth of the church and its penetration of mainstream America. The Mormon church spends roughly $550 million per year on its missionary efforts.[52] This breaks down to over $10 million spent each week on its missionary program. A lot of this money goes into media efforts that reach some 357.4 million people in a single year.[53]

The *New York Times* reports that the church "pays for an extensive campaign of television commercials that deal with everyday issues, like the demands of parenting, rather than heavy-handed religious appeals."[54] By focusing on family-related issues in a positive and uplifting way, the church has succeeded in drawing attention away from its cultic doctrine and onto its mainstream image.

Other strategies Mormons have used in past decades to attain respectability and give the appearance of being a mainstream Christian denomination include:

- Eliminating the controversial doctrine of polygamy from the church;

- Allowing blacks to be in the priesthood (they were formerly barred); and

- Taking part in humanitarian efforts when catastrophes occur—such as the community service rendered to people in Utah during the time of severe flooding in the mid-1980s.[55]

## Mormons and the Interfaith Movement

The Mormons have become increasingly involved with the interfaith movement in America. By so doing, they are attempting to position themselves as being on the same level of legitimacy as Protestants, Catholics, and Jews. In fact, in 1988 the Mormons joined with 22 groups—including Protestant, Catholic, and Jewish—in the National Interfaith Cable Coalition producing religious and values-oriented programs on the VISN television network.[56]

As well, an Associated Press article entitled "Mormons Forge Links with Other Faiths" shows that the Mormons have a history of interfaith involvement in the past decade and a half:

In 1986, Mormons became part of the Religious Alliance Against Pornography, a wide ecumenical cross-section. In 1984, they affiliated with Religion in American Life involving most major U.S. denominations in seeking to stimulate weekly worship. Also in the mid-80s, Mormons entered into interreligious relief work, including aid to the homeless. They contributed about $5 million to relief efforts in famine-ravaged central Africa, much of it through Catholic Relief Services and the American Red Cross.[57]

Dallin H. Oaks, a member of the Mormon church's ruling Council of Twelve, said, "I think the outlook for our being involved with others is good. . . . I think other groups need us, and we need other groups."[58] The trend toward interfaith involvement contributes immeasurably to the Mormon church's goal of being perceived in America as a mainstream Christian denomination.

## The Only True Church?

Mormons recognize that it would be difficult for them to continue being involved with Protestants, Catholics, and others as long as they hold fast to their historical claim that *theirs* is the only true church and all others are apostate. In view of this, the Mormon church has sought to soften its stance on this issue. Indeed, some Mormon leaders are now denying that Mormonism has the harsh view of orthodox Christianity for which it is reputed.[59]

In order to make this denial plausible, however, Mormon leaders and scholars have had to adopt strained interpretations of founder Joseph Smith's "only true church" statements.[60] For example, according to the canonized version of Joseph Smith's account of his first vision (in which he allegedly beheld God the Father and Jesus Christ), Smith reports what he was told in response to his inquiry regarding which church he should join:

> I was answered that I must join none of them, for they were all wrong; and the Personage who addressed me said that all their creeds were an abomination in his sight, that those professors were all corrupt; that: "they draw near to me with their lips, but their hearts are far from me, they teach for doctrines the commandments of men, having a form of godliness but they deny the power thereof."[61]

One Mormon leader offered the following explanation of Joseph Smith's words: "By reading the passage carefully, we find that the Lord Jesus Christ was referring only to that particular group of ministers in the Prophet Joseph Smith's community who were quarreling and arguing about which church was true."[62]

But if this were so, all Joseph Smith had to do was move to a neighboring community and seek out a minister who wasn't corrupt! It wouldn't have been necessary to "restore" the church of Jesus Christ on earth by founding the Mormon church.[63]

### Are Mormons Christians?

In 1992 Stephen Robinson—chairman of the Department of Ancient Scripture at Brigham Young University (a Mormon university)—wrote a book entitled _Are Mormons Christians?_ Among a host of recent efforts by Mormons to gain respectability and acceptance for their church as Christian, this book is surely the most important and sophisticated. In this work, Robinson seeks to prove that "arguments used to exclude Latter-day Saints [Mormons] from the 'Christian' world are flawed."[64]

In chapter 1 of the book, Robinson offers a generic definition of "Christianity" that is so inclusive that it appears Mormons indeed _are_ Christians.[65] Robinson's primary definition of a Christian is derived from _Webster's Third New International Dictionary:_ "One who believes or professes or is assumed to believe in Jesus Christ and the truth as taught by him; an adherent of Christianity; one who has accepted the Christian religious and moral principles of life; one who has faith in and has pledged allegiance to God thought of as revealed in Christ; one whose life is conformed to the doctrines of Christ."[66]

|| **_We should not assume that all who call Jesus "Lord" are really Christians._** ||

But are Mormons Christians in the sense that the _Bible_ defines Christians? Bible scholar Gordon Lewis is right when he says that Robinson's approach to legitimizing Mormonism "can only succeed if a Christian does not need to believe in one personal, transcendent God, one incarnate Christ, the completed atonement, and one gospel of grace through faith alone [Mormons _do not_ believe these things]. For mere descriptive purposes, historians may classify every group that calls itself Christian as Christian. Jesus Christ, however, did not do this. Jesus taught that 'the way' was narrow and that we should not assume that all who call Jesus 'Lord' are really Christians (Matthew 5:20; 7:13-23)."[67]

In a section entitled "Conclusions," Robinson gets to the heart of his belief that Mormons are Christians: "Of all the various arguments against Latter-day Saints [Mormons] being considered Christians, not one—not a single one—claims that Latter-day Saints don't acknowledge Jesus Christ as Lord. Consider the enormous implications of this fact. The only issue that really matters is the only issue that is carefully avoided!"[68]

The discerning Christian recognizes, however, that though the Mormons acknowledge Jesus as "Lord," they so redefine "Lord" as to completely change its meaning. Robinson's "Lord Jesus" is a *creature* who had a beginning in time. Robinson's "Lord Jesus" is not the Creator-God who is worthy of our worship.[69]

Gordon Lewis appropriately responds to Robinson's argument this way:

> If the Christ of a Mormon is not the one true God (John 17:3) who is eternal (John 1:1; Hebrews 1:8-12; 5:6; 13:8), the object of worship is a creature and worship itself becomes idolatry. If the Christ of a Mormon is a spirit-child who has been procreated—like countless other spirit children by the flesh-and-bone Father and one of his wives—then he is not uniquely of the same nature as the Father, as the Bible and the historic church teach. If the [Mormon] Christ is our finite brother, not different in kind from us, he is therefore not uniquely Immanuel—"God with us" (Matthew 1:23). The Christ of the Bible is the unique God-man—incarnate, crucified, and risen once-for-all. Only if He was infinite God in human flesh could His blood have infinite value for the justification of all the billions of people who have ever sinned.[70]

We must emphasize that the Scriptures grant the right to be called "Christian" *only* to those who receive Jesus (John 1:12) as the eternal (not just preexistent) Word who was continuously and personally *with* the one true God and *was* the one true God (John 1:1) who became flesh (John 1:14).[71] Hence, the Mormon attempt to appear Christian based on their commitment to Christ "the Lord" backfires, for theirs is "another Jesus" who is not Christian at all (2 Corinthians 11:4).

## The Unification Church:
## Mainstreaming Through "Front Groups"

When I was a young boy I remember seeing a particular episode of _The Twilight Zone_ in which planet earth was visited by some apparently friendly aliens who wished to help humankind. In what seemed to be an act of goodwill, the aliens gave a copy of a book—written in the alien language—to human leaders as a gift.

Scholars were soon able to translate the title of the book: _How to Serve Man_. This gave earth's leaders a great deal of confidence. After all, if these aliens wanted to serve humankind so much that they wrote a book about it, then we humans can surely trust them, right?

As the story goes, the aliens invited a group of human beings to visit their home planet. So, a group of people were selected and they boarded the spaceship, looking forward to the journey. Just as the doors on the spaceship were bolted shut and its engines were ignited, a person rushed onto the scene, screaming in a panic, "Don't go, don't go—we've finished translating the book and it's a _cookbook!_" It contained recipes on different ways of serving people _as meals_. What a deception these aliens had pulled: Without even being aware of the danger, a bunch of humans had gotten blindly sucked into a situation that spelled their doom.

This may seem like an unusual way to begin a section on the Unification Church. But bear with me; I want to make a point.

> **_The ultimate aim of "front groups" is the conversion and indoctrination of people into a cult._**

All over this country, there are people in various walks of life who are being blindly sucked into situations that spell their doom—_spiritual_ doom. More specifically, there are numerous people who become affiliated with some "professional" or "academic" organization—an activist group on a college campus, for example—yet are unaware that some of these organizations are actually "front groups" for various cults. And these people end up getting lured into a cult through the back door. Such front groups are a key means some cults use in their attempt to penetrate mainstream America.

An example of this is the Reverend Sun Myung Moon's Unification Church, which offers a wide array of front organizations—estimated at over 200 in the United States alone.[72] The church's ultimate aim with these organizations is the conversion and indoctrination of people into the cult.[73]

Here's a brief sampling of Unification front groups:

- The International Federation for Victory over Communism

- Freedom Leadership Foundation

- World Freedom Institute

- American Youth for a Just Peace

- International Cultural Foundation

- One World Crusade

- Project Unity

- Creative Community Project

- Professors Academy for World Peace

- Committee for Responsible Dialogue

- The Collegiate Association for the Research of Principles[74]

Many of these groups sound quite inviting and beneficial. Tragically, however, unsuspecting people have been sucked into the Unification Church by joining up with one or another of these organizations. As a case study, let us consider one of these groups in greater detail.

## The Collegiate Association for the Research of Principles (CARP)

The Collegiate Association for the Research of Principles (CARP) was first established in the United States at Columbia University in 1973.[75] Through this organization, numerous youth in America have been introduced to the teachings of Reverend Sun Myung Moon. The organization boasts having penetrated over 300 campuses in the States.[76]

A promotional brochure published by the Unification Church tells us:

CARP was established to revitalize the founding spirit of Christianity, based on the "Divine Principle," proclaimed by the founder of Unification Church International, Rev. Sun Myung Moon, to seek harmonious and functional integration of religion and science; to promote cultural exchange of East and West; to formulate a new system of universal ethics; to offer critique and counterproposal to atheistic Marxist-Leninism; and to evaluate systems of higher education so that it may contribute in the development of the whole person.[77]

## The "Divine Principle"

What is the "divine principle" mentioned above? Actually, this is the heart of Unification theology. Researcher J. Isamu Yamamoto explains it this way:

The specific teaching of the _Divine Principle_ can best be divided into three areas: the first Adam, the second Adam, and the Lord of the Second Advent. The first Adam and Eve were God's initial human creations who fell into sin. The second Adam was Jesus Christ who died on the cross because of the faithlessness of the Jews. The Lord of the Second Advent is the Messiah who must come to establish the Kingdom of Heaven here on earth. These three Adams comprise God's plan for fulfilling the original goals of creation.[78]

In Moon's theology, Jesus was not able to complete the work of redemption. Yes, He _was_ able to provide _spiritual_ redemption to humankind, but not _physical_ redemption. Why not? Because "he was crucified by the Jews and because he was unable to meet his perfect mate and establish the Kingdom of Heaven on earth."[79]

You see, if Jesus hadn't been crucified, He would have eventually found a perfect mate and begun God's _perfect family_ on earth. This would mean He would have accomplished both spiritual and physical salvation for humankind. As it was, however, He was killed before He could finish His work.[80]

In view of this, the Messiah or Lord of the Second Advent must come to complete God's goal for creation. This "Messiah" is Reverend Sun Myung Moon. (Moon doesn't come right out and say this, though he has implied it at Unification conferences, as we will see in the next chapter.)

Unificationists set forth a twisted interpretation of Jesus' words in John 16:12,13: "I have much more to say to you, more than you can now bear. But when he, the Spirit of truth, comes, he will guide you into all truth. He will not speak on his own; he will speak only what he hears, and he will tell you what is yet to come." Unificationists say that the words Jesus left unuttered are presently being revealed through the Holy Spirit as "new truth" (i.e., through Moon's teachings). This new truth will "elucidate the fundamental contents of the Bible so clearly that everyone can recognize and agree with it."[81]

Since at CARP workshops and seminars "the basic philosophy of CARP, the Unification Principle, is explained at length,"[82] it is clear that the organization is ultimately used to indoctrinate students in Moon's theology. There is no way to estimate just how many students have been drawn into the Unification Church through CARP. But this organization—along with numerous other Unification front groups—has been of great benefit to Moon in his ongoing efforts to bring his church into America's mainstream.

### Christians Confronting Front Groups

Earlier I mentioned a television program in which some unfortunate people had been deceptively lured into an alien spacecraft to be served as the main course for hungry aliens. We can assume they met with a swift end; there was nothing anyone could do to rescue them.

But with regard to people getting lured into the cults through front groups, there *is* something Christians can do if they are committed enough to get involved. For example:

- Christians can make sure they stay abreast of the tactics of cults that use front groups. They can do this by (among other things) subscribing to relevant publications such as the *Spiritual Counterfeits Project Journal*[83] and the *Christian Research Journal*.[84] (The latter publication is produced by the Christian Research Institute, the countercult organization founded by Walter Martin.)

- Christians can point their finger and identify such cultic front groups should they surface in the local community.

- Christians can design and put into action Christian alternatives to some of these groups.

- Christians can, via local churches, unite in their stand against cultic intrusions, knowing that a rope of many strands is not easily broken.

## Cultic Mainstreaming
## in the 1990s and Beyond

At the beginning of this chapter I quoted James M. Dunn, who said, "History teaches that today's 'cults' may become tomorrow's mainstream religions."[85] The words seem prophetic. The New Age movement, Mormonism, and the Unification Church (just three of many possible examples) were once cultic groups on the outer periphery of the religious landscape in America. But now they are aggressively jostling for the spotlight on center stage. It would seem that for these and other such cults, mainstreaming has become the central agenda for the 1990s.

# 7

# Media Savvy and the Culting of America

*Suppose someone invented an instrument, a convenient little talking tube which, say, could be heard over the whole land . . . I wonder if the police would not forbid it, fearing that the whole country would become mentally deranged if it were used.*[1]

—Sören Kierkegaard (1813-1855)

POPULAR TELEVISION JOURNALIST Bill Moyers once asked whether television could be "a force in the central issue of our time, the search to signify and affirm meaning, open our souls to others," and be a channel for the "biggest story of the century, the struggle to define what it means to be spiritual." That "little screen," Moyers said, is "the largest classroom, perhaps the largest chapel, God has given us in a long, long time."[2]

Moyers is right when he speaks of the power of television. As powerful as television is, however, it is not the only media. Also powerful is the radio and the print media. Combined, these three outlets exercise tremendous influence on the minds of Americans, as evidenced in the following statistics:

- Some 97 percent of Americans own televisions.[3] About 98 percent of these watch television regularly.[4]

- Americans average about four hours *a day* of television viewing.[5]

- This means that over the past year, the typical American adult spent an equivalent of two full months (24 hours a day for 61 days) watching television.[6]

- Scholarly studies reveal that "kids draw most of their information from the television, spending an average of more than 10,000 hours watching it by the time they reach age eighteen. (That, by the way, represents more than one entire year—24-hour days, seven days a week—absorbing the messages broadcast by television producers.) The typical child in the preschool through sixth-grade age group watches in excess of thirty hours of television programming per week."[7]

- There are some 350 million radios in America—we have more radios than people.[8]

- Some 124 million Americans read a newspaper every day.[9]

In view of such staggering numbers, can anyone doubt why the cults seek to purchase, manage, and influence the media in America? The media represents the single most effective means of reaching large numbers of people in a quick, efficient way.

In this chapter we will look at the same three representative cultic groups (Mormons, New Agers, and the Unification Church) discussed in chapter 6, "Mainstreaming: Cultic Agenda for the 1990s." We will see that a primary means of attaining mainstream status in America has been the effective use of the media.

First, however, let us look briefly at how the American media has contributed to the religious confusion in this country by giving a national platform to liberal Christian scholars who consistently call into question the words and works of Jesus Christ. (These scholars are liberal in the sense that they typically deny the inerrancy of the Bible as well as the supernatural and miraculous in the Bible. Conservative Bible scholars, by contrast, hold to the inerrancy of the Bible.)

## Jesus in the Media

The so-called "Jesus Seminar" consists of a 200-member group of liberal biblical scholars from all over the country that receives *constant* media coverage. This group first met in 1985 and has stirred controversy from the very beginning.[10] The Jesus Seminar has concluded that over half of the sayings attributed to Jesus were put into His mouth by the Gospel writers and early believers. Among the rejected sayings are the following:[11]

- *Matthew 5:11:* "Blessed are you when people insult you, persecute you and falsely say all kinds of evil against you because of me."

- *Mark 10:33,34:* "We are going up to Jerusalem," he said, "and the Son of Man will be betrayed to the chief priests and teachers of the law. They will condemn him to death and will hand him over to the Gentiles, who will mock him and spit on him, flog him and kill him. Three days later he will rise."

- *Mark 13:26,30:* "At that time men will see the Son of Man coming in clouds with great power and glory. . . . I tell you the truth, this generation will certainly not pass away until all these things have happened."

- *John 3:16:* "For God so loved the world that he gave his one and only Son, that whoever believes in him shall not perish but have eternal life."

- *John 14:6:* "Jesus answered, 'I am the way and the truth and the life. No one comes to the Father except through me.'"

How did this group come to its conclusions regarding which words of Jesus were authentic and which were not? Actually it's quite simple. Seminar participants subjectively *voted* on each respective saying of Jesus by using a different-colored bead—red, pink, gray, or black.[12]

Some 31 of the sayings in the four gospels fell into the "red" category, thus indicating that these sayings were viewed as authentic. Another 200 sayings fell into the "pink" category, indicating the conclusion that Jesus said something similar to the recorded words. The red and pink categories together constitute about 20 percent of the total.[13] About 30 percent of the sayings fell into the "gray" category, indicating the conclusion that some of the ideas may have roots in Jesus, but not the words that were recorded. That leaves about 50 percent that fell into the "black" category, indicating that these sayings were rejected altogether.[14] Amazingly, *all* of Jesus' sayings in the Gospel of John were voted down.[15]

A newspaper report on the Jesus Seminar led one conservative biblical scholar to write a letter to the editor, saying, "Theirs is not a quest for the historical Jesus, but a quest for the *intellectually respectable* Jesus, free of such features, embarrassing to modern intellectuals, as demons, miracles, and predictions about the future—all of which were commonplace features of First-Century thinking, Jewish and Gentile."[16]

What is disconcerting is that the Jesus Seminar has continually received heavy media coverage in a great many of our nation's leading newspapers and magazines. The false impression left with people is that many (if not a majority) of the nation's top scholars believe that a significant portion of the words attributed to Jesus in the New Testament were made up and do not belong there. In contrast, conservative biblical scholars who provide convincing evidence for the full authenticity of Jesus' New Testament sayings are rarely mentioned or reported on in the media.

When reports of the Jesus Seminar are combined with other media reports—such as those dealing with the alleged connection of the Dead Sea Scrolls with Jesus and the emergence of Christianity, and (Episcopal) Bishop Spong's homosexual-oriented interpretation of the Bible—one cannot deny that the media has influenced the general public's perception of who Jesus is and what Christianity is all about.

> *Negative media coverage about Jesus functions as a fertilizer on the weed of cultism in America.*

I don't believe it's merely a coincidence that many Americans today have a diminished view of Jesus Christ. A 1993 poll, for example, reveals that "Americans are nearly evenly divided on whether or not Christ was perfect. Although 47% say He was perfect, 44% argue that while He was on earth He made mistakes. . . . To a large segment of our population He had His fair share of faults and failures during His earthly tenure."[17]

Negative media coverage about Jesus functions as a fertilizer on the weed of cultism in America. Such reports set the stage for the cults to offer their own distortions of the person and work of Christ.

### Mormons and the Media

The Latter-day Saints (LDS) own a $300-million-a-year media conglomerate. And the church spends roughly $550 million per year on media for its worldwide missionary efforts. It is estimated that church-owned radio and television outlets reach more than 2.3 million adults per day.[18] Talk about effective use of media!

In an article entitled "LDS Media Empire: A Voice for Mormon Values" in the *Las Vegas Review Journal*, we are told that television and radio stations "are just part of the [Mormon] church's media empire, which includes a newspaper publishing company, an advertising agency, a book publishing and retail sales company, and television production companies."[19] The media indeed serves as a "voice" for Mormon values.

## Dealing with Image via the Media

Researchers who have studied the Mormons' use of media say the church "responds to public relations problems as quickly as any image-conscious corporation. It commands a powerful public relations apparatus that smoothly markets Mormonism to the world."[20]

In a massive public-relations campaign—including a series of television, radio, and magazine ads that began in 1971—the Mormon church has marketed itself as "a bastion of domestic strength and middle-class respectability."[21] This media campaign has paid rich dividends for the church, not only in terms of people joining it but also in terms of how the church is perceived by the average American.

For many years the Mormon church has also purchased advertisements in popular publications such as *Reader's Digest* and *TV Guide*. These ads typically portray the church as a wholesome, all-American institution—focusing on their apparent virtuous lifestyles instead of setting forth their cultic doctrines.[22] These ads offer a free copy of the Book of Mormon,[23] and Mormon publications report that the ads "are bringing significant increases in missionary work."[24]

## Mormonism and Videos

Videos have been very effectively used by the Mormon church to attract new members. Indeed, a Mormon publication reports that "in all countries, videos introduce many more people to the [Mormon] gospel than traditional tracting and contacting do, and missionary work is reaping great benefits."[25]

Dale L. Gardner, a Mormon leader in Kentucky, said that "the media support is really having an impact on people. . . . Responses of viewers to the videos have been overwhelming, and this gives the missionaries great confidence and enthusiasm."[26] We can expect the Mormon use of videos to continue and even increase in coming years.

## Mormonism and Television

An example of how the Mormons have used television would be the church-produced program "Together Forever." At one time this program was broadcast in every city in the United States that had a Mormon missionary headquarters. The result of the program, according to Mormon leaders, was "increasing success for missionaries."[27]

Commenting on the program, Mormon elder Robert L. Backman of the Missionary Executive Committee said response to the program was "gratifying."[28] The program was intended to introduce nonmembers to Mormon values and was "just one part of a Church effort to use mass media to spread the [Mormon] gospel."[29]

Seasonal Mormon television programming has included "Mr. Kreuger's Christmas," "The Other Wise Man," and "The Last Leaf." LDS-produced Christmas programs and public-service announcements are claimed to be viewed by hundreds of millions of people in some 25 countries.[30]

The Mormons have also made heavy use of television commercials. On various cable television stations—including TNT, CNN, Headline News, and Ted Turner's WTBS—the Mormons have purchased commercial time for what they consider to be "straightforward" messages, according to the *Church News* supplement of the Mormon-owned *Deseret News*.[31]

What are these commercials like? As described by Christian journalist William Alnor, "In one of the new Mormon commercials, an attractive female librarian is pictured saying that of all the great books written by great authors, she prefers to read about the Savior. She then explains that, besides the Bible, there's another testament of Jesus Christ—the Book of Mormon."[32]

Another major Mormon commercial "portrays Christ as a baby and then continues with His life until the crucifixion. It concludes that after Christ's resurrection His ministry continued and it didn't end with the Bible—it ended with the Book of Mormon."[33]

Still another series of Mormon television ads are called "Homefront." These ads show poignant and humorous vignettes of domestic life. "Encouraging patience and understanding between parents and children, they end with: 'A thought from The Church of Jesus Christ of Latter-day Saints—The Mormons.' "[34]

Many Mormon commercials give toll-free phone numbers that viewers can call to receive a free copy of the Book of Mormon.[35] And, of course, people love to call in for free books!

The question is, how effective have these commercials been? The *Church News* reports that the results are "impressive."[36] Mormon leaders say the commercials make it much easier for church missionaries to accomplish their task in local communities. People seem to be more receptive to the missionaries after having viewed the wholesome, positive commercials.

## Mormonism and Radio

At any given moment during the day, we are told, millions of adults across America are listening to Mormon-owned radio stations.[37] Major markets include New York City, Los Angeles, Dallas, Seattle, Chicago, Kansas City, San Francisco, Salt Lake City, and Phoenix.[38] As well, Mormon leaders say, radio announcements about the Book of Mormon aired on various stations across the country are bringing many, many responses.[39]

> *A total of 357 + million people are reached in a single year through Mormon public service programs.*

Countless radio listeners from coast to coast are learning more about Mormon views and they don't even know it.[40] How so? By the airing of a series of in-depth public-service announcements called "Times and Seasons."[41]

The programs do not mention the Mormon church outright, but the views presented on them are consistent with the tenets of the church.[42] The tapes "are labeled with a copyright from the church, but some make no mention that the production comes from the Mormons. Forty-eight segments have been produced since 1988."[43]

"The Mormon connection is downplayed deliberately," said Gerry Pond, manager of the church's Radio News and Feature Services.[44] "We have gone overboard, bent backward to make sure they are public affairs," he said.[45]

One radio programmer liked the series so much that she decided to use it as "part of her station's Sunday Christian programming."[46] Such receptivity delights the Mormon church to no end because it has been attempting for years to be accepted as a mainstream "Christian" body.

## The Mormons' Effective Use of the Media

An article in _The Salt Lake Tribune_ reported that effective media use and advertising has contributed to a sharp upsurge in Mormon converts and missionary effectiveness.[47] According to the article, "In an address before 1,100 at BYU [the Mormons' Brigham Young University] . . . Elder Russell M. Ballard of the Quorum of the Twelve Apostles said the Mormon church will step up its use of advertising as well as radio and television productions and community service programs throughout the United States as well as communist countries in the next decade."[48]

The article quotes Ballard as saying, "Media activities have been instrumental in the growth experienced by the church's missionary program. Each year, the number of people reached by the media increases."[49] Ballard said "baptisms by LDS missionaries have increased by 7 percent in the U.S. and missionary productivity by 16 percent in LDS missions through radio and television."[50] Ballard estimated that a total of 357.4 million people are reached in a single year through public service programs.[51]

In short, the Mormons have media muscle and they're not shy about flexing it in their endeavor to penetrate mainstream America.

## The New Age Movement and the Media

The New Age movement includes a wide spectrum of individuals such as reincarnationists, psychics, astrologers, goddess worshipers, holistic-health professionals, ecologists, political activists, educationists, and much more. All of these New Age practitioners utilize the media in one form or another to bring their ideas before the public. Let's take a brief look at some representative examples.

### The New Age Movement and Television

The New Age movement has penetrated both adult and children's television programming. Perhaps the best-known adult New Age television event was Shirley MacLaine's miniseries "Out on a Limb," which aired January 18-19, 1987. With blockbuster ratings, this series introduced people all over America to New Age occultism—including MacLaine's experiences with reincarnation, UFOs, astral travel (out-of-body experiences), and channeling (spiritism). The week following the broadcast, sales of New Age books virtually skyrocketed all across the country.

Since then, New Age themes (and New Age guests) have regularly surfaced on some of today's most popular television shows—including "Star Trek: The Next Generation," "Kung Fu: The Legend Continues," and talk shows such as "Oprah Winfrey," "Phil Donahue," and "Geraldo." New Agers have also been featured on major news programs such as ABC's

"20/20" (channeler J.Z. Knight) and interview programs such as "Bill Moyers" on the Public Broadcasting System (Moyers interviewed the late Joseph Campbell).

Many children's television shows are also permeated with New Age concepts—including "Thunder Cats," "She-Ra," "He-man," and "Masters of the Universe."[52] In these and other similar shows, children are introduced to psychic powers, communication with spirits from the other side, occultic symbols, yoga, and a variety of other Eastern ideas.[53]

Cable station HBO (Home Box Office) featured episodes of "Fraggle Rock," created by the late Muppet master Jim Henson. Among the New Age ideas discernible in this series are Zen philosophy, an emphasis on the harmony and oneness of all things, and intuition over rationality.[54] Such ideas are vintage New Age.

New Age ideas can also be found in television commercials designed for major manufacturers. For example, in 1993 Mitsubishi ran a series of ads for one of its new cars—the Gallant. It portrayed a stage at the center of a room with people on all sides of the stage. The people in the room are pictured imagining the best possible car, concentrating on every feature they ever wanted or hoped for in a car. And as they visualize this perfect car, it begins to take physical shape before our very eyes. This has definite New Age overtones, for New Agers believe that visualization with the human mind can bring about the things one desires in the physical world.

### The New Age Movement and Telephone Hotlines

_Body Mind & Spirit_, a popular New Age magazine, is presently featuring ads for its own "psychic hotline" through which people can get in contact with "America's top professional psychics, now standing by to unlock the secrets of your inner self and forecast your future."[55]

The ads ask, "Are you ready to seek the answers to your most pressing questions, the solutions to your greatest problems? Are you ready to receive real, practical advice that could make your life HAPPIER and HEALTHIER? To take the vital steps on your Spiritual Journey leading at last to true PEACE, PROSPERITY, ROMANCE, and JOY?"[56] If so, "then, you're ready to call the new _BODY MIND & SPIRIT_ LIVE PSYCHIC HOTLINE. The only psychic hotline in America featuring certified, accurate psychics approved by _BODY MIND & SPIRIT_."[57]

We are told that the staff of _Body Mind & Spirit_ spent months interviewing America's top psychics before selecting the very best to be a part of its hotline.[58] "Now, with a single phone call, you can choose for yourself from among the country's leading Master Psychics, including: ASTROLOGERS ...NUMEROLOGISTS...DREAM INTERPRETERS...TAROT READERS...CHANNELERS...PAST LIFE THERAPISTS...CLAIRVOYANTS...AURA READERS...and HEALERS."[59]

Readers of this New Age publication are told that they'll be amazed at the "remarkably revealing insights into the past and present. And inspired by their incredibly accurate forecasts of your future."[60] All of this is available for a mere $3.95 per minute on a convenient 900 number.[61] The world of New Age occultism is just a phone call away!

## The New Age Movement and Videos

Videos are another means used by New Agers to promote their mystical ideas. Again, it is Shirley MacLaine who helped give momentum to this form of media as a New Age educational tool. In an article entitled "Videos for a New Age" published in *Video Business*, we are told that "Shirley MacLaine's *Inner Workout* can be credited with giving the [New Age video] genre a much welcome shot of star power."[62]

MacLaine's video publisher said that "the publicity has been all over the place, and the tape has been selling everywhere, from New Age stores to video stores and mass merchants."[63] This has opened the door for many other New Agers to promote New Age ideas through video.

Hot-selling New Age videos in recent years include "Lilias: Alive with Yoga," "Meetings with Remarkable Men: Life of Gurdjieff," "Joseph Campbell: The Power of Myth," "Tai Chi with Nancy Kwan," "An Evening with Bernie Siegel," "Louise Hay: You Can Heal Your Life," and "Relax with Dennis Weaver."[64] The New Age video market is alive and well in America!

## The New Age Movement and Print Media

In April 1982, a full-page ad appeared in 14 prominent newspapers around the world—from Rome to Jerusalem, from Kuwait to Karachi, from New York to Los Angeles—proclaiming that "The Christ Is Now Here." The ad, sponsored by the (New Age) Tara Center in Los Angeles, California, affirmed that "within the next two months [the Christ] will speak to humanity through a worldwide television and radio broadcast. His message will be heard inwardly, telepathically, by all people in their own language."[65]

The ad claimed this would take place by the end of spring 1982 on the "Day of Declaration," after which would commence a new era of peace and happiness. This Christ would come not as a religious, political, economic, or social leader, but as an "educationalist" who would solve all the world's problems in these areas and usher in a New Age of love, peace, and shared wealth. This information about the appearance of the Christ was alleged to have been revealed to a self-proclaimed prophet of the Christ, Benjamin Creme, founder of the Tara Center.[66]

The year 1982 came and went with no appearance by the Christ. The most common explanation for the Christ's no-show (at least ten explanations have been offered) is that the media prevented it. Since the media represents humanity at large, Creme says, its apathy is indicative of the broader apathy of humanity. And since the Christ's manifestation cannot occur against man's wishes (according to some cosmic law), his coming has been delayed.[67]

From 1982 to 1990, Creme has continued to maintain that the Christ will soon reveal himself to humanity. In April 1990, the Tara Center distributed a press release alleging that a man claiming to be Maitreya presented his credentials as the messiah before 200 media representatives and world leaders at a conference in London, England. The meeting was advertised in many prominent newspapers the month prior to the event.[68]

It is not known precisely where this event took place or who the 200 conference participants were. Fifty of them were said to be reporters, though not a single article ever appeared in any publication documenting, mentioning, or even alluding to the meeting. Apparently, the media's apathy toward Creme's Christ has not diminished.[69]

Reminiscent of the 1982 ads in which Creme claimed that the Christ would present his credentials to all humanity on the Day of Declaration "by the end of spring 1982," he is now saying that the April 1990 conference was a prelude to the Day of Declaration, though the date of that "declaration" has not been revealed.[70]

Creme is also using the radio as much as he can to promote his occultic message. I have been on several radio programs with Creme, defending Christianity against his New Age distortions of the person and work of Christ. Understandably, he was less than enthused about the issues I raise in _The Counterfeit Christ of the New Age Movement_ (Baker Book House, 1990).

## Transcendental Meditation and Its Deceptive Use of the Media

Representatives of Transcendental Meditation have not only attempted to use the media but have made misleading public statements via the media to advance TM's cause. _The Cult Observer_ reported that "TM has made many incorrect or distorted public announcements to advance its programs."[71]

The article notes as an example that "leading TM spokesman Deepak Chopra, M.D., claimed publicly that the Massachusetts Board of Education had virtually decided to accredit the Maharishi Vedic University's graduate degree programs. The state said it had merely received an *application* for such accreditation."[72]

Ex-members say that TM teaches followers to use this type of deception to further Maharishi's cause. "I was taught to lie and to get around the petty rules of the 'unenlightened' in order to get favorable reports into the media,"[73] the *Cult Observer* article quotes one former TMer as saying. "We were taught how to exploit the reporters' gullibility and fascination with the exotic, especially that [which] comes from the East. We thought we weren't doing anything wrong because we were told it was often necessary to deceive the unenlightened to advance our guru's plan to save the world."[74]

## The Unification Church and Direct-Mail Media

A common tactic used by the Unification Church to lend respectability to itself and gain members is sponsoring conferences. Cult watcher Ruth Tucker, professor at Trinity Evangelical Divinity School in Deerfield, Illinois, is correct in saying that "through scientific, philosophical, and religious conferences offered free of charge to ministers and educators at posh resorts, the organization has been able to win influential friends that would not otherwise have offered support."[75]

The Unification Church spares no expense with these conferences because Moon is seeking mainstream status for his church in America, and he has a lot of money to spend in accomplishing this goal.[76]

Regarding the Unification Church's attempt at legitimacy in America, an article in *Christianity Today* commented, "The most-publicized legitimation tactic is probably the Moonie professional conferences. Most are organized under the auspices of the church's New Ecumenical Research Association (New ERA). The Moonies have convened with evangelicals, scientists, lawyers, and journalists."[77]

How do pastors and ministers get coaxed into attending such meetings? By direct mail! The following excerpts from a Unification letter sent to church leaders shows how effective direct mail can be:

> *Dear Pastor:*
>
> *We are pleased to invite you to attend one of our upcoming four-day seminars on "Unification Theology and Christian Renewal: Implications for Ecumenism and Social Action."*

> _The purpose of these seminars is to afford an understanding of the Unification movement—its insights and values—relating in particular to ecumenical and social action now proceeding with this movement and many Christian churches. These seminars are part of an ongoing series, which has already hosted more than two thousand ministers with responses that have been quite positive._[78]

Now, here's the clincher: The letter informs the pastor/minister that the Unification Church will cover all the expenses for this conference—including airfare, accommodations, and meals:

> _You are invited to join us at one of the above seminars as a guest of Interdenominational Conferences for Clergy. You as a participant will be provided transportation at our expense. We will cover room and board cost for spouses as well, although we will not cover their air fare. You may also recommend an associate pastor, although we cannot pay air fare for more than one person per congregation._[79]

One such conference—promoted via direct mail—was sponsored by the Assembly of the World Religions in 1991. Moon provided a lavish, all-expenses-paid conference at the San Francisco Airport Hyatt Regency for religious leaders across the world—and he did this to influence them in his attempt to go mainstream.[80] The _Orange County Register_ reported that during this meeting, Reverend Moon hinted to the eclectic gathering—including swamis, scholars, lamas, and imams—that he is the new world Messiah.[81]

Moon also said humanity must find its "true parent" and free itself from the grips of Satan. "This person is the Messiah," the _Orange County Register_ cited the Reverend as saying. "To help fulfill this very purpose I have been called upon by God. . . . I have suffered persecution and confronted death with only one purpose in mind, so that I can live with the heart of true parents to love races of all colors in the world."[82] Longtime church members said the speech was Moon's most direct public pronouncement that he sees himself as the new world Messiah.

## Warning America

There are hundreds of other examples that could be cited to demonstrate how the cults are making effective use of various media in the culting of America. But the above is sufficient to show that through the media, the cults have brought their religious appeal into the very living rooms (and workplaces) of the nation.

Obviously, America—the land of religious freedom (a freedom for which I am thankful and a freedom that I defend)—has no Theological Federal Communications Commission, nor is there a Spiritual Pure Food and Drug Administration.[83] However, the Christian church can and must play a role in warning the American public of the spiritual cyanide being disseminated by the megadose through various media, luring souls to an eternity apart from God. The church cannot afford to remain silent.

# 8

# The Hollywood Connection

*Hollywood didn't abandon the church. The church abandoned Hollywood.*[1]

—Ted Baehr

HOLLYWOOD IS THE MOTION picture and television capital of the world. To make it big in this city—the "city of stars"—brings worldwide fame and superstardom. There are many who have achieved such status in this city; it is a fact that there are more famous people per square mile in Hollywood than anywhere else in the world.

Understandably, various cults and religions have been very open about their affiliation with one or more Hollywood stars. Such an affiliation has great public-relations value for the cult. The Mormon church, for example, has gotten no small amount of favorable public exposure as a result of its connection with the Osmonds. The Jehovah's Witnesses sect has reaped great benefit from its ties with the Jacksons (though superstar Michael Jackson defected some years ago). The Church of Scientology has likewise received heavy publicity due to the growing number of Hollywood celebrities joining the church—including Tom Cruise, Kirstie Alley, Mimi Rogers, Anne Archer, Sonny Bono, John Travolta, and Chick Corea.[2] Nichiren Shoshu Buddhism (a "name it and claim it" form of Buddhism) has benefited as a result of its association with actor Patrick Duffy (of "Dallas" fame), musician Herbie Hancock, and rock star Tina Turner.[3] Nichiren Shoshu Buddhism has been called one of the fastest-growing religions in America.

Another form of Buddhism—Tibetan Buddhism—has received tremendous publicity as a result of star Richard Gere's affiliation with the religion.[4] Gere is a committed follower of the Dalai Lama, the spiritual and temporal leader of Tibetan Buddhism. Gere has personally organized numerous press conferences for the Dalai Lama, often appearing side by side with the spiritual leader.[5] Gere is presently seeking financial backing for a movie in which he would play Buddha on the silver screen.[6]

As you might expect, there are far more celebrity cultists than there is room to write about them all in a single chapter. My goal, in view of this, is not to discuss every single celebrity who is involved in a cult or false religion, but simply to look at some representative examples that will help us better understand the "Hollywood connection" in the culting of America.

Because the New Age movement is so prevalent and influential in Hollywood, and because Hollywood celebrities often grace the front covers of popular New Age magazines, I will limit my attention in the first half of this chapter to representative New Age celebrities. Then in the second half, I will shift my attention to major motion pictures and how they have contributed to altering the religious landscape of America. (Good sources are available for those interested in fuller discussions of various celebrities as related to the cults.)[7]

## The New Age Movement and Hollywood

### Shirley MacLaine: New Age Prophetess

Shirley MacLaine is obviously a major player when it comes to a discussion of the Hollywood connection and the culting of America. Jon Klimo once commented, "Critics and fans alike concur that MacLaine has done more than any other single person in recent times to soften the ground for people to believe and participate in things they once avoided for fear of being thought 'flaky.' "[8]

MacLaine's New Age book *Out on a Limb* was on the *New York Times* bestseller list for fifteen straight weeks—with over three million copies sold. As noted in the previous chapter, MacLaine's television miniseries "Out on a Limb," based on the book, aired January 18-19, 1987. With blockbuster ratings, this series introduced people all over America to New Age occultism—including MacLaine's experiences with reincarnation, UFOs, astral travel (out-of-body experiences), and channeling.

MacLaine followed her success from *Out on a Limb* with another book—*Dancing in the Light*, which sold a whopping 2.2 million copies. A third book, _It's All in the Playing_, sold just as well, indicating a tremendous market for books containing New Age ideas.[9]

New Age critic Douglas Groothuis comments that "MacLaine's last three books (not counting her two pre-New Age autobiographies) and her countless media appearances [not to mention her television miniseries, "Out on a Limb"] have amounted to a massive endorsement for trance-channeling (mediumship), yoga, reincarnation, past-life regression, psychic abilities, UFO contacts, occult literature, and more. _And people are buying the message._"[10]

> ║ _**Many leaders in the church are unaware of the threat New Age beliefs pose to Christian orthodoxy.**_ ║

MacLaine's theology (her message) is New Age to the core—and she promotes that theology by every avenue open to her. Her view of God, for example, is clearly pantheistic (all is God). In _Out on a Limb_, she refers to God as the "God Force, of which all things are a part."[11]

In keeping with this view of God, MacLaine also views human beings as God: "You are God. You know you are Divine. But you must continually remember your Divinity and, most important, act accordingly."[12] She affirms that "I am God, because all energy is plugged in to the same source. We are each aspects of that source. We are all part of God. We are all individualized reflections of the God source. God is us and we are God."[13] She also says that "each soul is its own God. You must never worship anyone or anything other than self. For you are God. To love self is to love God."[14]

Because man is ultimately God, humans are viewed by MacLaine as having virtually unlimited potential. She affirms that "it's all inside of you. Just listen to your feelings and trust them. You are unlimited. You just don't realize it."[15]

Man's biggest problem, MacLaine believes, is ignorance of his divinity: "The tragedy of the human race was that we had forgotten we were each Divine."[16] Hence, "if everyone was taught one basic spiritual law, your world would be a happier, healthier place. And that law is this: Everyone is God. Everyone. The greatest threat to Earth is spiritual ignorance."[17]

MacLaine is also a reincarnationist. She once said that "reincarnation is like show business. You just keep doing it until you get it right."[18] For

MacLaine, reincarnation is a form of self-salvation. She confidently affirms that "if you are good and faithful in your struggle in *this* life, the *next* one will be easier."[19]

Is MacLaine having an impact on people's theology? It would seem so. Pollster George Barna, in his book *The Barna Report 1992-93*, says it is clear that Shirley MacLaine and other New Age prophets and gurus are making a substantial impact on Americans. Barna warns, "Make no mistake about it: the appeal of New Age ideas and practices is continuing to grow. Millions of Christians espouse New Age beliefs without realizing what they are doing. Many leaders in the church are poorly informed and unaware of this subtle threat to Christian orthodoxy."[20]

## Linda Evans: New Age Channeling Advocate

Most Americans are familiar with Linda Evans because of her role on the popular television show "Dynasty." But she is also well known for the many cosmetic commercials she does. She is considered one of the most glamorous celebrities in Hollywood.

Evans has become very close friends with one of today's better-known New Age channelers—J.Z. Knight, who channels (or acts as a mouthpiece for) a spirit entity known as Ramtha, an alleged 35,000-year-old Lemurian warrior who communicates from "the other side." Evans very much values her relationship with Knight. "A lot of the freedom I have in my life today is the result of J.Z. Knight's courage to do what she does," Evans said in a 1992 interview.[21]

Knight says, "I met Linda between Ramtha sessions, when I came back to my body during a break." According to an interview, Knight "recalled coming out of a trance and seeing Evans sitting quietly nearby, tears streaming down her cheeks. 'She looked like an angel,' J.Z. said softly, staring out the window at the mist drifting over the pastureland. 'I didn't know her as "Linda Evans the star," but there was a pure beauty that just emanated from her like light. And I connected with it right away.' "[22]

Linda Evans concedes that while she was deeply moved by her first encounter with J.Z. Knight and the spirit entity known as Ramtha, she was troubled by doubt regarding the unexplainable phenomenon. "In the beginning, I was totally suspicious. Being an actress and understanding acting, I wanted to see if this 'channeling' was trickery. I wanted to know if I could be fooled, so that I could protect myself. Who wants to be misled?"[23] But Evans eventually had all her doubts dispelled and she fully accepted Knight and her channeling.

Through J.Z. Knight, the entity known as Ramtha communicates the same old New Age lies: You are your own god, you create your own reality, and there is no death. Sadly, with an endorsement from the likes of Linda Evans, many people across the United States and around the world are now much more open to such "revelations" from the world of channeling.

Evans said that some of her close associates were upset when she first became interested in J.Z. Knight's channeling. "My business manager and my agent are just horrified with this entire situation," Linda Evans said, laughing. "But they're also my friends, and they're pleased that I'm happy."[24]

Related to all this, a 1992 article in the New Age magazine *Body Mind & Spirit* speaks of Evans's apparent desertion of Hollywood to spend more time with Knight:

> When *Dynasty* ended, many fans expected Linda Evans to continue being Linda Evans—the glamorous star who graced magazine covers, headlined Movies of the Week, and would probably soon slip into her own TV series. Instead, Evans dropped out of sight. The tabloids tracked her to a five-acre, lakefront estate outside Tacoma, Washington, where, they reported, she'd abandoned her Hollywood friends and career to be closer to "cult leader" Knight and Ramtha.[25]

"What many people are afraid of," Evans said, "is that I've gone off and given myself to this channeled person, and that the world has somehow lost me to this confusing idea. Well, I'm more in the world and happier within myself than I've ever been. Besides," Evans laughs, "Ramtha doesn't *want* me. He wouldn't know what to do with me if I gave myself to him. He doesn't want followers."[26]

Evans stood solidly with her friend J.Z. Knight when the media turned on the channeler. A series of media reports accused Knight of channeling for money, of "taking a cosmic nap [closing her eyes to engage in a channeling session] when she needed a little cash," and practicing mass hypnosis. Matters worsened when Knight was trying to explain reincarnation to a "20/20" reporter by asking, "If we're immortal, how can murder be wrong?" Knight was portrayed as "a female Charles Manson."[27]

Evans defended Knight in a *Redbook* magazine interview, which ended up being syndicated worldwide. She did so at the risk of grave damage to her career.[28] "Linda is my tower of strength," Knight said. "She's never been afraid to say she loves me as a friend."[29]

Are Evans and Knight still close today? "Absolutely!" confirms Knight. "We have a wonderful sisterhood, an intimacy as the best of pals. I trust this woman. And you can't say that about many people in the public eye because they have to be whatever the public wants them to be. Linda may be the beautiful darling of the world, but she has the ability to effect dynamic change. The world can benefit not just from her beauty, but from her wisdom."[30]

What is the "wisdom" Evans communicates to the world? Among other things, she proclaims the "wisdom" of being open to revelations from spirit entities who speak through New Age channelers. And just as cosmetic corporations reap great benefit from a television commercial featuring Linda Evans, so the whole field of New Age channeling has reaped enormous benefit from Evans's glowing endorsement of J.Z. Knight.

## Marianne Williamson: Hollywood's Glitzy New Age Guru

In Hollywood there are a number of gurus who not only communicate their cultic ideas to the stars but have also penetrated mainstream America because of their association with the stars. A classic example of this is Marianne Williamson.

Every Saturday morning Williamson steps up to a pulpit and speaks to a packed house. For a suggested offering of seven dollars a head, people crowd in to hear New Age metaphysical messages from Hollywood's favorite guru, who is impeccably groomed and clad in designer clothes.[31]

The celebrities who soak up metaphysical wisdom from Williamson include Anthony Perkins, Lesley Ann Warren, Tommy Tune, Cher, Roy Scheider, David Geffen, Barbra Streisand, Dawn Steel, Oprah Winfrey, Raquel Welch, and Rosanne Arquette.[32] And her influence is growing with each passing week.

As reported in *Newsweek* magazine, Williamson draws most of her material from *A Course in Miracles*, an occultic bestseller in New Age circles. This 1,200-page spiritual/psychological tome was written in the 1960s by now-deceased Jewish psychologist Helen Schucman. By a process called "automatic handwriting" (in which a spirit entity guides the hand), Schucman wrote this hefty volume, and she claims the source of the words was Jesus Himself.

This "Jesus," however, is not the Jesus of the Bible—for her Jesus' teachings are completely at odds with what the Jesus of the New Testament taught.[33] The Jesus of *A Course in Miracles* is open to the "truth" in all religions. As Williamson puts it, "No religion has a monopoly on the greatest story ever told."[34]

Williamson claims that _A Course in Miracles_ was her personal "path out of hell." Since its first printing in 1976, it has sold some 850,000 copies and has spawned over 1,000 study groups in the United States and abroad.[35] I spoke to some folks at the Bodhi Tree, a New Age bookstore in Hollywood, and they say _Course_ is among the very top-selling books offered at their store. The book gained further publicity when it was featured in April 1993 on the popular television news program "20/20."

The source of unhappiness, _Course_ teaches, is the mistaken sense of separateness from others that is imposed by the "illusion" of our separate and distinct physical bodies. That, in turn, causes us to hate and condemn others.[36] The way to happiness—the "miracle"—is a mere change in perception. _A Course in Miracles_ teaches people how to change their perception. Marianne Williamson explains the proper spiritual "perception" this way:

> If you go deeply enough into your mind and my mind, we have the same mind. The concept of a divine, or "Christ" mind, is the idea that, at our core, we are not just identical, but actually the same being. "There is only one begotten Son" doesn't mean that someone else was it, and we're not. It means we're all it. . . .
>
> Christ refers to the common thread of divine love that is the core and essence of every human mind. . . .
>
> The love in one of us is the love in all of us. There's actually no place where God stops and you start, and no place where you stop and I start. Love is energy, an infinite continuum. . . .
>
> _A Course in Miracles_ likens us to sunbeams thinking we're separate from the sun, or waves thinking we're separate from the ocean. Just as a sunbeam can't separate itself from the sun, and a wave can't separate itself from the ocean, we can't separate ourselves from one another. We are all part of a vast sea of love, one indivisible divine mind.[37]

Our ultimate reality, then—_the core of who we are_—is a single undivided essence. We're not just similar in our essential nature, Williamson says; we're the _same stuff._[38]

Because of her popularity among the stars, Williamson has been described as "the latest mystical sensation in Hollywood, where many work assiduously to cultivate their souls, often with the same devotion they apply to their physiques."[39] An expert on new religious movements in California suggests that Williamson is "an expression of the entertainment industry—fueled by the fame and the desire to be a star."[40]

Williamson appeared on the popular "Oprah Winfrey Show," and Winfrey said she *loved* Williamson's book *A Return to Love*. "Loved it so much, in fact, she gave it a grand Oprah-size plug . . . announcing she'd personally bought 1,000 copies for distribution to the spiritually needy. That was enough to send the book soaring to the top of the *New York Times* 'how-to' heap," *Newsweek* magazine reports.[41] The book became the fifth-best-selling nonfiction work of 1992,[42] and it is a prime example of how a guru's affiliation with a star can enable that guru to penetrate mainstream America.

### LeVar Burton: From the Priesthood to the New Age

LeVar Burton is featured on "Star Trek: The Next Generation" as Lt. Geordi LaForge, the chief engineer. This television series is one of the most popular—and one of the most expensive—in Hollywood history, and it has catapulted Burton into worldwide stardom.

Burton says that while he was in his teens, he was a seminary student at St. Pius in Northern California studying for the Catholic priesthood.[43] But things changed in a very big way. Why did he quit seminary and come to Hollywood?

> Instinct. I listen to that small inner voice 98 percent of the time. The two percent I don't, I wish I had. Without knowing why, I made a decision that led me to the point of coming here. Originally I had gone to St. Pius to study for the priesthood. That decision was leading me to other decisions. I had imagined myself, envisioned myself, being a priest since I was eight years old. But that did not mean that the dream couldn't change. . . . I was brought up Catholic, but that was due to circumstances.[44]

According to a popular New Age magazine, Burton is today known in the Hollywood area for his interest in yoga and crystals: "I see them as tools to get me where I want to go,"[45] Burton says. "The driving force of this goal of mine is to really align myself with the Spirit that connects me to all things, the Spirit that I have in common with every other atom that exists."[46]

> *People are much more open to these*
> *practices when they learn that their*
> *favorite Hollywood heroes endorse them.*

We noted in the previous chapter that yoga is a spiritual discipline by which one conditions the self at all levels—physical, psychical, and spiritual. The ultimate goal is a state of well-being, the loss of self-identity, and absorption into union with "the Absolute." Burton admits he uses yoga to "align" himself with the "Spirit that connects me to all things." This is clearly New Age thinking.

And why all the interest in crystals? New Agers believe crystals contain incredible healing and energizing powers. New Age critic Elliot Miller notes that the capacities New Agers attribute to crystals (without scientific basis) seem endless:

> They can attract desirable and repel undesirable forces. They can store information that New Agers psychically program into them, and then radiate these "positive images" back to the New Agers to help them achieve goals like weight loss or confidence. They can absorb, stimulate, amplify, and focus every spiritual and healing force, and thus are used to aid a variety of New Age therapies. . . . They are also used to enhance meditation, visualization, magic, "astral" or "soul travel," channeling, and various forms of divination. They are worn on the body to attract prosperity, the opposite sex, and general good luck, and are even placed on or near plants to help them grow, carburetors to keep them running, and refrigerators to bring electric bills down.[47]

*Crystals have certainly made a believer out of LeVar Burton!*
Burton adds that "meditation is a part of my process . . . as are things like fire-walking a part of my process. Rebirthing [a New Age practice] is [also] a part of my process."[48] In other words, Burton is an advocate of many different New Age practices. And he is not shy about letting the world hear about it.[49]

As was the case with MacLaine and Evans, when young fans read about Burton's involvement with yoga, crystals, meditation, fire-walking, rebirthing, and the like, credibility is immediately given to these practices. People are much more open to these practices when they learn that their favorite Hollywood heroes endorse them.

### Stephanie Kramer: Long-Time New Ager

Stephanie Kramer attained stardom in America as a result of her role in the popular television series "Hunter." Kramer is very open about her belief in the cosmic power of crystals. "I use them because I believe that they are empowered with enormous energies of high vibration. They can be used during meditation as channels for healing, to complete and maintain a balance. They are most effective tools. I wear them occasionally."[50]

Kramer says that when laying down, "I put them [crystals] in a particular pattern on the body that aligns with the chakras to help bring the body into balance."[51] What are "chakras"? According to yoga philosophy, they are seven centers of spiritual energy situated in the "subtle body" which permeates the physical body. "Normally quiescent, by special disciplines of body and mind, it is claimed the chakras can become active and convey psychic powers."[52]

Kramer says her spiritual life is important to her. "I've been involved in metaphysics since I was a little girl. At the age of seven I started reading about [psychic] Edgar Cayce, [French occultist] Nostradamus, psychic phenomena, the paranormal, anything I could find. And I went on from there."[53]

She claims to read about seven metaphysical (New Age/occult) books each week. During an interview, she said that among the books she was currently reading were *Spirit Song* by Mary Summer Rain, *Indian Medicine Power* by Brad Steiger, *The Reappearance of the Christ and the Masters of Wisdom* by Benjamin Creme, and *A Course in Miracles*.[54] These books are extremely popular in New Age circles. (I've read the latter two, and they are virtually permeated with New Age occultism.)

Kramer also believes in reincarnation. "God only knows how many lives I've had. I believe we've all had many more than we care to remember. I think I've been interesting more than once, but I've not been any famous historical characters."[55]

There are no doubt many people who now respect and embrace certain New Age practices because of Kramer's glowing endorsement of them. When it is realized that MacLaine, Evans, Burton, and Kramer are just *four among many* celebrities in Hollywood voicing support for New Age practices—and when this is combined with the fact that there are many other celebrities voicing support for other cultic groups—the Hollywood connection as related to the culting of America becomes painfully clear.

## Motion Pictures and the Culting of America

### Star Wars: The Power of the Force

George Lucas has produced some of the most popular films of all time, including the world-renowned _Star Wars_ trilogy. In accepting a lifetime achievement award at the Academy Awards ceremony in 1992, Lucas made the statement, "I've always tried to be aware of what I say in my films because all of us who make motion pictures are teachers, teachers with very loud voices."[56] Lucas was exactly right! Motion pictures and their directors _are_ teachers with very loud voices.

Lucas believes that movies have an incredible influence on today's culture. As he related to _American Film_ magazine,

> Film and [other] visual entertainment are a pervasively important part of our culture, an extremely significant influence on the way our society operates. People in the film industry don't want to accept the responsibility that they had a hand in the way the world is loused up. But, for better or worse, the influence of the church, which used to be all-powerful, has been usurped by film. Films and television tell us the way we conduct our lives, what is right and wrong. When Burt Reynolds is drunk on beer in _Hooper_ and racing cops in his rocket car, that reinforces the recklessness of the kids who've been drawn to the movie in the first place and are probably sitting in the theater drinking beer.[57]

Has Lucas tried to communicate messages to the viewing public through his films? Most definitely! Take _Star Wars_ as an example. (The _Star Wars_ phenomenon is still relevant in the 1990s, as evidenced by the recent release of a new trilogy of _Star Wars_ books—authorized by Lucasfilm—that have all made the _New York Times_ bestseller list. Moreover, a 1994 article in _Parade_ magazine reports that by 1997 George Lucas will present the first of three new _Star Wars_ movies.[58])

What message was Lucas attempting to convey through _Star Wars_? _Time_ magazine reports these words from Lucas: "I was trying to say in a very simple way, knowing that the film was made for a young audience, that there is a God and there is both a good side and a bad side. You have a choice between them, but the world works better if you're on the good side. It's just that simple."[59] Clearly, this does not sound like the Christian concept of God.

Lucas's biography said that "Lucas wanted to instill in children a belief in a supreme being . . . a universal deity that he named the Force, a cosmic energy source that incorporates and consumes all living things."[60] What is this "Force"? Lucas admits that he got this idea from Carlos Castaneda's *Tales of Power,* which chronicles the story of Don Juan, a Mexican Indian sorcerer who speaks of a "life force."[61]

It is also highly revealing that Irvin Kershner, the director of *The Empire Strikes Back* (the second *Star Wars* movie), is a Zen Buddhist. His admission of religious intent in this movie is quite explicit: "I wanna introduce some Zen here because I don't want the kids to walk away just feeling that everything is shoot-em-up, but that there's also a little something to think about here in terms of yourself and your surroundings." Kershner spoke of Yoda, the Jedi trainer, as a "Zen Master."[62]

We need not go into great detail in analyzing *Star Wars*. It is sufficient to simply note that the *Star Wars* phenomenon has served to put an exclamation point on many of the Eastern concepts that began flooding into the West in the 1960s.

### The Rise of the Devil in Hollywood

At one time in Hollywood's history, people in movies acknowledged God's existence and the fact that He is the Sovereign Governor of the universe. At one time in Hollywood's history, the devil always got what was coming to him (that is, he always lost in the battle between himself and God).

Today, however, contemporary horror movies often give evil in general and the devil in particular the upper hand. As one critic put it, "You just can't keep the Devil down for very long, especially in Hollywood."[63]

In view of this rising prominence of the devil and the occult in Hollywood, Gary DeMar suggests that "something happened at the movies beginning in the sixties when the occult entered the real world. The [seven] dwarfs were out, and the Devil, the real Devil, was in. Hollywood made the occult mainstream in the enormously popular *Rosemary's Baby* (1968)."[64]

DeMar laments, "The frightening thing about *Rosemary's Baby* is how normal everyone seems. There are no outward signs that these people are in league with the Devil. No brooms or black hats. No pentagrams etched on the forehead. Your next-door neighbor could be a Satan worshipper. This is truly frightening."[65]

Other movies that have glorified the devil in recent decades include *The Exorcist* (1973), *The Exorcist II: The Heretic* (1977), *The Amityville Horror* (1979), and *Poltergeist* (1982) just to name a few. All these movies—and many more that continue to be produced on into the 1990s—make the devil seem all-powerful. Let's consider _The Exorcist_ as an example:

> _The Exorcist_ made it to the big screen in 1973. In this block-buster movie, the Devil seems to get the upper hand once again. Numerous attempts at exorcism fail. The Christian faith is made to look powerless. The movie ends with the Devil leaving the possessed girl, only to enter and destroy the exorcist. After seeing Father Karras hurl himself out the window in a final act of desperation, the audience is left with the impression that the Devil won the battle, and the church is left broken and bloodied on the sidewalk below. The Devil, of course, rises again in _Exorcist II_.[66]

## The Demise of Christ in Hollywood

While the devil is exalted and glorified in Hollywood, Christ is demoted and shamed. One example of this is Martin Scorsese's film, _The Last Temptation of Christ_.[67] In this movie, we find an objectionable, highly offensive portrayal of Christ the Lord.

As Christian writer Joseph Gudel notes,

> For many Christians, the most repugnant elements in the movie are those in the hallucination sequence in which Jesus, while suffering on the cross, envisions himself as having denied the road to Calvary and having lived a "normal" life instead. He visualizes himself as having married Mary Magdalene and having sexual relations with her. She then dies abruptly and he marries the other Mary, Martha's sister. Later, when this Mary is out of the house, Jesus has an adulterous affair with Martha.[68]

At the beginning of the movie, Jesus is portrayed as a coward and a traitor, making crosses for the Romans to use for their many crucifixions. Judas—portrayed as an honorable figure in the film—rebukes Jesus for this:

> _Judas:_ You're a disgrace. Romans can't find anybody else to make crosses, except for you. You do it. You're worse than them! You're a Jew killing Jews. You're a coward! How will you ever pay for your sins?

*Jesus:* With my life. Judas. I don't have anything else.[69]

This portrayal of Jesus as a sinner like other men is a thread that runs through the entire movie. On different occasions, Jesus is seen confessing His sins and asking various people to forgive Him. In one particular scene in the movie, Jesus is portrayed in the desert confessing to a group of ascetics:

> I'm a liar, a hypocrite; I'm afraid of everything. I don't ever tell the truth, I don't have the courage. . . . I don't steal, I don't fight, I don't kill—not because I don't want to—but because I'm afraid. I want to rebel against you, against everything, against God, but I'm afraid. You want to know who my mother and father is? You want to know who my God is? Fear! You look inside me and that's all you'll find.[70]

Gudel's analysis of this film is penetrating. The Jesus of this movie is simply a man, "someone chosen by God to become the Messiah, the Christ. He is not God, but slowly becomes divine by following God's will. He is portrayed as a weak, mentally-tormented, sin-ridden person. This Jesus seems to teach universalism, that everyone will be saved. And he plots his own martyrdom with Judas, much against Judas's wishes, so that he can become the Savior."[71]

Can anyone seriously question that the glorification of the devil and the simultaneous shaming of Jesus in Hollywood have not had a significant impact on the religious landscape of America?

## *Ghost:* A New Age Blockbuster

A cover story in the New Age magazine *Body Mind & Spirit* featured an interview with the writer and the director of *Ghost*. In the article, we read that *"Ghost* has made it big because it reawakens us powerfully and passionately to who we really are as multidimensional beings. Its depiction of death and the astral world breathes magic back into our daily lives."[72] (New Age occultists believe the "astral world" is a dimension or level of being that lies just beyond the physical world.)

*Ghost* is a story about a young man (played by Patrick Swayze) who is "suddenly ripped out of his 'Earth suit' [physical body], yet stays around on the Earth plane long enough to solve the mystery of his murder."[73] He then "reconnects" with his girlfriend (played by Demi Moore), and educates himself (and the audience) to the "realities" of being a real-live ghost.

> *Movies can serve as an incredibly*
> *powerful promotional vehicle*
> *for New Age doctrines.*

Bruce Joel Rubin, the writer of the *Ghost* screenplay, is described in the article as "an enormously talented 'bridge' writer—that is, he is able to translate sophisticated metaphysical ideas into highly attractive mainstream art."[74] When asked where he got the inspiration to write the screenplay, Rubin responded, "From my own spiritual life. . . . I want to give people a sense that there is a larger universe than their conscious minds allow them to perceive. The sensory realities around us are limited realities, and . . . if we can expand our consciousness, we can begin to see that there is infinitely more going on in the universe we inhabit. I want to make movies about that."[75]

*Ghost* was directed by veteran director Jerry Zucker. When asked why he wanted to do this film, Zucker responded by saying, "It was the first script to take the issue of the spiritual world seriously."[76]

When asked if he believed in reincarnation, Zucker said, "Yes, yes I do. . . . the idea that life is a continuum makes sense—that the purpose of life is to grow and learn—and that we have many lives in various different physical bodies. . . . It's hard to find a reason for having only one life, especially given how little we accomplish in one life."[77]

When we consider that *Ghost* was one of the top-grossing films of all time, it becomes clear that this movie has served as an incredibly powerful promotional vehicle for New Age doctrines. When I attended the Whole Life Expo (a New Age superconvention attended by tens of thousands of New Agers) in Southern California, the editor of *Body Mind & Spirit* magazine asked an auditorium full of New Agers how they liked the movie *Ghost*. The instant applause and affirmative shouts were near deafening.

## Cleaning Up Hollywood

It is highly significant that at one time the church was involved in the Hollywood scene. At that time, the church had an influence on the films that were being produced.

In 1933, for example, the Catholic Legion of Decency was founded to help Hollywood keep its act clean. Some 15 years later they were joined by the Protestant Film Office, supported by the National Council of Churches (NCC). For three decades, representatives from these organizations read every movie script from every major studio to make sure it conformed to the strict moral standards of the Motion Picture Code.[78]

How did all that change? According to one researcher, "in 1966 the churches voluntarily closed their film offices and withdrew from the entertainment industry. Worse yet, that same year the National Council of Churches' Film Awards Committee turned down a film on the life of Christ in its recommendations for an Academy Award nomination, and instead gave support to two movies containing nudity and blasphemy. Executives of the film studios were shocked, as was the Motion Picture Code Administration."[79]

> *Hollywood didn't abandon the church.*
> *The church abandoned Hollywood.*

According to Ted Baehr, chairman of Good News Communications, just a few months after the Protestant Film Office shut down in 1966, the Church of Satan Film Office opened. Soon after this, "gay and lesbian activists, radical feminists, Marxists and other groups also opened film offices to lobby the mass media for their points of view."[80]

Within a few years of the church's withdrawal from Hollywood, movies that glorified satanism *(Rosemary's Baby)*, homosexuality *(Midnight Cowboy)*, and excessive violence *(The Wild Bunch)* began showing on the big screen. Since that time, the entertainment industry has been on a fast slide into the sewer.[81] "Today, more than 60 percent of the movies are R-rated, most of them brimming with sex and gore."[82]

Sadly, Ted Baehr says his toughest challenge is not getting people in Hollywood to see the light, but getting the church to acknowledge that there is a problem. His goal is to move Christians "from denial to discernment."[83] "Hollywood," Baehr says wistfully, "didn't abandon the church. The church abandoned Hollywood."[84]

Baehr says that "the church has been retreating, wringing its hands but doing little to change the situation. To make matters worse, surveys such as the Barna Research Poll show little or no difference in viewing habits between Christians and non-Christians in America. This is especially true of Christian teens, who average the same 50 R-rated films per year as their secular counterparts."[85]

The challenge before the Christian church is clear. The question is, will the church choose to _act_, or will it continue wringing its hands as a lame spectator on the sidelines? In other words, will the church be a part of the _solution_, or will it continue to be a part of the _problem?_

# Part 3

# *Enticing Mainstream America*

# 9

# Conquering America with 26 Letters

*Of making many books there is no end.*[1]
—Solomon

"GIVE ME 26 LETTERS and I'll conquer the world." I'm not sure who originally coined this statement, but it's packed with meaning. It points to the tremendous persuasive influence of literature on the masses of people in the world. It is certainly not surprising that one of the primary means cultists have used in their attempt to win people to their respective causes is the widespread distribution of cultic literature.

Though there are many cultic organizations that produce mass quantities of literature, we will limit our attention in this chapter to two representative groups—the Jehovah's Witnesses and the New Age movement. These two best illustrate the point I want to make. After reading this chapter, I think you'll agree that the proliferation of cultic literature in America is one of the greatest and most unrelenting challenges before the church today.

## The Jehovah's Witnesses:
## Over 10 Billion Pieces of Literature

Former Jehovah's Witness David Reed, in his 1993 book *Jehovah's Witness Literature*, said, "At some point during the late 1980s, Jehovah's Witnesses published their 10-billionth (10,000,000,000th) piece of literature. It took more than one hundred years to produce all those books, booklets, magazines, and tracts since the first *Watchtower* magazine [the Jehovah's

Witnesses' primary magazine] rolled off the press in the summer of 1879, but the next 10 billion pieces of literature may take little more than a decade, if the sect continues to grow at its present rate."[2]

Reed also points out that with a twice-monthly printing in excess of 16 million copies per issue, *The Watchtower* magazine "now approaches the circulation of such all-time favorites as *Reader's Digest* and *TV Guide* and easily outsells the combined total of *Time*, *Newsweek*, and *U.S. News & World Report.*"[3] Make no mistake about it: The Watchtower Society is a well-oiled publication machine that is cranking out cultic literature faster than Christians can keep up with it.

It is noteworthy that the Watchtower Society's main "Bethel" plant in Brooklyn, New York, prints on almost 1,000 miles of paper—or 61 million pages—*per day* and turns out more than three million *New World Translation* Bibles per month.[4] To date, the Watchtower Society has produced some 47 million copies of the book *You Can Live Forever in Paradise on Earth* (in 94 languages).[5]

The Watchtower's *1991 Yearbook of Jehovah's Witnesses* reports that there are "more than eleven thousand full-time factory and office workers (up from five thousand in 1980)."[6] As well, the January 1, 1993, *Watchtower* reports "nearly 4.5 million active participants in the work of distributing literature from house to house worldwide. Some 11.5 million people can be found at kingdom halls studying Watchtower literature."[7]

## The Watchtower Society: God's Voice to Humankind?

The Jehovah's Witnesses believe that God personally set up the Watchtower Society as His visible representative on earth. It is through this organization and no other that God allegedly teaches the Bible to humankind today.

Without the Watchtower Society and its vast literature, people are said to be utterly unable to ascertain the true meaning of Scripture. Jehovah's Witnesses are reminded of this over and over again in Watchtower publications. For example, in various past issues of *The Watchtower* magazine, we read:

> • "The Watch Tower Bible and Tract Society is the greatest corporation in the world, because from the time of its organization until now the Lord has used it as his channel through which to make known the glad tidings."[8]

- "Is not the Watch Tower Bible and Tract Society the one and only channel which the Lord has used in dispensing his truth continually since the beginning of the harvest period?"[9]

- "Jehovah's organization has a visible part on earth which represents the Lord and is under his direct supervision."[10]

- "We must not lose sight of the fact that God is directing his organization."[11]

- "Jehovah's organization alone, in all the earth, is directed by God's holy spirit or active force."[12]

## The Authority of the Watchtower Society

Jehovah's Witnesses believe that the Watchtower Society, as God's visible representative on earth, exercises authority over all true believers. And Jehovah's Witnesses are expected to obey the Society—whose instructions are communicated via literature—as *the voice of God*.[13]

If there is a conflict between what the Society says and what the government says, Jehovah's Witnesses are instructed to unquestioningly obey the Society. So, for example, if the government calls upon a young man to be drafted into the military, he must obey the Watchtower Society rather than the government and refuse to do military service.

Jehovah's Witnesses believe that the teachings of the Watchtower Society are all-encompassing and should affect every area of life. One issue of *The Watchtower* magazine refers to the Society as "an organization to direct the minds of God's people."[14] Another issue says that "Jehovah's organization . . . should influence our every decision."[15] In fact, *The Watchtower* goes so far as to say that "we must recognize not only Jehovah God as our Father but his organization as our Mother."[16]

Even reading the Bible is considered insufficient *in and of itself* in learning the things of God. *The Watchtower* tells us, "Unless we are in touch with this channel of communication that God is using, we will not progress along the road to life, no matter how much Bible reading we do."[17]

## No Private Interpretations Allowed

Watchtower literature is replete with admonitions to "dependent" Bible interpretation—that is, dependent on the Watchtower Society's literature.

Jehovah's Witnesses are not to "think for themselves" in terms of interpreting the Bible. They are to submit their minds to the Watchtower Society. In various Watchtower publications we read:

- "God has not arranged for [His] Word to speak independently or to shine forth life-giving truths by itself. It is through his organization God provides this light."[18]

- "Avoid independent thinking . . . questioning the counsel that is provided by God's visible organization."[19]

- "Fight against independent thinking."[20]

- "We should seek for dependent Bible study, rather than for independent Bible study."[21]

- "The Bible cannot be properly understood without Jehovah's visible organization in mind."[22]

- "If we have love for Jehovah and for the organization of his people we shall not be suspicious, but shall, as the Bible says, 'believe all things,' all the things that *The Watchtower* brings out."[23]

- "He does not impart his holy spirit and an understanding and appreciation of his Word apart from his visible organization."[24]

In view of all the above, it is clear that the literature of the Watchtower Society wields tremendous control over a vast number of people. And that number is growing all the time, as evidenced in the following statistics:

- In 1940, there were 58,009 "peak" (active, baptized) Jehovah's Witnesses in the United States.

- This figure jumped to 108,144 by 1950; 205,900 by 1960; 416,789 by 1970; 565,309 by 1980; 850,120 by 1990; 892,551 by 1991; and is now approaching one million.

- The statistics for the growth of this cult around the world are even more alarming. By the end of 1992, there were almost 4.5 million active, baptized Jehovah's Witnesses globally. By comparison, in 1940 there were only 95,327 Jehovah's Witnesses in the world.[25]

## The *New World Translation*

The *New World Translation* is an incredibly *biased* translation of Scripture. An examination of this translation makes it utterly clear that a primary goal of its translating committee was to strip from the Bible any vestige of Jesus Christ's identification with Yahweh.[26] Consider the following side-by-side comparisons of the *New World Translation* with the New International Version (an orthodox translation), and note especially the emphasized words:

| *New World Translation* | *New International Version* |
|---|---|

### Acts 20:28

| | |
|---|---|
| Pay attention to yourselves and to all the flock, among which the holy spirit has appointed you overseers, to shepherd the congregation of *God, which he purchased with the blood of his own [Son]*. | Keep watch over yourselves and all the flock of which the Holy Spirit has made you overseers. Be shepherds of the church of *God, which he bought with his own blood*. |

### Colossians 1:16,17

| | |
|---|---|
| By means of him *all [other] things* were created in the heavens and upon the earth, the things visible and the things invisible, no matter whether they are thrones or lordships or governments or authorities. *All [other] things* have been created through him and for him. Also, he is before *all [other] things* and by means of him *all [other] things* were made to exist. | For by him *all things* were created: things in heaven and on earth, visible and invisible, whether thrones or powers or rulers or authorities; *all things* were created by him and for him. He is before *all things*, and in him *all things* hold together. |

### Colossians 2:9

| | |
|---|---|
| Because it is in him that all the *fullness of the divine quality* dwells bodily. | For in Christ all the *fulness of the Deity* lives in bodily form. |

Do you see the obvious bias in this translation against the full deity of Jesus Christ? Dr. Robert Countess, who wrote a doctoral dissertation on the Greek "scholarship" of the *New World Translation*, concluded that the translation "has been sharply unsuccessful in keeping doctrinal considerations from influencing the actual translation. . . . It must be viewed as a radically biased piece of work. At some points it is actually dishonest. At others it is neither modern nor scholarly."[27] No wonder British scholar H.H. Rowley asserted, "From beginning to end this volume is a shining example of how the Bible should not be translated."[28] Indeed, Rowley said, this translation is "an insult to the Word of God."[29]

Are Drs. Countess and Rowley alone in their assessment of the *New World Translation?* By no means! Dr. Julius Mantey, author of *A Manual Grammar of the Greek New Testament*, calls the *New World Translation* "a shocking mistranslation."[30] Dr. Bruce M. Metzger, professor of New Testament studies at Princeton University, calls the *New World Translation* "a frightful mistranslation," "erroneous," "pernicious," and "reprehensible."[31] Dr. William Barclay concluded that "the deliberate distortion of truth by this sect is seen in their New Testament translation. . . . It is abundantly clear that a sect which can translate the New Testament like that is intellectually dishonest."[32]

> *It must have been utterly embarrassing for the Watchtower Society when it became public who the translators were.*

Now, in view of this universal "thumbs down" by legitimate biblical scholars, it is highly revealing that the Watchtower Society has always resisted efforts to identify members of the *New World Translation* committee. The claim was that they preferred to remain anonymous and humble, giving God the credit and glory for this translation. However, as former Jehovah's Witness David Reed notes, "an unbiased observer will quickly note that such anonymity also shields the translators from any blame for errors or distortions in their renderings. And it prevents scholars from checking their credentials."[33]

It must have been utterly embarrassing for the Watchtower Society when it became public who the translators of the *New World Translation* were. The reason for this is that the translation committee was completely unqualified for the task. Four of the five men on the committee had no Hebrew or Greek training whatsoever (they had only a high-school education). The fifth—Fred W. Franz—claimed to know Hebrew and Greek, but upon examination under oath in a court of law in Edinburgh, Scotland, was found to fail a simple Hebrew test.

Note the following cross-examination, which took place November 24, 1954, in this court:

> "Have you also made yourself familiar with Hebrew?"
>
> _"Yes."_
>
> "So that you have a substantial linguistic apparatus at your command?"
>
> _"Yes, for use in my biblical work."_
>
> "I think you are able to read and follow the Bible in Hebrew, Greek, Latin, Spanish, Portuguese, German, and French?"
>
> _"Yes."_[34]

The following day, Franz was put on the stand again, and the following interview took place:

> "You, yourself, read and speak Hebrew, do you?"
>
> _"I do not speak Hebrew."_
>
> "You do not?"
>
> _"No."_
>
> "Can you translate that into Hebrew?"
>
> _"Which?"_
>
> "That fourth verse of the second chapter of Genesis?"
>
> _"You mean here?"_
>
> "Yes."
>
> _"No."_[35]

The truth of the matter is that Franz—like the others in the *New World Translation* committee—cannot translate Hebrew or Greek. In fact, Franz dropped out of the University of Cincinnati after his sophomore year—and even while there, he had not been studying anything related to theological issues.

In view of the above facts, it is horrifying to ponder that over three million copies of the *New World Translation* are published each and every month by the Watchtower Society. What a travesty!

If the average Jehovah's Witness only knew the true history of the translation he holds so dearly. . . .

## The New Age Movement: A Literature Explosion

In 1980 prominent New Ager Marilyn Ferguson affirmed that "there are New Age publications of all kinds: radio programs and newsletters, directories of organizations, lists of resources, Yellow Pages and handbooks, and new journals about consciousness, myth, transformation, and the future. Thousands of spiritual titles roll off the presses in inexpensive editions."[36]

Since 1980, the New Age publishing industry has virtually exploded. Indeed, there are now some 2,500 occult and New Age bookstores in the United States and over 3,000 publishers of occult and New Age books, journals, and magazines.[37]

Even major secular publishing houses like Bantam and Ballantine have New Age divisions. The vice-president of Bantam books, Stuart Applebaum, said that metaphysical books are "one of our strongest categories" and are "getting even stronger."[38]

|| *There are over 3,000 publishers of occult and New Age literature.* ||

We have already touched on the phenomenal success of certain New Age books—including those of Shirley MacLaine, Marianne Williamson's *A Return to Love*, and *A Course in Miracles*. Below we shall examine a representative sampling of other New Age books that have made a significant impact in recent years.

## Kevin Ryerson: High-Profile New Age Channeler

Kevin Ryerson attained notoriety as Shirley MacLaine's channeler and even played himself in MacLaine's movie, *Out on a Limb*. Ryerson teamed up with Stephanie Harolde and wrote a book, *Spirit Communication: The Soul's Path*, in an effort to teach people all over the world how they can become channelers of spirit entities. The work was published and promoted by Bantam Books, a major player in the publishing world.

In this book, which Shirley MacLaine praises as the clearest and most comprehensive book on channeling she has read, Ryerson compares channeling to a radio broadcast. If two different radio stations are competing for the same frequency, by slightly adjusting the dial we can tune one frequency down and the other will come in more clearly. Kevin Ryerson, he tells us, is the channel that gets tuned down; this allows the other frequency (spirit entities from the other side) to come through. Ryerson furnishes readers with guidelines on how to "adjust the tuning" so that they—like he—can become channels.[39]

Over half of the book is a collection of the central teachings of the entities who communicate through Ryerson. These entities repeat the same old lies that are popular in the New Age movement: You are God, you have unlimited potential, you create your own reality, and there is no death.[40]

Regarding the possibility of demon possession, Ryerson asserts, "I personally believe there's a psychic lock on the frequency or vibration of each person's physical body that only we, ourselves, can match. It would be impossible for someone else to 'inhabit' our vibration." Besides, says Ryerson, "I trust the transformative process of the inner divine. . . . I believe that God acts as our personal bodyguard."[41]

God, of course, is not the "bodyguard" of the channel or medium, for He detests mediums: "Let no one be found among you . . . who is a medium or spiritist or who consults the dead. Anyone who does these things is detestable to the LORD" (Deuteronomy 18:10-12). Scripture attests not only that demonic possessions can occur (Matthew 8:28), but that "Satan himself masquerades as an angel of light" (2 Corinthians 11:14)—and is hence capable of impersonating benevolent spirit entities.[42] *(See* my book *The New Age Movement* [Zondervan, 1994] for more on the issue of New Age channeling.)

## Matthew Fox: *The Coming of the Cosmic Christ*

Another prominent New Ager who has influenced millions with his writings is the controversial Matthew Fox. Fox has long been an advocate of what he calls "Creation Spirituality"—a blend of mysticism, panentheism (a word meaning "all is in God and God is in all"), feminism, and environmentalism.

In his recent book, *The Coming of the Cosmic Christ* (a million-plus bestseller published by Harper & Row), Fox suggests that there is a major religious transformation currently underway, rooted in a "rediscovery" of the "Cosmic Christ." This transformation allegedly signals the beginning of a spiritual renaissance that can heal the pain caused by "the crucifixion [or ecological destruction] of Mother Earth."[43]

Fox begins the book by arguing that "Mother Earth is dying."[44] He then points to mysticism as "a resurrection story for our times."[45] Among other things, mysticism can enable people to enjoy union with the whole of creation (including Mother Earth). Indeed, Mother Earth may be saved by man's return to the mystical.

Fox's mystical orientation leads him to suggest that we abandon any further quest for the "historical Jesus" and refocus our attention on a "quest for the Cosmic Christ." He provides several definitions of the Cosmic Christ, the most important being "the pattern that connects."[46] The Cosmic Christ allegedly connects "heaven and earth, past and future, divinity and humanity, all of creation."[47]

Fox calls for a *deep ecumenism*, by which he means a genuine coming together of all persons of all religions at a mystical level.[48] This, of course, is made possible by the Cosmic Christ, "the pattern that connects." We must realize, declares Fox, that the *Kingdom/Queendom of God* is within us all.[49] This is not a surprising statement since as a panentheist Fox sees "all things in God and God in all things."[50] In order for people to come together at a mystical level, however, Fox believes they must become more right-brain oriented. This is because the right lobe of the brain is (allegedly) where man's mystical ability resides.[51]

For most Christians, Fox's many deviations from orthodoxy will be apparent. However, new Christians (or those who are biblically illiterate) could conceivably read his book and be led to believe that the ideas contained therein are compatible with Christianity. This would be tragic, for Fox's writings represent a radical departure from the historic faith. (Incidentally, Fox's book is endorsed on the back cover by *People of the Lie* author M. Scott Peck.)

Following are just a few of Fox's more blatant deviations: He completely robs Jesus Christ of His uniqueness; portrays Jesus as merely one of many enlightened individuals who have incarnated the Cosmic Christ; reduces Christianity to one of many viable options in the smorgasbord of world religions; argues that we must move from a "personal Savior" Christianity to a Cosmic Christ Christianity; chastises those who have stood against the goddess religions of the native peoples of the world; maternalizes the nature of God; exalts the cosmos to deity; superimposes New Age interpretations on countless biblical texts; devalues (denies?) man's sin problem; proposes a "cosmic redemption" based on a revival of mysticism rather than the work of the historical Jesus; and flatly denies the biblical teaching that homosexual acts are sinful, affirming instead that heterosexuality and homosexuality are equally acceptable to the Cosmic Christ.

Fox's Christianity is not just a _distortion_ of biblical faith; it bears no resemblance to it. His "Christ" is completely foreign to the pages of the New Testament, which is the only authentic source for knowledge about Christ and the Christian faith.

Though some of his ecological concerns are legitimate, Fox's cosmos-oriented Christianity must be likened to spiritual quicksand which can potentially swallow up innocent victims unaware of the dangerous ground on which they tread.

## Joseph Campbell: Posthumous New Age Prophet

It is estimated that more than 34 million people have watched "The Power of Myth" on television, a series of conversations that television host Bill Moyers taped with Joseph Campbell shortly before Campbell's death in 1986. A book with the same title—based on the television series—anchored itself on the _New York Times_ bestseller list for some 45 weeks. Moyers says he has received over 100,000 personal letters in response to the series.[52]

"The response to Campbell . . . has been the most phenomenal response to anything I have done in 18 years of television," Moyers said. "It is evidence of this profound search going on in this alienated world, looking for an experience of belief."[53]

A cursory scan through the _Power of Myth_ book shows that it is antagonistic toward Christianity and strongly favorable to New Age ideas about God and man. Campbell says that certain religious myths should be rejected as "out of date"—particularly the idea of a personal lawgiver God of the Jews and Christians. He believes that biblical cosmology does not "accord with our concept of either the universe or of the dignity of man. It belongs entirely somewhere else."[54] His New Age inclinations are also evident in the statement, "We are all manifestations of Buddha consciousness, or Christ consciousness, only we don't know it."[55]

Campbell is particularly bothered by the Christian concept of sin because he believes it stifles human potential. The very act of confessing sins makes a person a sinner, he says, while a confession of greatness makes one great.[56] The "idea of sin puts you in a servile position throughout your life."[57] Campbell later redefines sin as simply a lack of knowledge, not as a transgression against a moral and holy God. "Sin is simply a limiting factor that limits your consciousness and fixes it in an inappropriate condition."[58]

Campbell is adamant that the Christian Bible should not be interpreted in a literal sense. He refers to the biblical creation account as "artificialism," for example, and he reproves Bill Moyers for speaking of the resurrection of Christ in historic terms.[59] Moreover, Campbell says that Jesus' ascension into heaven, metaphorically interpreted, means that "he has gone inward—not into outer space but into inward space, to . . . the consciousness that is the source of all things, the kingdom of heaven within."[60]

Of course, by denying the physical resurrection of Christ, Campbell has driven a stake through the very heart of historic Christianity. One might recall that the apostle Paul said that if Christ be not raised, our Christian faith is in vain (1 Corinthians 15:14). If the doctrine of the resurrection is not true, then the apostles preached falsehoods, Christians are hopelessly left to wallow in their sin, believers who have died have truly perished forever, and followers of Christ are the most pitiful of all people because of their misplaced faith in a so-called resurrected Messiah (verses 15-19).

In response to Campbell, New Age critic Douglas Groothuis is right on target in saying that "Paul had no mere mythic symbol in mind here. Neither would the early Christians have died martyrs' deaths for metaphors. The apostle Peter, in his second epistle (1:16), went so far as to say that 'we did not follow cleverly invented stories when we told you about the power and coming of our Lord Jesus Christ, but we were eyewitnesses of his majesty.' "[61]

What are we to make of Joseph Campbell? Groothuis assesses him this way: "Campbell may not have countenanced it, but it may befall him to become a posthumous prophet for New Age sentiments. Although more of an academic than a popularizer, his world view is in basic agreement with New Age celebrities like Shirley MacLaine, Werner Erhard, and John Denver: All is one; God is an impersonal and amoral force in which we participate; supernatural revelation and redemption are not needed."[62]

Unfortunately, virtually millions of Americans have been influenced by the views of Joseph Campbell. There is no telling just how many people have been sucked into a New Age worldview as a result of reading *The Power of Myth,* or seeing its television counterpart.

## Al Gore's *Earth in the Balance*

In 1992 Vice President Al Gore published a book entitled *Earth in the Balance: Ecology and the Human Spirit* (Houghton Mifflin). The title to the book is based on an illustration used by the White House for a 1990 conference on the environment. As described by world religions specialist Dean Halverson, who reviewed Gore's book for the *Christian Research Journal*, "the illustration depicted a balance with the earth on one side and six gold bars on the other. Gore interpreted the illustration to mean that the Bush administration was trying to convince the world that the environment faces no serious dangers and that the wisdom of any effort to rescue it is outweighed by the cost."[63]

As indicated by the book's subtitle—*Ecology and the Human Spirit*—Gore believes that the current ecological crisis is actually a *spiritual* problem. Gore writes: "The more deeply I search for the roots of the global environmental crisis, the more I am convinced that it is an outer manifestation of an inner crisis that is, for lack of a better word, spiritual."[64]

What does Gore mean by "spiritual"? He defines it as "the collection of values and assumptions that determine our basic understanding of how we fit into the universe."[65] The key word here is "collection." Indeed, Gore *collects* his "values and assumptions" not only from Christianity (which is his professed religion), but from other sources as well—including the New Age movement.[66]

No one denies that Gore claims to be a Christian. In an interview with *Christianity Today*, Gore said, "The foundation of all of my work on the environment is my faith in Jesus Christ."[67]

However, there is also a heavy dose of New Age in Gore's worldview. An example would be Gore's openness to the idea that truth is found in *all* the religions of the world. Gore's language infers that he believes choosing a religion is simply a matter of personal preference and that Christianity is no more true than are other religions. One gets the idea that it's fine to choose Christianity, but choosing any other religion is equally fine *(see* pages 202, 244, and 368 in Gore's book).[68] Gore understands religious faith to be simply a matter of personal preference; *objective truth is not an issue.*[69]

In his book, Gore also seems to "divinize" humanity and the earth by saying that they share the same essence as God. He speaks of an interrelated "web of life" that closely resembles the pantheistic oneness of Hinduism and the New Age. All of us are "connected" to each other and to the Earth through this "web of life."

"This sense of being connected with all things," Dean Halverson observes, "is the essence of what Gore means by 'spiritual.' But such an understanding of 'spiritual' reveals how Gore's spirituality is aimed in the wrong direction—*toward the creation* rather than *toward the Creator.* Gore is concerned more with humanity's sense of separation from the earth than from God."[70]

Gore recommends the New Age concept of earth-centered oneness. He writes, "A modern prayer of the Onadanga tribe offers another beautiful expression of our essential connection to the earth: 'O Great Spirit, whose breath gives life to the world and whose voice is heard in the soft breeze . . . make us wise so that we may understand what you have taught us."[71] Gore then points to the world's Mother Earth religions—ancient goddess worship, Hinduism, European witchcraft, and the like—as models for living in harmony with nature.[72] Though Gore claims to be a Christian, his book essentially constitutes a strong endorsement of the New Age movement.

### New Age Books Go Mainstream

Because New Age books are becoming so popular, it is expected that in coming years, the purely New Age bookstore will become a thing of the past. A 1992 article entitled "Horizon 2000" in *Publishers Weekly* tells us that *"mainstreaming* is the byword for what [alternative booksellers] generally see happening to the [New Age] category in the next decade, as general trade publishers and general-interest book-sellers, in response to growing demand, continue to embrace the kinds of books now found on New Age bookstore shelves."[73]

> *The powers of darkness have declared literary war, and there will no doubt be many casualites.*

In other words, New Age bookstores will become a thing of the past because the books that have been traditionally sold in them will increasingly be carried by major distributors such as Waldenbooks and B. Dalton Books.

### Saints Alive!

We have just examined the ways in which the culting of America has been facilitated and accelerated by a cultic use of the 26 letters in the English alphabet. A tidal wave of cultic literature is literally engulfing the West.

As never before, then, Christians must equip themselves so they can shine as lights in a world of darkness. The powers of darkness have declared literary war, and there will no doubt be many casualties in the years to come. Unless Christians come alive and actively involve themselves in the battle, the West may be lost.

You and I are called by God to "contend for the faith that was once for all entrusted to the saints" (Jude 3). Joined together—as an army of contenders— you and I can make a difference, and we'll see more on just how we can do that in an upcoming chapter.

# 10

# The Culting of American Education, Business, and Health

*Iowa third-graders chant prayers to Mother Earth and practice Medicine Wheel Astrology. Connecticut fourth-graders use guided imagery to "experience" Indian tribal life and meet "wise" spirit helpers.*[1]

—Berit Kjos

*Dozens of major U.S. companies . . . are spending millions of dollars on so-called New Age workshops.*[2]

—The Wall Street Journal

*Holistic (New Age) health has been "legitimized by federal and state programs, endorsed by politicians, urged and underwritten by insurance companies, co-opted in terminology (if not always in practice) by many physicians, and adopted by medical students."*[3]

—Marilyn Ferguson

EDUCATION, BUSINESS, AND HEALTH—THESE three fields encompass a huge chunk of the American public. Consider for a moment: Education encompasses our nation's children, parents, and teachers; business embraces the men and women who make up our nation's work force; and health includes virtually all of us (we *all* get sick).

One way the culting of America has been facilitated and accelerated has been through the cultic penetration of these three fields, with the greatest influence coming from the New Age movement. In fact, as we will see below, millions of people have been introduced to the New Age worldview either at school, work, or the doctor's office.

> *New Agers recognize that public schools are* **the** *platform for indoctrinating massive numbers of young people with New Age ideas.*

## The Culting of American Education

New Agers, for one, recognize that if they are to succeed in bringing about an age of enlightenment and harmony, they must penetrate the educational institutions of the world. They recognize that the public school system is *the* primary platform for indoctrinating massive numbers of young people with New Age ideas. This is why they expend so much effort in influencing public school policies.

From elementary schools to advanced institutions of learning, the New Age movement has thoroughly penetrated the educational system in our country. In a *Washington Post* article, for example, we read of "pagans at the Harvard Divinity School. A Goddess-centered ritual at the University of Pennsylvania. A feminist seder [commemorative feast] in Silver Spring. New moon groups at a rabbinical seminary. Women's spirituality sessions at Appalachian State University."[4] The article asks, with obvious justification, "What on earth is going on?"[5]

One woman—a student of elementary education at one of the California State University campuses—had to read a number of pagan books as part of her curriculum. These included *When God Was a Woman*, *Return of the Goddess*, and *The Once and Future Goddess*.[6]

Christian author Berit Kjos speaks of the invasion of paganism into elementary schools: "Iowa third-graders chant prayers to Mother Earth and practice Medicine Wheel Astrology. Connecticut fourth-graders use guided imagery to 'experience' Indian tribal life and meet 'wise' spirit helpers. Oregon students celebrate Winter Solstice by acting the roles of the Sun God, Moon Goddess, drummers, and animal spirits."[7]

Christian parents have every reason to be concerned about what is going on in public schools across the country. Our children are being taught things that not only contradict but _stand against_ what they have learned as Christians.

## Curriculum Books Stripped of Christianity

Paul Vitz, in his important book _Censorship: Evidence of Bias in Our Children's Textbooks_, shows that Christianity and Christian values have been systematically stripped from our children's curriculum books.[8] It is highly revealing that while children's textbooks are silent on Christianity, many of them teach about Buddhism, Hinduism, Eastern meditation, magic, Indian spirituality, and yoga.[9]

Since Christianity and Christian values are omitted from the textbooks, it is implied that these are irrelevant and unimportant.[10] By contrast, New Age ideas—such as globalism, mysticism, Indian spirituality, the higher self, inner divinity, and much more—are viewed as necessary for "educational awareness" and have found their way into many school curriculums.

It is well known that students spend some 75 percent of classroom time and 90 percent of homework time with textbooks. It is therefore understandable why New Agers have made great efforts to get their ideas included in textbooks.[11]

## New Age Agenda for American Education

New Agers have a definite agenda for what they see as important for schoolchildren. New Ager Marilyn Ferguson shares her insights on the New Age educational curriculum: "Altered states of consciousness are taken seriously: 'centering' exercises, meditation, relaxation, and fantasy are used to keep the intuitive pathways open and the whole brain learning. Students are encouraged to 'tune in,' imagine, and identify the special feeling of peak experiences. There are techniques to encourage body awareness: breathing, relaxation, yoga, movements, and biofeedback."[12]

The New Age educational curriculum stresses personal autonomy and responsibility. Now, while these can be positive attributes, New Agers divorce them from the beliefs and values handed down by parents—and this includes values that Christian parents base on Scripture. Ferguson tells us, "A major ambition of the curriculum is autonomy. This is based on the belief that if our children are to be free, they must be free even from us, from our limiting beliefs and our acquired tastes and habits. At times this means teaching for healthy, appropriate rebellion, not conformity."[13]

## Distinctives of New Age Education

The distinctives of New Age education include—among many other things—right-brain learning, guided imagery, Values Clarification, and globalism. To get a better feel for what New Age education is like, let's take a brief look at each of these.

*Right-Brain Learning.* Educators say that the right side of the brain governs man's creative and intuitive abilities. The right-brain/left-brain distinction is not necessarily New Age in and of itself, but New Agers have appropriated the distinction as a means of justifying the introduction of "right-brain learning techniques" into the classroom.

Certainly I'm all for artistic creativity. But what bothers me about all this right-brain talk is that New Agers relate it to mysticism. New Ager Matthew Fox, for example, says the right portion of the brain is where man's mystical ability resides.[14] Shirley MacLaine agrees, and adds, "A person who thinks . . . with the right hemisphere is capable of seeing a broader connectedness to events that would be little more than a contradictory puzzle to a left-brained Westerner. . . . Eastern thinkers are more open to intuitive thinking."[15]

By including right-brain learning techniques, New Agers hope to accomplish what they call whole-brain learning as opposed to strictly left-brain (objective) learning. Right-brain learning techniques include various practices such as yoga, meditation, chanting, and visualization. By such practices, children are led to have mystical experiences. These practices have already entered a number of public schools around the country.

*Guided Imagery.* Guided imagery is also called "visualization." It is sometimes used to help students meet an inner "helper," "spirit guide," or "higher self."[16]

One case I'm aware of involved Susan Pinkston, a pastor's wife in California, who wrote about her ten-year-old son's experience as he was led through a guided imagery session by his teacher:

> He said she had them lie on the floor, close their eyes, breathe deeply, and count backward from ten. She then described a journey in which they were walking through a lovely meadow. They walked up the hillside and sprouted wings out their backs. They flew away to a cave; they walked into the cave and saw three doors. They opened one door and the room was filled with their 'heart's desire.' That room was to go to anytime [they were] under stress.[17]

Now, the imagination (which God Himself gave humans) _can_ be used in a positive way to create great music, art, books, and the like. But the human imagination can also be used _wrongly_—with damaging results. One must recognize that man's imagination has been marred by sin (Genesis 6:5). It is also important to realize that guided imagery sessions can induce an altered state of consciousness that can have extremely dangerous consequences.[18] The fact is, _any_ kind of activity that leads to an altered state of consciousness can open a person to demonic affliction.

_Values Clarification._ Values Clarification, as you might recall from my brief discussion in chapter 5, seeks to help students discover _their own_ values. The idea is that values are not to be imposed from _without_ (such as from Scripture or parents) but must be discovered _within._ The underlying assumption is that there are no absolute truths or values.[19] This thinking has penetrated the public school system on a wide level.[20]

One mother in Kenosha, Wisconsin, expressed great dismay at the Values Clarification her children learned in school. She said:

> By the time my first two children had reached third grade, I realized something was wrong. The child I took to school in the morning was not the child I picked up after school in the afternoon. If this change had been a positive change, reflecting academic progress, I would have been delighted. However, the change I noticed was in their value system. They seemed to be desensitized to the morals I had been trying to instill in them as their mother, and I thought that I had failed. . . . I failed because I had assumed that the schools my children were attending were like the schools I had attended. . . . I found instead that the thrust of schools had turned from education to indoctrination. I found the values I instilled in my children were not reinforced or respected by the schools, but were systematically challenged in the classroom.[21]

_Global Education._ This is a prominent aspect of the educational process among New Agers. It involves educating students to think of themselves as global citizens, in keeping with the New Age political agenda.[22]

In his book _Confronting the New Age_, Douglas Groothuis suggests five salient features of global education: 1) a desire to politicize children starting as early as possible in the child's life; 2) a liberal/pacifistic internationalism that stresses disarmament as the only appropriate approach to conflict; 3) an ethical and moral relativism; 4) moral equivalence ("all nations are morally equal"); and 5) the need for a one-world government.[23] Ideas such as these have made their way into a number of public school curriculums.

School textbooks that set forth globalism call for a *raised consciousness* among students. William Bennett, the former U.S. secretary of education, notes that curriculum guides for global education are "shot through with calls for 'raised consciousness,' for students and teachers to view themselves 'as passengers on a small cosmic spaceship,' for classroom activities involving 'intuiting,' 'imaging,' or 'visioning' a 'preferred future.' "[24]

Globalism is clearly rooted in the monistic ("all is one") and pantheistic ("all is God") worldview of the New Age movement. In his book on global education, *New Genesis: Shaping a Global Spirituality*, Robert Müller said:

> On a universal scale, humankind is seeking no less than its reunion with the "divine," its transcendence into ever higher forms of life. Hindus call our earth Brahma, or God, for they rightly see no difference between our earth and the divine. This ancient simple truth is slowly dawning again upon humanity . . . as we are about to enter our cosmic age and to become what we were always meant to be: the planet of God.[25]

## What Is a Parent to Do?

Because our children are surrounded by influences alien to their very beings, we as parents have a sobering responsibility to guard their welfare and to lead them in the ways of the Lord. We must equip them to recognize and resist subtle New Age deceptions in the classroom.

How can we do this? There are a number of steps that you, as a parent, can take.[26] For example:

- *You can become educated about the various New Age influences in the public school system.* For parents who want more information on this subject I recommend the book *Your Child and the New Age* by Berit Kjos (Victor Books).

- *You can keep abreast of what your child is learning in school.* Talk with your child about what he or she is learning. Be sure to scan through his or her textbooks and watch for any religious or anti-Christian elements. It is also wise and helpful to volunteer in your child's classroom as often as you can. By doing this, you can provide much-needed assistance, establish a positive relationship with the teacher and school, and observe firsthand what your child's learning environment is like.

- *You can learn about and exercise your rights as a parent.* For example, you can become familiar with *The Protection of Pupil Rights (Hatch) Amendment,* which says that public school instructional materials can be inspected by parents. You can also become familiar with the "equal protection" clause of the fourteenth amendment, which affirms that New Age educators have no more right to promote their beliefs in school than do Christians to promote their beliefs.

- *You can mobilize your efforts with other Christian families.* Remember, a rope of many strands is not easily broken. By uniting with other Christians who hold the same convictions you do, your voice becomes greatly amplified. There is strength in numbers!

- *You can equip your child to recognize spiritual deception.* Go over important New Age buzzwords like "meditation," "centering," "visualization," "guided imagery," "higher self," and "globalism." Warn your child *in advance* of the dangers of these practices and ideas. And be sure your child knows what the Bible has to say about God, Jesus Christ, man, and salvation.

By taking steps such as these, you can go a long way toward insulating your child from the influences of the New Age movement.

## The Culting of American Business

The business community in America has also been thoroughly penetrated by the New Age movement. A *Wall Street Journal* article reported that "business after business is putting its managers into 'New Age seminars' . . . all promise 'consciousness-raising' and nonreligious conversion resulting in a 'changed person.' "[27] Companies that have utilized the services of New Age seminars include Ford, Proctor & Gamble, TRW, Polaroid, and Pacific Telesis Group.[28]

Richard Watring, personnel director of Budget Rent-a-Car, polled 780 personnel directors in 1984. He found that 45 percent of them had "seen or used" one or more "psychotechnologies" of New Age consciousness-raising.[29] This percentage has risen significantly since that time. As I point out in *The New Age Movement* (Zondervan, 1994), "One reason so many

Fortune 500 companies have been eager to use New Age seminars is that they promise increased productivity, better employee relations, more creativity among workers, and—bottom line—*more sales*."[30]

### Coercion to Attend New Age Seminars

In recent years, many employees have complained about company leaders who coerced them to attend New Age seminars against their wishes. In 1989 *The Wall Street Journal* reported, "There is nothing voluntary, as a rule, in company-ordered group-psychology sessions. In most cases managers are simply told to attend. . . . They are ordered to attend a session aimed at 'changing their personality' because somebody claims that it's likely to be good for them or, maybe, good for the company—no one quite knows. Company ordered psychological [New Age] seminars of this kind are, in other words, an invasion of privacy that is not justified by company needs."[31]

Similarly, an article in *Fortune* magazine asserted, "It's one thing if an individual walks in off the street and signs up for a course, but quite another if your boss sends you. Then there's a level of coercion. Does my boss have the right to put me through training that conflicts with my religion and world view?"[32]

In the early 1990s, lawsuits began to be filed against employers who forced employees to attend New Age seminars. Lawsuits have also been filed against the seminars themselves. According to the *Los Angeles Times*, these lawsuits are part of "an emerging backlash against employers who try to boost productivity by requiring workers to take part in so-called human potential seminars, motivational programs designed to change workers' values, attitudes, and self-esteem."[33]

Many of the complaints against New Age seminars have been filed with the U.S. Equal Employment Opportunity Commission (EEOC), a government agency that investigates job discrimination claims. Because of increased complaints against New Age seminars, the EEOC ended up circulating a policy notice to commission employees to help them deal with this growing problem.

The policy notice cites Title VII of the Civil Rights Act, which protects employees from religious discrimination. The law requires employers to provide "reasonable accommodation" for an employee's religious beliefs unless it creates "undue hardship."[34]

The EEOC policy notice also says, "While there may be some disagreement over whether the training programs themselves are religious, an employee need only demonstrate that participation in the program in some manner conflicts with *his/her* personal religious beliefs." Those who do this are exempted from having to attend the seminar.[35]

## The Goal of New Age Seminars

Attend a New Age seminar, and you will hear that you are your own God, you can create your own reality, and you have unlimited potential. These three concepts may be considered the hallmark of such seminars.

In terms of methodology, the seminar leaders typically first attempt to shred the attendee's present worldview (or way of looking at reality). Then they endeavor to trigger an altered state of consciousness in hopes of inducing a mystical experience so powerful that it will cause the participant to question his or her previous understanding of reality.

The participant is then exposed to a New Age explanation that makes sense of the mystical experience. He or she is introduced to a *new* worldview which says that you are your own God and you can create your own reality.[36]

## *Est:* **Over 500,000 Attendees**

One of the more popular New Age seminars in years past has been *est*, founded by the controversial Werner Erhard. Though *est* is no longer around today (it's been repackaged with a new name—see the next section), over 500,000 people attended this training seminar.

*Est* taught people that they were their own gods and could create their own realities and remake their world. They were told that they were *totally responsible* for their circumstances—both good and bad—and could control their futures with godlike powers. Their potential was said to be unlimited.

Leaders of *est* seminars first sought to strip away the participants' worldview. New Age critic Tal Brooke comments, "Layers of cherished memories, beliefs, intimate secrets, and foundational presuppositions about reality were peeled back and shredded like someone hacking away at a raw onion. *Est* seminar attendees were systematically undone, shocked, as barriers were broken."[37] Once a person's former worldview was demolished, it was replaced with a new, mystical worldview in which he or she could act as his or her own god.

Suzanne Perkins, a former *est* worker, said that during her *est* training she was deprived of food and sleep as her worldview was attacked. "They broke down my moral and emotional standards." Indeed, "they said it was all right to sleep with your friend's husband because you can create the feeling of being guilty or feeling fine. You are your own God."[38]

## "The Forum" and "Transformational Technologies"—*Est* Repackaged

*Est* was later repackaged as The Forum, and then Transformational Technologies (or Trans Tech). The new versions of the seminar are milder, more professional, and sleeker—making them all the more appealing to a broader base of companies and businesses.

The Forum emphasizes getting in touch with "being": "Being is that dimension of ourselves that shapes our actions, our performance, and ultimately determines what we accomplish."[39] By getting in touch with "being," people learn to take action and improve their performance. This is one reason the seminar is popular among businesses. After all, improved performance ultimately means more money for the company. Like *est*, The Forum says you are your own god and you can create your own reality. Your potential is virtually unlimited.

Over the past decades, many companies have utilized the services of either *est*, The Forum, or Transformational Technologies. Among the companies that have sponsored *est* or The Forum are Allstate, Sears, General Dynamics, The Federal Aviation Administration, IBM, Boeing Aerospace, and Lockheed.[40] Transformational Technologies has penetrated about 100 of the Fortune 500 group of companies—including Ford, TRW, General Electric, McDonald's, and RCA.[41]

## Other Representative New Age Seminars

There are a number of other New Age seminars that have attained prominence in the business community. These include the Esalen Institute, Lifespring, and Pacific Institute.

*Esalen Institute.* This is a human potential group that offers a variety of seminars and workshops for "mind, body, and soul" at its Big Sur, California, headquarters. Michael Murphy founded the institute in 1962 after studying at an ashram (a religious community headed by a guru) in India.

The Esalen Institute has been called the "Harvard of the human potential movement."[42] Among the Eastern-styled seminars offered by the institute are ones dealing with guided imagery/visualization and sensory awakening.

*Lifespring.* This New Age consciousness-raising group teaches that human beings are perfect and good just the way they are, and promises its clients enlightenment. Lifespring teaches that all human beings already have everything necessary to achieve and be all that they want in their lives.

Lifespring emphasizes that people can create their own reality. Promotional literature for the seminar says that "we literally create our experience of life based upon our beliefs about ourselves and how we expect the universe to react to us."[43]

In Lifespring, "self" practically becomes an object of veneration. A promotional item urges: "Come and experience beyond self-esteem and self-worth to a sense of awe and veneration for who you are just as self-life is the greatest love."[44]

Lifespring also involves Eastern religion. "The seminars make use of the most effective principles, intellectual concepts, and techniques of parapsychology and Eastern disciplines."[45]

*Pacific Institute.* This institute is another human potential group that emphasizes self-actualization through visualization and affirmation (positive self-statements). This group stresses the intrinsic goodness and perfection of each person. Clients include many Fortune 500 companies—including ABC-TV, NASA, Eastman Kodak, AT&T, and IBM.

## Signposts for Identifying New Age Seminars

Since business seminars have been a primary means of bringing new converts into the New Age movement, Christians at the workplace have every reason to be concerned. But how can a New Age seminar be recognized?

Douglas Groothuis, in his book *Confronting the New Age*, has identified seven signposts for identifying such a seminar:

1) the use of visualization to create reality;

2) the use of positive affirmations (self-talk);

3) the use of some form of Eastern meditation or other "psycho-technologies";

4) extravagant promises regarding how the seminar can forever "change your life";

5) outrageous costs;

6) secrecy regarding the content of the seminars;

7) excessively long hours.[46]

Signposts such as these should raise a red flag in the minds of those who are thinking about attending a seminar. *Christians beware!* And *remember your rights!* You cannot be forced to attend a seminar that conflicts with your personal religious beliefs.

## The Culting of American Health

The New Age movement has also thoroughly penetrated the health field via what has come to be called "holistic health"—a New Age form of alternative medicine that has mushroomed in popularity over the last decade.

The word "holistic," when applied to health care, refers to an approach "that respects the interaction of mind, body, and environment."[47] Indeed, holistic health endeavors to focus on the *whole* person and his surroundings. As well, holistic medicine views "physical problems as having possibly mental or spiritual origin, besides organic. That is, the individual is looked at in a holistic way, as a body, mind, and spirit, not only the physical body."[48]

> *A significant percentage of Christians believe certain New Age practices are compatible with Christianity.*

Some aspects of holistic health are quite reasonable and are hence acceptable to the Christian. As we will see below, however, many New Age health therapies betray an unchristian worldview and lack scientific basis.

### How Popular Are New Age Health Therapies?

*Time* magazine reported in 1991 that alternative (New Age) medicine is "now a $27 billion-a-year industry." The magazine noted that 30 percent of the people it polled had tried an unconventional therapy.[49] A 1993 *Newsweek* article pointed out that Dr. David Eisenberg and colleagues "reported that 34 percent of the people they surveyed had used at least one unconventional therapy in the past year. . . . That works out to 61 million Americans."[50]

These statistics are of great concern. The fact is, many people—even Christians—have been introduced to the New Age worldview by being treated with a holistic therapy. Sad to say, a significant percentage of Christians are of the opinion that certain New Age practices are compatible with Christianity.[51] Indeed, some 23 percent of Protestants and 59 percent of Catholics indicated they thought certain New Age practices were compatible with Christianity.[52]

**Energetic Medicine**

The New Age model of holistic health—encompassing a variety of "energetic" healing therapies—is based primarily on energy, not matter. Parapsychologist Thelma Moss, who has done extensive research on alleged healing energies, says, "Is there a common thread that can be discerned through these various phenomena of healing? I believe so. The Hindus call it 'prana,' the Hawaiians 'mana,' the Chinese 'ch'i,' and Hippocrates called it the 'heat oozing out of my hand.' Mesmer 'animal magnetism,' and Quimby 'mind force.' I believe they were all referring to the _same invisible energy_."[53]

This is not a scientifically explainable or physical energy (like electricity). Rather, New Agers speak of a "cosmic" or "universal" energy that is based on their monistic (all is one) and pantheistic (all is God) worldview.[54] Douglas Groothuis explains, "The universal energy of which we are all a part is frequently cited as the source of healing. We are not clumps of dead matter but configurations of active energy. To increase the flow of healing energy we must attune ourselves to it and realize our unity with all things."[55]

New Age critic Elliot Miller points to the strong connection between occultism and energetic medicine: "Wherever it has appeared—in ancient paganism, modern occultism, or parapsychological research—this 'life force' has been accompanied by altered states of consciousness, psychic phenomena, and contact with spirits. Additionally, those who are capable of perceiving, and adept at manipulating, this force invariably are shamans (e.g., witch doctors), 'sensitives,' or psychics, thoroughly immersed in the pagan/occult world."[56]

Many holistic health therapies seek to enhance the flow of "healing energy" in the body. Unfortunately, by engaging in such practices, many people have been sucked headlong into New Age occultism. Indeed, as Miller puts it, "my wide-ranging research of occultism emboldens me to suggest that this energy is part and parcel of the occult—where the occult appears, it can be found; where it is found, the occult will inevitably appear."[57]

Now, it is beyond the scope of this chapter to provide a full explanation of the various New Age holistic health therapies. But I do want to mention four of the more popular ones to give you a feel for the kinds of energetic therapies I'm talking about. (Good sources are available for those interested in more detailed study.)[58]

_Therapeutic Touch._ This is a therapy in which the practitioner "channels" the "universal life energy" for the ailing patient (by touch) and then helps him or her to assimilate this energy. This assimilation allegedly brings healing to the body.

*Rolfing.* This therapy is based on the assumption that sickness is caused by energy blockages in the body. Rolfing seeks to relieve such energy blockages by applying deep pressure or massage to the body. It has been described as "massage with a vengeance."

*Acupuncture/Acupressure.* Both of these therapies seek to unblock and redirect energy flow in the body as a means of healing.

*Chiropractic.* Some chiropractors are New Agers. In their treatments they typically combine spinal adjustments with some form of "energy balancing" to treat various bodily ailments.[59] I must point out, however, that a number of chiropractors are *not* New Agers. They do not subscribe to the New Age worldview—disavowing any use of "energy balancing"[60]—and simply use chiropractic as a therapy for neuromusculoskeletal disorders (such as backaches).

These and a number of other New Age health therapies have served to introduce virtually millions of Americans to a New Age worldview. New Age medicine—with its heavy emphasis on energy balancing—is truly a gateway into the New Age.

## Christians Beware!

How should the Christian view New Age energetic medicine? In answering this question, Elliot Miller has rightly pointed out that if this energy is inherently occultic (and thus demonic), then Christians involved with it may become confused and compromised. "Continued involvement could gradually lead to further involvement with the occult, and the deterioration of Christian faith and life. I am aware of cases where this scenario has indeed been lived out, and I find no assurance that the same will not ultimately hold true for all who become deeply involved with this energy."[61]

Hence, Miller warns, "Christians who believe in the supreme authority of Scripture must also believe in the biblical doctrine of Satan and his pervasive influence in this present world system. If 'the whole world lies in the power of the evil one' (1 John 5:19), how much more the kingdom of the occult, his unique domain! Thus Christians have reason to be cautious concerning phenomena that has had a long and strong connection to the realm of occultism and paganism."[62]

# 11

## The Lure of Money, Sex, and Power

*The Bible says that [Jesus] has left us an example that we should follow His steps. That's the reason why I drive a Rolls Royce. I'm following Jesus' steps.*[1]

—Frederick K.C. Price

*We have a sexy God and a sexy religion. . . . Salvation sets us free from the curse of clothing and the shame of nakedness! We're as free as Adam and Eve in the Garden before they ever sinned! . . . Be liberated tonight! Hallelujah!*[2]

—"Moses" David Berg

*If we accept the basic premise that our thoughts create our reality, it means that we need to take responsibility for creating all of our reality—the parts we like and the parts we don't like.*[3]

—David Gershon and Gail Straub

DO YOU KNOW ANYONE who can be lured by money? Seduced by sex? Enticed by power? Most of the human race, you say? You're probably right.

I think I'm safe in saying that few issues touch us more profoundly or universally than money, sex, and power. Indeed, no topics stir greater controversy. And no human realities have a greater potential to bring either a blessing or a curse to people.[4]

In this chapter, we will see that a wrong and perverted use of money, sex, and power have played a definite role in luring people into cultic groups and *keeping* them there. To illustrate this, we will focus our attention on the Word-Faith movement, the Children of God, and a key element of the New Age movement.

## For the Love of Money: The Word-Faith Movement

"Name it and claim it" has become a household phrase in millions of homes across America. Why is this so? Word-Faith teachers like Kenneth Hagin, Kenneth Copeland, Frederick Price, John Avanzini, Robert Tilton, Marilyn Hickey, Paul Yonggi Cho, Charles Capps, Jerry Savelle, Morris Cerullo, and Paul Crouch all teach this doctrine on the powerful platform of the Trinity Broadcasting Network (TBN)—watched by millions every evening.[5]

Just about every night on TBN a person can tune in and learn how to gain wealth by following the prosperity formulas of Word-Faith teachers. These formulas, however, have more in common with cultic metaphysics than with Christianity.

Word-Faith teachers are indebted to Phineas P. Quimby's metaphysical school of thought, which came to be known as "New Thought." Quimby taught his followers that they could create their own reality through the power of positive affirmation. By using creative visualization, one can allegedly transform intangible images into tangible reality.[6] I discussed this aspect of New Thought in my book, *The Counterfeit Christ of the New Age Movement:*

> According to New Thought, human beings can experience health, success, and abundant life by using their thoughts to define the condition of their lives. New Thought proponents subscribe to the "law of attraction." This law says that just as like attracts like, so our thoughts can attract the things they want or expect. Negative thoughts are believed to attract dismal circumstances; positive thoughts attract more desirable circumstances. Our thoughts can be either creative or destructive. New Thought sets out to teach people how to use their thoughts creatively.[7]

### The Prosperity Gospel of the Word-Faith Teachers

The Word-Faith teachers set forth a gospel of greed and avarice. It is not the gospel of the Bible (1 Corinthians 15:1-4). Their gospel is commonly known as the "prosperity gospel"—setting forth the idea that it is God's will that all Christians be wealthy. Let's touch on some key elements of this deviant theology.

*God desires His children to be wealthy.* Kenneth Hagin says that God not only wants to deliver believers from poverty, "He [also] wants His children to eat the best, He wants them to wear the best clothing, He wants them to drive the best cars, and He wants them to have the best of everything."[8] Frederick Price likewise boasts, "If the Mafia can ride around in Lincoln Continental town cars, why can't the King's Kids?"[9]

*It is a sin to be poor.* Word-Faith teachers often communicate the idea that it is sinful to be in a state of poverty. Robert Tilton is representative: "Not only is worrying a sin, but being poor is a sin when God promises prosperity!"[10]

One wonders whether Tilton and other Word-Faith teachers have read their Bibles recently! Did not Jesus say, "Blessed are you who are poor" (Luke 6:20)?

*God doesn't expect us to serve Him for free.* Frederick Price explains that "most employers at least have enough common decency about them that they don't ask somebody to work for them *for free.* . . . If a man has enough nicety about him to do that, can't you at least believe that the Father God is not asking you to serve Him *for free* either?"[11]

*Jesus is our example, and He was not poor.* Jesus' alleged wealth is a favorite theme among Word-Faith teachers. Consider the following:

- Frederick Price says he's trying "to get you out of this malaise of thinking that Jesus and the disciples were poor. . . . The Bible says that He has left us an example that we should follow His steps. That's the reason why I drive a Rolls Royce. I'm following Jesus' steps."[12]

- John Avanzini attacks apologists and theologians for teaching that Jesus was poor. Outraged, he snorts, "I don't know where these goofy traditions creep in at, but one of the goofiest ones is that Jesus and His disciples were poor. Now there's no Bible to substantiate that."[13]

- Avanzini adds, "John 19 tells us that Jesus wore designer clothes. Well, what else you gonna call it? Designer clothes—that's blasphemy. No, that's what we call them today. I mean, you didn't get the stuff He wore off the rack. It wasn't a one-size-fits-all deal. No, this was custom stuff. It was the kind of a garment that kings and rich merchants wore. Kings and rich merchants wore that garment."[14]

▪ Avanzini elsewhere boasted, "Jesus had a nice house, a big house—big enough to have company stay the night with Him at the house. Let me show you His house. Go over to John the first chapter and I'll show you His house. Now, child of God, that's a house big enough to have company stay the night in. There's His house."[15]

▪ Avanzini further claimed that "Jesus was handling big money because that treasurer He had was a thief. Now you can't tell me that a ministry with a treasurer that's a thief can operate on a few pennies. It took big money to operate that ministry because Judas was stealing out of that bag."[16]

▪ In like manner, Frederick Price said:

> The Bible says that He [Jesus] had a treasurer—a treasury (they called it "the bag"); that they had one man who was the treasurer, named Judas Iscariot; and the rascal was stealing out of the bag for three-and-a-half years and nobody knew that he was stealing. You know why? Because there was so much in it. . . . Nobody could tell that anything was missing. . . . Besides that, if Jesus didn't have anything, what do you need a treasury for? A treasury is for surplus. It's not for that which you're spending. It's only for surplus—to hold it until you need to spend it. Therefore, He must have had a whole lot that needed to be held in advance that He wasn't spending. So He must have had more than He was living on.[17]

*God sets forth laws of prosperity in the Bible.* Kenneth Copeland is representative in teaching that "there are certain laws governing prosperity in God's Word. Faith causes them to function. . . . The success formulas in the Word of God produce results when used as directed."[18] Copeland and others teach these laws to millions on the Trinity Broadcasting Network.

*Positive confession is the key to gaining wealth.* If we want wealth, all we have to do is *speak* it into existence. Marilyn Hickey often affirms on her television show that *confession brings possession.*[19]

Kenneth Copeland likewise says:

*You can have what you say!* In fact, what you are saying is exactly what you are getting now. If you are living in poverty and lack and want, change what you are saying. It will change what you have. . . . Discipline your vocabulary. Discipline everything you do, everything you say, and everything you think to agree with what God does, what God says, and what God thinks. God will be obligated to meet your needs because of His Word. . . . If you stand firmly on this, your needs will be met.[20]

*Giving money to God's work can yield a hundredfold increase.* Based on a complete distortion of Mark 10:30, Gloria Copeland—wife of the famous televangelist Kenneth Copeland—explains the "hundredfold return" this way:

> You give $1 for the Gospel's sake and $100 belongs to you; give $10 and receive $1,000; give $1,000 and receive $100,000. I know that you can multiply, but I want you to see it in black and white and see how tremendous the hundredfold return is. . . . Give one house and receive one hundred houses or one house worth one hundred times as much. Give one airplane and receive one hundred times the value of the airplane. Give one car and the return would furnish you a lifetime of cars. In short, Mark 10:30 is a very good deal.[21]

In his book *The Laws of Prosperity*, Kenneth Copeland similarly writes, "Do you want a hundredfold return on your money? Give and let God multiply it back to you."[22] He urges his supporters, "Invest heavily in God; the returns are staggering, 100 to 1!"[23] Again, "Every man who invests in the Gospel has a right to expect the staggering return of one hundredfold."[24]

*Giving liberally to TBN can get you out of debt.* Paul Crouch boasts, "If you're broke, if you're at your wit's end, if you're out of a job, out of work, let me tell ya. Not only are we gonna bless the world and preach Christ to millions and multitudes around the world, but you can be saved, yourself, by planting seed in this fertile soil called TBN."[25]

*Whatever you do, don't pray, "If it be Your will."* Kenneth Hagin urges his followers, "It is unscriptural to pray, 'If it is the will of God.' When you put an 'if' in your prayer, you are praying in doubt."[26]

How unbiblical can you get? First John 5:14 clearly says, "This is the confidence we have in approaching God: that *if* we ask anything *according to his will*, he hears us" (emphasis added; cf. Matthew 6:10; 26:39; James 4:15).

### Christians Enticed

Tragically, millions of Christians are being enticed into the cultic Word-Faith movement through this gospel of prosperity. They are being lured into seeking what is on the Master's table rather than seeking the Master's face.

> *It is impossible to calculate just how many lives have been shattered as a result of this deviant, cruel theology.*

I am even personally aware of elderly Christians who have given their life savings to ministries such as Robert Tilton's, in hopes of bringing financial blessing on themselves in their later years. Instead, they end up in bankruptcy. It is impossible to calculate just how many lives have been shattered as a result of this deviant, cruel theology.

### The Bible and the Pursuit of Financial Prosperity

It is not necessary to biblically refute each of the above elements of the prosperity message; this has been more than adequately done in other books.[27] However, a brief perusal of key passages relating to the overall perspective God desires us to have toward money and riches would be a helpful contrast to the Word-Faith distortions.

First, let's recognize that God does not condemn possessions or riches *per se*. It is not a sin to be wealthy! (Some very godly people in the Bible—Abraham and Job, for example—were quite wealthy.) But God does condemn a *love* of possessions or riches (Luke 16:13; 1 Timothy 6:10; Hebrews 13:5). A love of material things is a sure sign that a person is living according to a temporal perspective, not an eternal one.

Scripture tells us that a love of money and riches can lead to sure destruction. The apostle Paul flatly stated that "people who want to get rich fall into temptation and a trap and into many foolish and harmful desires that plunge men into ruin and destruction" (1 Timothy 6:9). Paul also warned that "there will be terrible times in the last days. People will be *lovers of themselves, lovers of money . . . lovers of pleasure* rather than lovers of God—having a form of godliness but denying its power" (2 Timothy 3:1-5, emphasis added).

Jesus understandably warned His followers, "Watch out! Be on your guard against all kinds of greed; a man's life does not consist in the abundance of his possessions" (Luke 12:15). He urged us to have an eternal perspective, exhorting, "Do not store up for yourselves treasures on earth, where moth and rust destroy, and where thieves break in and steal. But store up for yourselves treasures in heaven" (Matthew 6:19,20; cf. John 6:27).

In His famous Sermon on the Mount, we find these words of wisdom from Jesus:

> Therefore I tell you, do not worry about your life, what you will eat or drink; or about your body, what you will wear. Is not life more important than food, and the body more important than clothes? Look at the birds of the air; they do not sow or reap or store away in barns, and yet your heavenly Father feeds them. Are you not much more valuable than they? Who of you by worrying can add a single hour to his life? And why do you worry about clothes? See how the lilies of the field grow. They do not labor or spin. Yet I tell you that not even Solomon in all his splendor was dressed like one of these. If that is how God clothes the grass of the field, which is here today and tomorrow is thrown into the fire, will he not much more clothe you, O you of little faith? So do not worry, saying, "What shall we eat?" or "What shall we drink?" or "What shall we wear?" (Matthew 6:25-31).

In view of the above, Jesus urges, "Seek first his kingdom and his righteousness, and all these things will be given to you as well" (Matthew 6:33). In other words, living for God in a righteous way should be our top priority. When we do this, we can rest assured that God will provide us with the necessities of life. And if God in His sovereign grace should bless us with material wealth, as He did Abraham and Job, we can use it for His glory and for the extension of His kingdom. We can use such wealth as a channel of blessing for others.

Our attitude should be that whether we are rich or poor (or somewhere in between), we are simply stewards of what God has provided us. Our attitude should mirror that of the apostle Paul, who said, "I know what it is to be in need, and I know what it is to have plenty. I have learned the secret of being content in any and every situation, whether well fed or hungry, whether living in plenty or in want. I can do everything through him who gives me strength" (Philippians 4:12,13).

## Sexual Perversion in the Kingdom of the Cults

In his book *The Lure of the Cults*, sociologist Ron Enroth says that one of the hallmarks of false religion is "the corruption and distortion of human sexuality."[28] Perhaps this is nowhere better illustrated than with a cult known as the Children of God, also called "The Family," which I will discuss at length. I must warn you, however, that some of what follows may be offensive to sensitive readers. I include it not to be shocking or insensitive, but to show just how perverse a cultic view of sexuality can become and demonstrate what kind of damage can be done to families, especially children.

### The Children of God and "Flirty Fishing"

The Children of God have long used sex as a means of bringing people into their cult. The activity of drawing people into the cult this way has been called "flirty fishing," or "FFing." One Children of God document shockingly said, "May God help us all to be flirty little fishies for Jesus to save lost souls. . . . God bless and make you a flirty little Fishy for Jesus!"[29]

"Moses" David Berg, the founder of the cult, prayed for the typical Children of God witness this way: "Help her, O God, to catch men! Help her to catch men, be bold, unashamed and brazen, to use anything she has, O God, to catch men for Thee!—Even if it be through the flesh, the attractive lure, delicious flesh on a steel hook of Thy reality, the steel of Thy Spirit!"[30]

Berg instructed that potential converts "should fall in love with you first, and then with the Lord! Now you and your flesh and your spirit and your love and real affection are the bait. But particularly your flesh is the bait."[31]

The Children of God's 1979 annual report boasted, "Our dear Flirty Fishers are still going strong, God bless'm, having now witnessed to over a quarter-of-a-million souls, loved over 25,000 of them, and won nearly 19,000 to the Lord, along with about 35,000 new friends."[32]

Berg once said that "there is nothing wrong with a sexy conversion. We believe sex is a human necessity, and in certain cases we may go to bed with someone to show people God's love."[33] Notice how God's love is redefined by Berg to be *physical passion*.

Berg once said:

> We have a sexy God and a sexy religion with a very sexy leader with an extremely sexy young following! So if you don't like sex, you'd better get out while you can still save your bra!

> Salvation sets us free from the curse of clothing and the shame of nakedness! We're as free as Adam and Eve in the Garden before they ever sinned! If you're not, you're not fully saved! Come on Ma! Burn your bra! Be liberated tonight! Hallelujah![34]

Berg even blasphemes to the point of calling God a pimp who makes the church His prostitute.[35] He said, "The Lord showed me how he literally shares his wife, the Church, with the world to prove His Love. . . . God is a Pimp! How about that!—Boom! He's the biggest one there is—He uses His Church all the time to win souls and win hearts to Him to attract them to Him."[36]

## The Children of God and "Love" in the Family

An interview with ex-Children of God members in _Christianity Today_ magazine indicated that extramarital sex and wife-swapping were commonplace in this cult:

> Married couples were encouraged as a group to participate in "skinny-dipping"—swimming in the nude. It was considered unrevolutionary not to participate. . . . It was also policy for all married couples to attend evening "leadership training" sessions. . . . These sessions would be held by David Berg, and no matter what subject they started out about they always ended up on the subject of sex, with David Berg quite frequently leading the couples into a mass lovemaking session while he looked on.[37]

Berg believed that the injunction in Acts 2:44—concerning believers having "everything in common"—applied even to husbands and wives. This is scripture-twisting at its worst.[38]

Children were not exempt from Berg's sexual perversions. He even suggested that parents masturbate their young boys at bedtime and instructed young female followers in the art of luring men into the group: "Tease him, flirt with him, then screw him until he drops over," Berg is quoted as saying.[39]

Berg encouraged adults to play and sleep together nude among their children, allowing full sexual exploration and activity.[40] Berg wrote, "They should be encouraged in nude mixed bathing and nude mixed play where socially, legally, and climatically permissible, acceptable, and advisable.

They should also not be inhibited from mutual and self-sexual examination, experimentation, or interplay when playing or sleeping together where legally possible and social and housing conditions permit."[41]

## A Case Study: Dalva Lynch

Dalva Lynch spent some 15 years with the Children of God.[42] In her story, published in the *Christian Research Journal*, the sexual perversions of the Children of God become appallingly clear. She explains a typical Children of God scene:

> The guitars ring out happily as the young, smiling musicians play songs so the others can dance. Most of them are young, too, and a bit inhibited.[43]
>
> The music builds, faster and faster, in a rock rhythm. The blood begins to warm up, and inhibitions begin to drop. "Free, eternally free, every day, free, free through Jesus!" they sing in unison, more and more strongly.[44]
>
> Inhibitions finally evaporate as the loud, rhythmic singing continues. One girl starts to take off her blouse. Another follows suit. Everyone dances, their arms raised as they shout, "Hallelujah, Jesus, we're free!" As their clothing falls to the ground they begin caressing each other's bodies.[45]
>
> And so, this special night of the new disciples' "Basic Course" at the "Babe's Ranch" ends in success. Couples and threesomes lie on the ground, or divide themselves among the rooms, in fulfillment of the law of God to "love one another" (John 15:12) and begin at last to be "like the angels of God in heaven," who "neither marry, nor are given in marriage" (Matt. 22:30). They have finally reached the "glorious liberty of the children of God" (Rom. 8:21) and can now be truly considered Children of God.[46]

Sexual perversion such as this was also characteristic of young children in the cult. Dalva vividly recalls what things were like for children during her years with the Children of God:

> From earliest infancy, the cult's children are taught the basic principle of sexual freedom. Children are encouraged to stimulate each other sexually and to take part in sexual acts with

adults. In the past Moses David has vehemently denied that incest is practiced among them on the pretext that, legally, the word requires actual penetration (which is not permitted in the Children of God, since this could hurt the little girls). But everything else is permitted, and the fathers are free to lie with their little daughters to "play," and the mothers to maintain sexual relations with their little boys.[47]

"My little ones," Dalva recalls, "were introduced to the 'delights of sex.'" Indeed, "at night, under the supervision of an obliging adult, the children between three and ten years old said their prayers and were separated into their beds by pairs—_to make love before going to sleep._"[48]

"Once I found my oldest son all alone, crying," Dalva said. "'The girls don't want to make love to me,' he sobbed. I started to talk to him, but the [Children of God] Shepherdess brusquely swept me aside, knelt beside him, and explained: 'You have to be more aggressive, David, and take the initiative! Then they'll like it and want to make love with you!' My poor seven-year-old—so shy and withdrawn."[49]

The Children of God cult is now raising the next generation of members—the offspring _born_ in the cult—and is apparently reaping the whirlwind because of its libertinism.[50] "The consequences of such practices have been disastrous," Dalva says. "Because one-third of the [Children of God's] second generation is now between 12 and 18 years of age, promiscuity has become rampant, along with the problems which obviously follow. That is why they have created the 'Teen Ranches'—which are, in truth, simply centers for psychological recovery and indoctrination."[51]

At these teen ranches, Children of God girls—who were given questionnaires to gauge the effectiveness of their indoctrination—"responded almost unanimously that their greatest trauma was that of sexual sessions with their own fathers, or with other older male members, who physically imposed themselves on the girls with threats that if they refused they would be considered rebellious."[52]

Does the Children of God cult still focus on sex today? Dalva responds that

nearly all the educational literature for children and young people is _still_ sexually oriented. _(Heaven's Girl,_ for example, is about the adventures of a teenage girl with supernatural powers, and of her FFing [i.e., sexual] conquests and adventures.) In fact, a large section of one of the books most read to children tells of the adventures of "Grandpa" (Moses David) in heaven and in the spirit world, parts of which are little more than breathless descriptions of his sexual activities with deceased girls from the group.[53]

## Resurfacing in the United States

Under fire from deprogrammers and child-abuse authorities, the Children of God fled from the United States in the mid-1970s. However, they have recently resurfaced in the States renamed as "The Family," with members saying they have changed. But cult watchers and former cult members are very skeptical—and for good reason.[54]

A 1993 report in the *Christian Research Journal* quotes former Children of God member and family researcher Ruth Gordon as saying, "Part of their [present] plan is to lay a fresh groundwork as if [alleged past practices of child sexual abuse and sexual deviancy] never occurred. It is no different from a brand-name company changing their label but not their content."[55]

Recent police raids conducted against the Children of God would seem to confirm the cult's continued emphasis on perverted sex. In September of 1993, 180 police officials raided a complex of seven residences in an upscale Buenos Aires neighborhood which housed the Argentine headquarters of The Family. According to news reports, "authorities detained 30 adults, took 268 children into protective custody, and seized an undisclosed number of allegedly pornographic videos and other materials."[56]

As reported in the *Christian Research Newsletter*, "A Reuters news dispatch told of 'grisly details' emerging 'about hard-core videos of sex between adults and children' and Argentine officials' claims that 'at least some of the children appear to be mentally impaired.' The Brazilian newsweekly *Veja* reported that authorities apprehended at least one video showing scenes of boys masturbating before adults, and another depicting sexual acts between a father and his daughter."[57] In view of this, it is understandable why many are dismayed that the Children of God have returned to the United States.

## The Pursuit of Power

How would you like to have the power to attain everything you ever wished for in life? You can, according to David Gershon and Gail Straub. In their blockbuster New Age book, *Empowerment: The Art of Creating Your Life as*

_You Want It,_ Gershon and Straub tell us that "empowerment" is the key, for this will give you the ability to create your own reality by the power of your mind. What "manifests" in your life will be a direct result of the thoughts you affirm—either on a conscious or unconscious level.

Since the attainment of personal power is a common theme of New Age seminars, and since the Empowerment Workshop seminar is one of the more popular seminars among New Agers, we shall narrow our attention to this one workshop as a case study. We will see that Gershon and Straub's central idea is that empowerment "will free you from boundaries that have limited you in the past and show you your power to shape your own destiny. On this journey you will learn the art of creating your life as you want it."[58] Like other New Age seminars, the Empowerment Workshop is all about _power_ and how to get what you want in life.

You have probably already noticed how similar this sounds to the "name it and claim it" or "confession brings possession" doctrine of the Word-Faith movement. Make no mistake about it: there's a noticeable connection (_both_ camps derived their ideas from the metaphysical cults). While Gershon and Straub's seminar focuses more on personal power, practically speaking, there is not a whole lot of difference (at least at the root level) between what they say about empowerment and what Kenneth Hagin and other Word-Faith teachers say about the prosperity gospel.

## Creating Your Own Reality

The idea that a person's beliefs create his or her own reality forms the conceptual basis of Gershon and Straub's Empowerment Workshop.[59] They explain it this way: "Of all the knowledge pertaining to the evolution of the human condition that has come to light in this extraordinary time in which we live, none is more promising than this idea: _We make and shape our character and the conditions of our life by what we think._ What you think and believe will manifest in your life. By becoming adept at intelligently _directing_ your thought, you can become adept at creating the life that you want. You can take charge of your destiny."[60]

Gershon and Straub note that "we can't avoid creating our reality; each time we think a thought we are creating it. Every belief we hold is shaping what we experience in our life."[61] In view of this, "if we accept the basic premise that our thoughts create our reality, it means that we need to take responsibility for creating _all_ of our reality—the parts we like and the parts we don't like."[62]

## Dealing with Limiting Beliefs

What makes matters complicated, Gershon and Straub tell us, is that we are often not aware of what we believe, and of how ingrained negative thoughts can affect us in bad ways. "We indiscriminately accept many limiting beliefs and never realize how much of an effect they are having on our lives. Thoughts like 'I'm not good enough' or 'I don't have what it takes to have a loving relationship, prosperity, the work I want, peace of mind, etc.' profoundly influence the shape of our individual worlds. Most of our pain, fear, and suffering are caused by these unconscious, unexamined, self-limiting beliefs."[63]

To be able to create the new reality we desire, we must first clear out the old. "We can't effectively manifest a new belief if we are simultaneously holding on to an old, entrenched belief that opposes this new idea."[64]

## Affirmations and Visualizations

Gershon and Straub offer us a game plan for achieving empowerment that focuses on making effective use of *affirmations* (positive self-talk) and *visualizations* (mental pictures of what you want to create). Detailed guided-imagery exercises are provided in successive chapters for letting go of unhealthy emotions, enhancing personal relationships, enjoying sexuality, getting in tune with your body, and improving attitudes toward money, work, and spirituality. By using these affirmations and visualizations, Gershon and Straub assure us that we will attract the worldly "nutrients" needed to have our "mental seed" grow to "fruition."[65]

This New Age team also provides a list of "limiting beliefs" and accompanying "turnarounds." By affirming the turnarounds, we are told, we can dispose of unhealthy beliefs that limit us. Here are a few examples:

*Limiting belief:* God is a male figure with a lot of power who will punish me if I don't do the right thing.

*Turnaround:* I create God as a loving, kind, playful, wise, powerful friend. We play together co-creating the universe.[66]

*Limiting belief:* Spirituality means giving over control of my life to some higher power that's outside of me.

*Turnaround:* God's will is my own highest consciousness in this moment.[67]

*Limiting belief:* To be spiritual I must follow a code of conduct laid out by a religion/guru/writer of a spiritual book.

_Turnaround:_ My spirituality grows out of my own self-knowledge. I trust it and found my actions upon it.[68]

_Limiting belief:_ The world is full of corrupt, evil people who are leading it down a road of destruction.

_Turnaround:_ I take responsibility to create the world as a beautiful and sacred place filled with beings committed to their own and the planet's evolution.[69]

_Limiting belief:_ Working to earn money requires that I subjugate the spiritual and creative aspects of my life.

_Turnaround:_ I make earning money a creative and spiritual activity.[70]

By using positive affirmations such as these—combined with visualizations—our thoughts can allegedly begin to change the reality around us. By using our minds, we have true _power_.

## Ethics Anyone?

There are many ways a Christian could critique this idea of creating one's reality by the power of the mind. Here I simply want us to focus on the profound moral implications of this teaching.

As noted earlier, Gershon and Straub say that "if we accept the basic premise that our thoughts create our reality, it means that we need to take responsibility for creating all of our reality—_the parts we like and the parts we don't like_."[71] The point we need to make in response to this is that if man creates his own reality, then he cannot legitimately condemn individuals who inflict evil upon others.

For example, we must conclude that the millions of Jews who were executed under Hitler's regime _created their own reality_. Hence, Hitler's actions cannot be condemned as ethically wrong, since he was only part of a reality that the Jews themselves created. Similarly, we cannot condemn terrorists who blow up passenger jets because the people on those jets create their own reality.

## Dealing with the Problem of Evil

Gershon and Straub make a lame attempt to deal with the existence of evil in terms of reincarnation and karma. As reincarnationists, they believe that each human being experiences one life after another. _Karma_ refers to the "debt" a soul accumulates because of good or bad actions committed during one's life or past lives. If one accumulates good karma, he or she will allegedly be reincarnated into a desirable state. If one accumulates bad karma, he or she will be reincarnated into a less desirable state.

Now, with this backdrop in mind, consider Gershon and Straub's explanation of why horrible things happen to some people: "To account for an individual who is involved in a major calamity such as an earthquake, famine, war, or who has a birth defect, we must go to a subtler level to understand the cause. There are essentially two reasons: the choice of the soul before it incarnates to have a particular lesson or experience for its growth, and the coming to fruition of a belief held in a former lifetime (our beliefs create and are not limited by time)."[72]

In other words, one possible reason a calamity occurs is that the individual soul chose this calamity as a learning experience prior to incarnating into a physical body (yes, I know it sounds bizarre). Another possible explanation is that the calamity is a direct result of a wrong thought or belief held in a former lifetime.

Would Gershon and Straub have us believe that when soldiers in Ceylon shot a nursing mother and then shot off her baby's toes for target practice, this was the choice of the soul before it incarnated into a body to have a particular lesson or experience for its growth?[73] When Shiites in the Soviet Union ripped open the womb of a pregnant Armenian woman and tore the limbs from the fetus, do Gershon and Straub really expect us to buy their "wrong thought or belief" explanation instead of being morally outraged?[74] Where is the divine and the sacred in this?

> *How much better it is to trust in the sure promises of God rather than depending on your visualizing prowess.*

We must also observe that Gershon and Straub's mind-over-matter techniques are blatantly occultic and non-Christian. And, like other New Agers, they deny wholesale that man (including his imagination) is *fallen* (Genesis 6:5). Thus they are blinded to the reality that they are using faulty equipment that can lead them astray. How much better it is to trust in the sure promises of a loving God for provisions in life rather than having to depend on your visualizing prowess (*see* Matthew 6:30).

## The Christian Challenge

Money, sex, and power. We have seen that each of these have been used as a means of luring people into the kingdom of the cults. Of course, money, sex, and power are not evil in themselves. The kingdom of darkness has simply harnessed these items for its own use. To be sure, a *love* for money is evil; a *misuse* of sex is evil; and the *abuse* of power is evil. But these three items *can* be used righteously as well.

The challenge for the Christian church is not to outright deny the use of money, sex, and power. Rather, the church must communicate and provide a theological framework, based on Scripture, for a balanced view of money, a healthy sexuality (within the marriage relationship), and proper use of power. As Christians, we must shine as lights in a world of darkness by modeling how these three things can be used properly to glorify God and to bless humankind instead of being used to enslave people.

# 12

# Extraterrestrials and the Culting of America

*Something does seem to be happening out there. And it seems to be increasing in frequency as humankind presses toward the year A.D. 2000.*[1]

—William M. Alnor,
Christian UFO researcher

*In the last thirty years they have been accelerating their interaction with us in preparation for a fast-approaching time of transition and transformation.*[2]

—Brad Steiger, New Age UFO advocate

IT USED TO BE that talk of extraterrestrials and UFOs (Unidentified Flying Objects) caused people to question your sanity. Not anymore! In fact, UFOs have been spotted by the likes of former president Jimmy Carter and a number of American astronauts—reportedly including those who participated in the Gemini 7, Gemini 11, Apollo 11, Apollo 12, and Skylab 3 missions.[3] Such seemingly credible sightings have caused many to wonder if earth is truly being visited by aliens from another planet.

The modern UFO era began in the late 1940s when people all around the globe began reporting flying saucers whizzing across the sky at incredible speeds. In the 1950s, some people—considered as being on the "fringe"—claimed to be contactees for alien civilizations somewhere within our own solar system. The 1970s and 1980s witnessed increasing numbers of people in the United States and around the globe claiming to have been *abducted* by aliens. Some of these stories made headlines in some of the nation's most prominent newspapers. Then, in the late 1980s, UFO enthusiasts began finding a new respectability as the New Age movement grew in popularity and influence.[4]

Back in the 1940s people did not take UFOs too seriously. A 1947 Gallup poll found that "virtually no one considered the objects to be from outer space." Most people considered such sightings to be either hoaxes, secret weapons, illusions of some kind, or some phenomenon that could be scientifically explained.[5]

By the 1950s, a slight shift in public opinion became evident: 3.4 percent of the population in the United States now believed in UFOs manned by extraterrestrials.[6] By 1973, some 11 percent of Americans claimed to have seen a UFO.[7]

> *Americans are more open than ever to the idea that our planet is being visited by extraterrestrials.*

By 1987, according to a Gallup poll, some 50 percent of Americans believed in the existence of UFOs—the same percentage that considered extraterrestrials to be real.[8] One in eleven people (about 9 percent) reported that they had seen something they thought was a UFO.[9] Then, by 1990, some 14 percent of Americans claimed to have seen a UFO.[10] And today, because of the ever-increasing popularity and growth of the New Age movement, Americans are more open than ever to the idea that our planet is actually being visited by extraterrestrials.[11]

It appears that the UFO phenomenon has now penetrated mainstream America. And, as we will see, there is a definite connection between extraterrestrials and the culting of America. First, however, we must address the question as to *why* UFOs have grown to be so popular in our day.

## Why Are UFOs So Popular?

Interest in extraterrestrials and UFOs is spreading throughout all quarters of the New Age movement as well as mainstream society in America.[12] One must wonder how a phenomenon that used to raise eyebrows and evoke ridicule has grown to be so popular. How did it happen?

## People *Want* to Believe

First, it seems that many Americans *want* to believe in extraterrestrials and UFOs. As one UFO investigator put it, "There's something about human nature that wants to believe in flying saucers and extraterrestrial life."[13]

John Wiley, in the *Smithsonian*, commented, "Many people, I suspect, want the aliens to arrive for the sheer excitement and for the disruption of the routine of daily life."[14] Indeed, Wiley says, "we have a history of yearning for alien life. The popular response today to movies about lovable, or at least benign, aliens seems little different from the excitement of newspaper readers in 1835 over a phony report that Sir John F.W. Herschel had 'discovered' batlike people living on the moon. . . . The hoax could not have lasted as long as it did unless people wanted to believe it."[15]

## The Media's Shift in Perspective

It is undeniable that there has been a noticeable shift in the way extraterrestrials and UFOs are treated in the media, particularly in major motion pictures and television. In earlier decades, aliens from outer space were portrayed as diabolic invaders intent on conquering or destroying the earth. Movies of this type include *Invasion of the Body Snatchers*, *The Crawling Eye*, and *Invasion of the Flying Saucers*.

In more recent years we have seen a flurry of benevolent aliens portrayed on the silver screen. Such movies include *Close Encounters of the Third Kind*, *E.T.*, and *Starman*. I think it is safe to say that this shift in the way aliens are *portrayed* has influenced public opinion regarding how they are *perceived* by the general public.

## The Phenomenal Sales of UFO Books

Bestselling authors in the UFO genre include Erich von Daniken, Brad Steiger, Shirley MacLaine, and Whitley Strieber. Books by these and other authors seem to have struck a nerve with the American reading public.

*Erich von Daniken.* Erich von Daniken's controversial book *Chariots of the Gods?* has amazingly sold more than 45 million copies since its release in the late 1960s.[16] Von Daniken made a number of wild claims in his book. For example, he believed the Ark of the Covenant was actually a radio transmitter that enabled Moses to communicate to beings in a spaceship that guided the Israelites across the wilderness during the exodus (described by the Israelites as a "pillar of fire" and "clouds").

Von Daniken also suggested that the Old Testament prophet Ezekiel saw a flying saucer and described it in Ezekiel 1:4-6: "I looked, and I saw a windstorm coming out of the north—an immense cloud with flashing lightning and surrounded by brilliant light. The center of the fire looked like glowing metal, and in the fire was what looked like four living creatures. In appearance their form was that of a man, but each of them had four faces and four wings."

Did Ezekiel see a flying saucer? The context of this passage makes such a suggestion preposterous. Ezekiel simply saw a vision. Indeed, this portion of Scripture opens with the words, "the heavens were opened and *I saw visions of God*" (*see* verse 1, emphasis added).[17] Moreover, Ezekiel 10 makes it patently clear that the four creatures Ezekiel saw were cherubim (angels), not aliens from outer space.

Von Daniken also speculated that a mysterious series of markings in the Peruvian desert were actually a landing strip used by earth's ancient ancestors.[18] Such sensationalistic claims were widely reported in the media, thus catapulting von Daniken's book onto the bestseller lists and making him a UFO celebrity of sorts.

*Brad Steiger.* Brad Steiger is a New Ager whose 107 books on psychic phenomena—with sales topping 15 million—have become quite popular in recent years.[19] A number of Steiger's books deal specifically with UFOs and extraterrestrials, including *Gods of Aquarius*, *The Fellowship*, and *The UFO Abductors*.

In his books, Steiger says the aliens have informed human contactees that we are headed for a glorious New Age of harmony, but must first pass through a time of "cleansing" (Armageddon, or Judgment Day). The extraterrestrials allegedly seek to help humankind go through this difficult period, bringing about a world society of love and unity.

*Shirley MacLaine.* Shirley MacLaine hasn't written any books specifically dealing with extraterrestrials or UFOs, but she does at least touch on them in her bestselling books.[20] According to her book *Out on a Limb*, MacLaine was introduced to the idea of extraterrestrials and UFOs by her spiritual mentor David.

David claimed to have had contact with an extraterrestrial named "the Mayan." While David and MacLaine were on a trip to Peru (a spiritual pilgrimage of sorts), she had an opportunity to meditate. And during her meditation, she says a UFO flew over her head and "I began to have flashing feelings coming toward me in another language."[21] To make a long story short, MacLaine said that *Out on a Limb* was indirectly inspired by the

Mayan.[22] She also said she had been chosen by extraterrestrials to spread the word regarding the coming New Age.[23]

A reporter who is sympathetic to MacLaine, Antonio Huneeus, summarizes MacLaine's beliefs this way:

> An important part of Shirley MacLaine's message has to do with her conviction that we are not alone, and that extraterrestrial civilizations have visited Earth in the past, and continue to do so at an increasing pace. This realization came to her during a gradual process of becoming acquainted—and accepting—other non-mainstream ideas like reincarnation, spiritualism and channeling, eastern meditation, etc., which led to her experience of a divine cosmic energy, or God-force, which she says exists within all of us.[24]

_Whitley Strieber._ Whitley Strieber's book _Communion_ is without a doubt one of the bestselling UFO books ever published. This sensational book shot to the top of the _New York Times_ bestseller list and stayed there for almost a full year. The book was later made into a movie starring Christopher Walken (playing the role of Whitley Strieber).[25]

Some time later, Strieber came out with a sequel entitled _Transformation_. Because of the public interest in these two books, Strieber appeared on such television shows as "Good Morning America," "The Phil Donahue Show," and the "Tonight Show" with Johnny Carson.[26] Obviously, these books played a tremendous role in the resurgence of interest in UFOs in America.[27]

The book _Communion_ chronicled Strieber's alleged abductions by aliens—harrowing experiences he did not remember until he recalled them under hypnosis. The aliens—insectlike creatures with almond-shaped eyes—allegedly implanted something into his brain through one of his nostrils and inserted another object up his rectum.[28]

The aliens came to Strieber during the middle of the night, and their visits were often accompanied by weird lights in the sky. They seemed to treat Strieber as a specimen for examination, though they never asked permission to do this. Strieber claims he felt helpless and uncomfortable in the aliens' presence, and he felt violated.[29] Some of the experiences he suffered were sexual in nature.[30] The aliens typically left Strieber feeling frightened, depressed, suffering from nightmares, and fearing for his family's safety (a wife and young son).[31] More on Strieber shortly!

## The New Age Embrace of UFOs

The New Age acceptance of UFOs can best be illustrated in the life of a former New Ager—Randall Baer. After Baer became a Christian, he wrote a book entitled *Inside the New Age Nightmare* (1989). In this book, Baer says that over 75 percent of all New Agers hold to an absolutely unshakable belief in the reality of UFOs.[32] Baer says it is noteworthy "that the strong upsurge in this trend also parallels the crystal craze and the huge increases in channeling activities in the mid-to-late 80s."[33]

Baer states that among New Agers "the question of whether UFOs are real is rarely contested or questioned. This belief is part and parcel of much, though not all, of the New Age mentality. UFOs are involved quite heavily in their concepts of the world's deliverance from a time of suffering and tribulation into an enlightened 'One World United Government' (that is, the New Age)."[34]

> *In New Age circles, a person is considered a bit weird if he doesn't believe in highly evolved extraterrestrials and UFOs.*

New Agers believe extraterrestrials are already heavily involved in helping humanity. As Baer says,

> Most New Agers hold firmly to the view that hundreds, if not thousands, of UFOs already are deeply involved in rendering aid to planet Earth in subtle but highly significant ways. But, because of a kind of 'prime non-interference directive' (like on *Star Trek*), the extraterrestrials cannot intervene directly or render explicit assistance until humanity is ready for their help. These extraterrestrials are believed to have a highly evolved spiritual philosophy (akin to New Age philosophy) and extremely advanced technologies, both of which form the foundation for the New Age One World Order.[35]

Baer concedes that all this may sound a bit wacky to some people. However, he says millions of New Agers are absolutely convinced that these things are true. "In fact, in most New Age circles, a person is considered a bit weird or 'out of it' if he doesn't believe in all this."[36]

## Is There Any "Hard Evidence"?

UFOs are reported to appear seemingly out of nowhere, travel at phenomenal speeds across the sky, turn at impossible angles, and disappear without a trace. Scientifically, then, UFOs are very hard to explain. One researcher said "it is literally impossible to understand them within the space-time framework we use to interpret ordinary events."[37]

UFOs have been sighted virtually around the world. Based on detailed research, John Ankerberg and John Weldon comment that "no nation is free of UFO reports—and many major nations around the world have officially or secretly engaged in serious investigations of UFOs at the governmental/ military level."[38] In fact, "in the U.S. alone, tens of millions of dollars have been spent in official UFO investigations by the CIA, FBI, Defense Intelligence Agency, U.S. Air Force, U.S. Army Intelligence, Naval Intelligence, and other organizations."[39]

Now, many UFO sightings can be dismissed as mistakenly identified planets, rocket launchings, weather balloons, and various atmospheric phenomena. Sometimes, however, sightings cannot be so easily explained. Indeed, the Air Force's _Project Blue Book_ was not able to provide a rationale for 700 out of 12,600 cases of sightings between 1947 and 1969, when the project was abandoned.[40] Others tell us that somewhere between five to ten percent of all UFO sightings remain truly _unidentified_.[41]

Still, the hard evidence for extraterrestrials and UFO landings is missing. No incontrovertible evidence exists. There is no UFO or extraterrestrial anyplace that a person can go and examine. And there are no existing parts that scientists agree _without question_ came from a UFO.[42]

The scientific community remains skeptical, and understandably so. The United States government officially denies the existence or danger of extraterrestrials and UFOs. This has caused some to accuse the government of conspiracy. But there is no evidence for this either.

## The Message of the "Space Brothers"

Many people all over the world claim to receive revelations or messages from these extraterrestrials—often called "space brothers." These so-called revelations typically come through occultic means such as channeling (spiritism) or automatic handwriting (in which the alleged space brother takes control of the human being's hand and writes messages). But what do these revelations or messages consist of?

## A New Age Slant

New Ager David Icke believes that extraterrestrials are arriving on earth in large numbers to help us "make the giant leap in evolution into the Aquarian Age, when humankind, or those who are evolved enough to meet the challenge, will rise out of the abyss at last. They are here to guide us through tremendously difficult times with love, wisdom, and understanding, and we ignore them and reject what they say to our cost."[43] An examination of UFO literature indicates that Icke's view is not unique.

Brad Steiger, another New Ager, comments: "Contactees have been told that the Space Beings hope to guide Earth to a period of great unification, when all races will shun discriminatory separations and all of mankind will recognize its responsibility to every other life form existing on the planet. The Space Beings also seek to bring about a single, unified government, which will conduct itself on spiritual principles and permit all of its citizens to grow constructively in 'love.' "[44]

During his New Age training, Randall Baer reflects that mentors "told us to start to call out in our meditations to the 'Space Brothers,' who allegedly were highly advanced extraterrestrial intelligences stationed in our solar system. These 'Space Brothers' had come from a variety of galaxies, and were part of a collective 'Intergalactic Space Federation' working together to assist planets like earth to go through a 'purification process' preceding a quantum leap into a new evolutionary stage of human development—a New Age of 'Heaven-on-earth.' "[45]

## A Counterfeit Christianity?

In many ways there seems to be a counterfeit Christianity in the messages of the extraterrestrials. My friend William Alnor is a UFO researcher who published his findings in a book entitled *UFOs in the New Age*. In it, he explained,

> Most New Age UFO enthusiasts have definite opinions about the end times, and most of them believe the earth is in the last days before a coming New Age, even a near-future second coming. Most believe in an Armageddon, tribulation, or "cleansing"

time in which the wicked on earth will be punished, a coming UFO "rapture" of sorts (meaning the removal of good spiritual people from the earth during the coming troubles), and afterwards a blissful New Age in which UFO believers will see a new Jerusalem or cities of light. And although it is not a major theme with most UFO groups, a few of them even talk about a coming wicked Antichrist that will bring the world to ruin during the cleansing.[46]

Alnor's comments accurately portray the writings of various New Age UFO advocates. Brad Steiger, for example, says that in the last thirty years the extraterrestrials "have been accelerating their interaction with us in preparation for a fast-approaching time of transition and transformation. This period, we have been told, will be a difficult one; and for generations our prophets and revelators have been referring to it as The Great Cleansing, Judgment Day, Armageddon. But we have been promised that, after a season of cataclysmic changes on the Earth plane, a New Age consciousness will suffuse the planet. It is to this end that the gods have been utilizing the UFO as a transformative symbol."[47]

Likewise, Gabriel Green—the founder of one of the largest UFO groups in America, the Amalgamated Flying Saucer Club—said, "If Armageddon comes, so will the aliens, swooping down in spaceships to evacuate one-tenth of the population in what Christians call 'the rapture.' . . . Only one-tenth of the population will be spiritually qualified to live in an environment of harmony, and there are some limitations on their [the extraterrestrials'] ability to provide for us, to house us and so forth."[48]

> _New Agers are clearly seizing upon Christian terms and doctrines and pouring their own New Age meanings into them._

It is also intriguing to note that increasing numbers of New Age UFO advocates are claiming to be members of the chosen 144,000 mentioned in Revelation 7 and 14.[49] In context, however, the book of Revelation is referring to 144,000 witnesses of the Messiah during the future Tribulation period—12,000 from each of the 12 tribes of Israel. New Agers are clearly seizing upon Christian terms and doctrines and pouring their own New Age meanings into them.

Such statements as these have caused Alnor to legitimately ask, "Could it be that the similar end-times scenarios being spewed in the form of messages from the space brothers are deliberate attempts to fool humankind about Bible prophecy in the very era of Christ's return? Could the benevolent space brothers that the New Agers talk about actually be some of the 'angels of light' deliberately sent by Satan to deceive mankind whom the apostle Paul warned the early Christian church about (2 Cor. 11:14)?"[50] The discerning Christian must wonder the same.

Alnor's conclusion is chilling: "I have concluded that the emerging religion of the UFOnauts is part of a diabolical program of disinformation— perhaps the greatest in history. It involves a clever counterfeit of the Christian message and a retranslation of future events as seen by most in the church today."[51]

## Diabolical Visitors?

Though motion pictures like *E.T.* and *Close Encounters of the Third Kind* portray aliens as benevolent and kind, a considerable amount of evidence indicates that they (*whoever* or *whatever* they are) are in fact diabolical and evil. We find this illustrated in the alleged encounters Whitley Strieber had with alien visitors.

According to Strieber, the almond-eyed, insectlike aliens repeatedly frightened him during the night. They would appear uninvited and unannounced—often accompanied by strange rapping sounds. They occasionally punished him if he wasn't living the way they desired. Strieber referred to the visitors as "soul eaters" and "predators." "Mostly they terrified me," Strieber said. "One does not want to develop a relationship with a hungry panther."[52]

In 1990 Dr. Jacques Vallee—a world-renowned UFO researcher—wrote a book entitled *Confrontations: A Scientist's Search for Alien Contact,* in which he examined over 100 UFO incidents around the world.[53] In the book he pointed to the diabolical nature of the visitors. He said their " 'scientific' experiments [on abductees] are crude to the point of being grotesque. The 'medical examination' to which abductees are said to be subjected, often accompanied by sadistic sexual manipulation, is reminiscent of the medieval tales of encounters with demons."[54]

## The Alien Agenda:
## Changing the Way Humans Think

An examination of the evidence that is available seems to indicate beyond any doubt that a primary agenda of the visitors—whoever or whatever they are—is to change the way people think about God and His Word, and to replace exclusivistic Christianity with a religion of universalism.[55] As well, the visitors seem intent on drawing people deeper and deeper into various forms of occultism.

Jacques Vallee suggests that the visitors are purposely hoping to "change our belief systems" and are engaging in a "worldwide enterprise of 'subliminal seduction.' "[56] In his book *The Invisible College*, Vallee says that "human belief . . . is being controlled and conditioned," "man's concepts are being rearranged," and we may be headed for "a massive change of human attitudes toward paranormal abilities and extraterrestrial life."[57]

Whitley Strieber acknowledges that the visitors seem to be attempting to affect the way humans think. He says they appear to be "orchestrating our awareness of them very carefully," and seeking "a degree of influence or even control over us."[58] Strieber admits that the aliens "have caused me to slough off my old view of the world like the dismal skin that it was and seek a completely new vision of this magnificent, mysterious, and fiercely alive universe."[59]

John Weldon, a Christian researcher who has thoroughly investigated the UFO phenomenon, says the visitors seek "to deliberately move significant portions of an entire culture, or world, into acceptance of or involvement in the occult, and a collective alteration in world view. This is preparatory for and necessary to the events surrounding the rise of the anti-Christ."[60]

## UFOs and the Occult Connection

Christian UFO researchers have noted that individuals who are contacted by (or become abducted by) UFOs often have a strong prior involvement in some form of occultism. Brooks Alexander of the Spiritual Counterfeits Project said that "many of the reported cases show some kind of occult involvement prior to initial UFO contact."[61] John Weldon likewise notes that "UFO contactees often have a history of psychic abilities or an interest in the occult."[62]

We find this illustrated in the life of Whitley Strieber. Prior to his abduction experiences, Strieber was a 15-year follower of the occult mystic G.I. Gurdjieff (whose belief system included elements of Zen, witchcraft, and shamanism, among other things).[63] Strieber also experimented with worshiping the earth as a goddess/mother. At a conference in San Francisco, Strieber admitted, "I made choices a long time ago that brought me into this experience."[64]

Christian UFO investigator David Wimbish has also suggested that interest in UFOs can actually draw a person into the occult: "Many UFO investigators have followed a path that has taken them directly into the world of the occult. They believe they are rediscovering ancient spiritual truths and uncovering new realities about the universe. It's more likely that they are getting involved with some ancient deceptions."[65] Indeed, the UFO phenomenon "has led many to experiment with astral projection, to believe in reincarnation, and to get involved in other practices that directly oppose the historic teachings of the Christian church."[66]

Because of the strong occult connection with UFOs, discerning Christians have suggested that those who are involved in UFOs are in contact not with extraterrestrials or aliens but with deceptive demonic spirits intent on drawing people away from Christ. We will find further evidence for this view in the next section as we consider why it is unlikely that UFOs are from outer space.

## UFOs: Not Likely from Outer Space

Gordon Creighton, editor of the British journal *Flying Saucer Review*, admits that "there seems to be no evidence yet that any of these craft or beings originate from outer space."[67] Not only is there no scientific evidence that UFOs come from outer space, there are also scientific problems that make such a possibility highly unlikely.

Bernard Oliver, the chief of research for Hewlett-Packard, spoke at a symposium conducted by NASA. Researcher Mark Albrecht summarized Oliver's argument this way: "He pointed out that the nearest star, Alpha Centauri, which is four light years away, represents an 80,000-year round trip from earth with our present technology. Beyond that, it is unlikely that any star within 100 light years distance is stable enough to support biochemical evolution."[68] This would seem to militate against extraterrestrials visiting planet earth from outer space. The distance is just too vast to make this a feasible possibility.

Furthermore, as John Ankerberg and John Weldon point out, "in light of the messages given by the UFO entities, how credible is it to think that literally thousands of genuine extraterrestrials would fly millions or billions of light years simply to teach New Age philosophy, deny Christianity, and support the occult? *Why would they do this with the preponderance of such activity already occurring on this planet?* And why would the entities actually possess and inhabit people just like demons do if they were really advanced extraterrestrials? Why would they consistently lie about things we know are true and purposely deceive their contacts?"[69]

## Is There Life on Other Planets?

Related to our discussion as to whether UFOs are visiting us from outer space is the question of whether there is life on other planets. Though I can't be dogmatic about this, it seems that there are several good reasons to doubt that there is intelligent life on other planets.

First, though atheistic scientists would scoff at this, Scripture points to the centrality of planet earth and gives us no hint that life exists elsewhere. In my book *Christ Before the Manger: The Life and Times of the Preincarnate Christ* (Baker Book House), I point out the following:

> Relatively speaking, the earth is but an astronomical atom among the whirling constellations, only a tiny speck of dust among the ocean of stars and planets in the universe. To the naturalistic astronomer, the earth is but one of many planets in our small solar system, all of which are in orbit around the sun. But Planet Earth is nevertheless the center of God's work of salvation in the universe. On it the Highest presents Himself in solemn covenants and Divine appearances; on it the Son of God became man; on it stood the cross of the Redeemer of the world; and on it—though indeed on the new earth, yet still on the earth—will be at last the throne of God and the Lamb (Revelations 21:1, 2; 22:3).
>
> The centrality of the earth is also evident in the creation account, for God created the earth before He created the rest of the planets and stars. Bible scholar John Whitcomb thus asks this penetrating question: "Why did God create the sun, moon, and stars on the fourth day rather than the first day? One possible explanation is that in this way God has emphasized the supreme importance of the earth among all astronomical bodies in the universe. In spite of its comparative smallness of size, even among the nine planets, to say nothing of the stars themselves, it is nonetheless absolutely unique in God's eternal purposes."[70]

We might ask why God would create such a vast universe of stars and galaxies if He did not intend to populate them. Psalm 19:1 gives us the answer: "The heavens declare the glory of God; the skies proclaim the work of his hands." The sheer immensity of the physical universe points us to the greater vastness and infinity of God Himself.[71]

Related to the issue of possible life on other planets is the question of how unfallen beings (assuming the "aliens" are unfallen) could share the same universe with fallen ones (humans). Elliot Miller, my colleague at the Christian Research Institute, responds by pointing out that "the effects of Adam's sin seem to pervade the entire universe (Romans 8:19-22). (I believe the second law of thermodynamics—that all things tend toward disorganization and death—is the scientific description of the curse God pronounced on creation in Genesis 3:14-19.) It does not seem likely that God would allow the effects of sin to impact a world of unfallen creatures (e.g., Revelation 21:4)."[72]

In view of these and other factors, it seems that from a theological perspective it is improbable that there is intelligent life on other planets. Of course, if this is the case, any discussion of earth being visited by extraterrestrials from other planets is rendered moot.

## The Verdict:
## A Satanic Deception?

I noted earlier that many UFO sightings have a natural explanation. Some sightings may even involve deliberate hoaxes. Hence, I don't want to imply that every time someone sees an unidentified flying object that Satan is at work. However, I think a case can be made that those UFOs that remain *truly unidentifiable*—and especially those that make "contact" or communicate messages to human beings—are rooted in the work of Satan. Let me explain why I think this is a viable possibility.

### Anti-Christian/Pro-New Age Message

The messages communicated by the alleged extraterrestrials consistently go against biblical Christianity. As Ralph Rath puts it, "There is nothing in the UFO phenomena that leads to the belief in the one true God. There is much in the UFO phenomena, on the other hand, that contradicts the ideas of God as revealed in the Bible and Christian tradition."[73]

|| *The extraterrestrial visitors, at the very least,* ||
|| *are more interested in steering us away from* ||
|| *the truth of the Bible than toward it.* ||

David Wimbish agrees with Rath and affirms, "We cannot believe Jesus *and* the visitors because their claims contradict one another. There is no way to reconcile the two."[74] Indeed, Wimbish notes, "The visitors are perfectly in tune with what has become known as 'New Age' religion—Eastern mysticism, astral projection, the harmonic convergence, and so on. They are not at all in harmony, though, with Jesus Christ, who said, 'I am the way, the truth, and the life.' At the very least, they are more interested in steering us away from the truth of the Bible than toward it."[75]

## Ever-Present Occultism

We have already touched on the strong link between the UFO phenomenon and occultism. We have noted that the messages received from extraterrestrials typically come through occultic means—such as channeling or automatic handwriting.

UFO contactees and abductees are often involved in a number of other forms of occultism, including the Ouija board, tarot cards, psychometry (psychic messages from personal articles), palm reading, seances, aura reading, crystal-ball gazing, astrology, and much more. After encountering UFOs, people are often drawn even further into the world of the occult—becoming involved in activities such as out-of-body experiences.[76]

## Demons Against God

Experts who have long investigated UFOs—both Christian and non-Christian—have noted the strong similarities between the UFO experience and the typical manifestations of demonism. Brooks Alexander, of the Spiritual Counterfeits Project, commented on "The John Ankerberg Show": "A lot of the characteristics that attend UFO 'close encounters' are also highly characteristic of demonic encounters. . . . More than anything else, the thing that we came to understand was that these UFOs are not extraterrestrial space vehicles, but they are extra-dimensional beings."[77]

John Keel, a respected authority on UFOs, said, "The UFO manifestations seem to be, by and large, merely minor variations of the age-old demonological phenomenon," and "the manifestations and occurrences described in [the literature of demonology] are similar, if not entirely identical, to the UFO phenomenon itself. Victims of [demon] possession suffer the very same medical and emotional symptoms as the UFO contactees."[78]

Jacques Vallee, in his book *Messengers of Deception*, observes an "impressive parallel" between "UFO occupants and the popular conception of demons."[79] Vallee says that "the UFO beings of today belong to the same class of manifestation as the [occult] entities that were described in centuries past."[80]

In a U.S. government document entitled *UFOs and Related Subjects: An Annotated Bibliography*, Lynn E. Catoe said, "A large part of the available UFO literature is closely linked with mysticism and the metaphysical. It deals with subjects like mental telepathy, automatic writing, and invisible entities, as well as phenomena like poltergeist ["noisy spirit"] manifestations and possession. . . . Many of the UFO reports now being published in the popular press recount alleged incidents that are strikingly similar to demonic possession and psychic phenomena which has long been known to theologians and parapsychologists."[81]

Former New Ager Randall Baer likewise affirms, "From millions of New Agers' experiences, there is a profoundly potent force behind whatever the UFOs really are. That force is definitely demonic in nature and has extraordinary delusionary brainwashing effects on people. I believe that, whatever new information may be uncovered about this phenomena in the years ahead, UFOs are messengers of deception, nothing else."[82]

In support of the idea that UFOs may in fact be manifestations of Satan or demons is the belief by some individuals that the UFOs themselves are *alive*. Brad Steiger, for example, said, "I have even come to suspect that in some instances, what we have been calling 'spaceships' may actually be a form of higher intelligence rather than vehicles transporting occupants."[83] Likewise, John Keel noted that "over and over again, witnesses have told me in hushed tones, 'You know, I don't think that thing I saw was mechanical at all. I got the distinct impression that it was alive.'"[84]

## Heeding the Bible's Warnings

Jesus clearly warned about religious deception in the last days: "At that time many will turn away from the faith and will betray and hate each other, and many false prophets will appear and deceive many people" (Matthew 24:10,11). Earlier, Jesus advised His followers to "watch out for false prophets. They come to you in sheep's clothing, but inwardly they are ferocious wolves" (Matthew 7:15). Could it be that the so-called extraterrestrials seek to appear as benevolent "brothers," but in fact are ferocious demonic wolves who seek to lead us astray?

The apostle Paul sternly warned, "Satan himself masquerades as an angel of light. It is not surprising, then, if his servants masquerade as servants of righteousness" (2 Corinthians 11:14,15). The fact is, _appearances can be deceiving_. This is why we need to anchor ourselves in the absolute Word of God.

The apostle John instructs us, "Do not believe every spirit, but test the spirits to see whether they are from God, because many false prophets have gone out into the world. This is how you can recognize the Spirit of God: Every spirit that acknowledges that Jesus Christ has come in the flesh is from God, but every spirit that does not acknowledge Jesus is not from God. This is the spirit of the antichrist, which you have heard is coming and even now is already in the world" (1 John 4:1-3). By this test alone, the extraterrestrials fail in terms of being messengers from the true God.

# 13

# Millennial Madness and the Rise of Doomsday Shivers

*Book your mountaintop today. They're bound to be in short supply in the coming decade.*[1]

—Stanley Young

*A string of zeros on time's odometer suggest that global changes are coming, and they're going to be dramatic and sudden.*[2]

—Ted Daniels, founder of
Millennium Watch Institute

*The Millennium is entering the consciousness of mainstream America.*[3]

—Paul Saffo

IT SEEMS THAT PEOPLE have been predicting imminent doom—or glorious apocalypse—since the pharaohs ruled Egypt. One example of this is what allegedly occurred at the turn of the first millennium. Legend and lore has it that humanity became grievously afflicted with millennial fever. Consider the following account:

Toward the arrival of the last millennium—December 31, 999 A.D.—so many people in the Christian lands of that time actually thought that the world was coming to an end that they proceeded to act in an unaccustomed fashion. In their dealings with each other they became so brotherly, so charitable, so filled with self-abnegation and love for their neighbor that the true millennium, however briefly, seemed to be at hand.[4]

Men forgave their neighbors' debts; people confessed their infidelities and wrongdoings. Farm animals were freed as their owners prepared for the final judgment. . . . The churches were besieged by crowds demanding confession and absolution. Commerce was interrupted. Beggars were liberally fed by the more fortunate. Prisoners were freed, yet many remained—wishing to expiate their sins before the end. Pilgrims flocked to Jerusalem from Europe. Class differences were forgotten. Slaves were freed.

Nearing December, groups of flagellants roamed the countryside whipping each other.

Christmas passed with a splendid outpouring of love and piety. Food shops gave away food and merchants refused payment. Of course, when December 31st approached a general frenzy reached new heights. In Rome, Pope Sylvester II held midnight mass in the Basilica of St. Peters to a standing room only audience. But they weren't standing. All lay on their knees praying.

After the mass had been said, a deathly silence fell. The clock kept on ticking away its last minutes as Pope Sylvester raised his hands to the sky. The attendees at this time lay with their faces to the ground listening to the tick tick tick.

Suddenly the clock stopped. Several bodies, stricken by fear, dropped dead as the congregation began screaming in terror. Just as it had suddenly stopped ticking the clock resumed to meet the midnight hour. Deathly silence still reigned until the clock ticked past 12. Bells in the tower began to scream jubilantly. Pope Sylvester stretched out his hands and gave a blessing over his flock. When the *Te Deum* had been sung, men and women fell in each other's arms, laughing and crying and exchanging the kiss of peace.

Not long after the suspense at St. Peter's and elsewhere, life resumed its normal rhythm. Owners captured their once freed animals. Merchants ceased giving away their goods. Prisoners were captured to be placed back in the slammer. Debts were remembered. And life went on as if nothing happened.[5]

Did all of this really occur around A.D. 1000? A person might think so from all the articles and books that have appeared in recent years popularizing the idea.[6] However, when one digs deep for hard, indisputable historical evidence, one is less than satisfied.[7] The question that arises is this: If a widespread panic and hysteria had really occurred, wouldn't we have more than the surviving 12 or 13 accounts of what happened at the turn of the first millennium—only *half* of which mention apocalyptic panics?[8]

Raoul Glaber, a Burgundian monk born in the late tenth century, wrote *Histories*—considered by many to be a prime source for what went on at the turn of the millennium. His writings indicate a panic concerning the approaching end.[9] A number of historians, however, have disputed Glaber's work.[10]

Moreover, historians interpret Glaber and other available writings of the time (few though they be) in different ways. For example, some "antipanic" analysts cite the fact that "people of the time wrote wills and testaments, clearly indicating an awareness of a future. But, other analysts say, the opening clauses of many of the surviving wills begin with some version of, 'The end of the world being close, I hereby . . .' or, 'The world coming to its conclusion, I . . .' "[11] Who is to say what all that meant, since lines such as those were merely standard, boilerplate openers for legal documents of that day?[12]

Despite all the confusion, I think we can say with a fair degree of certainty that while there probably was no mass hysteria or panic at the close of the first millennium, there *was* widespread *concern* that the end of the world *may* be near. A number of highly respected scholars support this view, noting that people living at the close of the first millennium had a definite case of the "preapocalyptic shivers."

For example, Reformed scholar Louis Berkhof, in his *History of Christian Doctrines*, confirms that "in the tenth century there was a widespread expectation of the approaching end of the world . . . it was associated with the idea of the speedy coming of Antichrist. Christian art often chose its themes from eschatology. The hymn *Dies Irae* sounded the terrors of the coming judgment, painters depicted the end of the world on the canvas, and Dante gave a vivid description of hell in his *Divina Commedia*."[13]

Philip Schaff—in his highly esteemed *History of the Christian Church*—described the flavor of the times when he said that Pope Sylvester II (who lived around A.D. 1000) gave "the first impulse, though prematurely, to the crusades at a time when hundreds of pilgrims flocked to the Holy Land in expectation of the end of the world after the lapse of the first Christian millennium."[14]

Bible scholar Stanley J. Grenz, in his recent, well-received book *The Millennial Maze*, said,

> Repeatedly church history has witnessed times of increased speculation concerning the end and the advent of a golden age on earth. The approach of the year A.D. 1000, for example, caused a great stir of expectations. When both that year and A.D. 1033 (a thousand years after Christ's death) passed, interest turned to A.D. 1065, for in that year Good Friday coincided with the Day of the Annunciation. Multitudes journeyed to Jerusalem to await the Lord's return, some arriving already during the previous year and waiting in the Holy City until after Easter.[15]

Grenz also notes that "Augustine's various statements concerning the meaning of the millennium mentioned in Revelation 20 were not without some ambiguity." Indeed, Grenz says, "they could be (and were) readily understood to indicate that Christ's Second Coming should occur one thousand years after his first advent. This implicit prediction, carrying as it did the authority of the bishop of Hippa coupled both with the theme of the old age of the world and with a rise in political and natural disasters, resulted in a great sense of anticipation in parts of Christendom first as A.D. 1000 and then as A.D. 1033 approached."[16]

In his in-depth study entitled *The Year 1000*, Henri Focillon concluded, "We have established that in the middle of the tenth century there existed a movement, a groundswell of the belief that the world was drawing to a close."[17] And "once the terminal year of the millennium has passed, the belief in the end of the world spreads with renewed vigor in the course of the eleventh century."[18] Though recognizing this "groundswell," Focillon is careful to point out that there was no mass hysteria, as some of the legendary accounts of the time seem to indicate.

To sum up, then, at the turn of the first millennium there was no mass panic but there *definitely was* widespread concern by many people that the end of the world was approaching. And just as many people were concerned about the world coming to an end around A.D. 1000, so also many are *now* concerned about the approach of the year A.D. 2000. Some believe that the end of the world may be near; others believe a glorious utopia awaits us. Let us now turn our full attention to the approach of A.D. 2000.

## Millennial Madness A.D. 2000

The approach of the year A.D. 2000 has put the fear of God into a good many people.[19] Some today are predicting imminent doom, others a glorious utopia, and still others predict doom followed by utopia. Any way we look at it, millennial madness is on the rise, and I am sure we can expect that this particular form of madness will afflict a significant share of the human race over the next decade.

|| *Storm warnings, portents, hints of catastrophe haunt our times.* ||

I am not alone in this viewpoint. Cultural commentator Christopher Lasch says, "As the twentieth century approaches its end, the conviction grows that many other things are ending too. Storm warnings, portents, hints of catastrophe haunt our times. The 'sense of ending,' which has given shape to so much of twentieth century literature, now pervades the popular imagination as well."[20]

Stanley Grenz says, "At the close of the twentieth century the message of the doomsday preachers—once the brunt of jokes and the laughingstock of 'enlightened' citizens of the modern world—has become in the minds of many people a serious possibility and a genuine concern in a way unparalleled in prior decades. For the first time in recent history we sense that our civilization is tottering on the edge of a precipice peering into the abyss of self-destruction and chaos."[21]

## Nostradamus: Setting the Stage

Nostradamus (1503-1566) was a French astrologer and occultist who attained notoriety for his prophecies, many of which were vague, allusive, cryptic, enigmatic, and very difficult to understand. Were any of them accurate? Many Nostradamus sympathizers say yes—though a great deal of interpretive liberty is involved in how such prophecies are "read." Former *Los Angeles Times* religion editor Russell Chandler—in his recent book *Doomsday: The End of the World*—summarizes the alleged (I repeat, *alleged)* prophetic fulfillments this way:

[Nostradamus's] mystical poems have been used to predict the future history of France (including the rise of Napoleon and the French Revolution); the American Revolution; the era of World War II and Hitler ("Hister"), Mussolini, and Franklin Roosevelt; the assassinations of John and Robert Kennedy; the coming of such inventions as air travel, aerial balloons and air warfare, gas masks, submarines, periscopes, manned space stations, and the atomic bomb; such disasters as the London fire of 1666, the 1986 explosion of the Challenger spacecraft, and the Chernobyl nuclear plant accident; the epidemic of AIDS; the identity of three antichrists; the fall of the Roman Catholic Church and the decline of communism—to name but a few extrapolations.[22]

Chandler observes that "modern-day Nostradamians do a much better job of matching his predictions with historical events *after* they have happened rather than pinpointing beforehand exactly what the aristocratic astrologer had in mind."[23] This is in noted contrast to the biblical prophets, whose predictions were clearly understood *prior* to the predicted event. (It was clearly understood, for example, that the Messiah would be born *in Bethlehem* [Micah 5:2] from a *virgin* [Isaiah 7:14].)

In any event, a number of people believe Nostradamus set the stage for millennial madness—for the year A.D. 2000—some 450 years ago. For example, John Hogue, author of *Nostradamus and the Millennium*, says Nostradamus predicted that humanity had two alternative futures for the period between 1992 and 1999—one involving destruction, the other involving a utopia.

Hogue bases his view on Nostradamus's assertion that the "element" for the last seven years of the twentieth century is *fire*. Hence, man may either be *destroyed* by fire (nuclear?), or perhaps a *spiritual* fire will ignite his consciousness and lead to a utopian society.[24]

Other interpreters of Nostradamus say he predicted only doom for the decade preceding A.D. 2000. Rene Noorbergen, a former war correspondent and Nostradamus admirer, says the prophet gives a forecast of World War III. Here's what he interprets the sage to be saying: "Sometime before 1995, Russia and the United States will ally themselves against China, the Arab Middle East, and Latin America in the most destructive and terrifying war the world has ever experienced. In what may well become the last great war, conducted by conventional and nuclear weaponry as well as by biological warfare, no continent will escape devastation."[25] Dark days await us, according to Noorbergen's understanding of Nostradamus.

One thing can be counted on for sure: As we approach the year 1999, Nostradamus's most ominous riddle will undoubtedly give millennial jitters to innumerable people:

> In the year 1999 and seven months
> The great King of Terror will come from the sky.
> He will bring back to life the great king of the Mongols.
> Before and after war reigns happily unrestrained.[26]

## The Cults and Millennial Madness

### New Age Predictions

New Agers are among those who predict a utopia for the years ahead. Ken Carey, the author of several New Age handbooks, envisions A.D. 2000 as a kind of psychic watershed beyond which lies "a realizable utopian society" in which people will have "a real sense of a new beginning."[27]

David Spangler, another New Ager, agrees and points to a Central American prophecy connected with the Mayan and Aztec civilizations that predicts a time of great cleansing in our era. Following this, a New Age of harmony and wholeness will emerge. Spangler says, "The Hopi Indians of the American Southwest have a similar prophecy, also focused on the period from 1980 to 2000 A.D. as a time of transition into a new cycle of cooperation."[28]

Elizabeth Clare Prophet, the controversial New Age leader of the Church Universal and Triumphant (CUT), says she has been informed by an "Ascended Master" that catastrophe awaits the world. She has been saying for years that Russia will invade the United States. Prophet said the period around 1994 will be particularly dangerous: "I believe that anytime between now and 2002 there is a high probability, a likelihood, of a war between the United States and the Soviet Union."[29]

In view of this, Prophet and her followers have built large bomb shelters to house the faithful. Church members can purchase room in the shelters for a mere six to ten thousand dollars apiece.[30] Mrs. Prophet likens the shelters to Noah's Ark in the earth.[31]

### Millennial Madness and New Age Books

Many observers believe that interest in cultic/metaphysical books will increase as we draw near to the year 2000. In an article entitled "Horizon

2000," a December 1992 issue of *Publishers Weekly* magazine focused on what publishers of metaphysical books expect in their field as we approach A.D. 2000. A few common themes emerged in the interviews. "Chief among them is these publishers' sense that, as one millennium yields to another, Western societies are undergoing a period of profound change. While taking care to eschew the millennialism associated with, say, fundamentalist Christians, they speak of the year 2000—or, strictly speaking, 2001—as an authentic cultural milestone."[32]

Sam Bercholz, the president and editor-in-chief of Shambhala Publications, is quoted as saying that "the millennium seems to bring on an interest in the genuinely spiritual—and also in the bizarrely occult and the metaphysical."[33] Shambhala produces a wide array of Eastern spiritual texts and has recently begun publishing "classics" in the mystical tradition, such as the works of Meister Eckhart and Hildegard of Bingen.[34]

Interest in Native American culture and spirituality is also on the rise. Indeed, "books about Native American culture and spirituality have become a strong-selling publishing subcategory, garnering their own section in many West Coast bookstores. . . . there is little evidence that interest in Native American culture has peaked."[35]

## The Jehovah's Witnesses

Throughout its history, the Watchtower Society has claimed to be God's prophet on earth today. In view of this, it is highly revealing that the Society now admits it was wrong in its 1874 prediction of the second coming of Christ, its 1925 prediction of the coming of select Old Testament saints to earth, its 1975 prediction of the end of human history, and other similar prophecies.[36]

Yet, in the Watchtower's *1975 Yearbook* the Society makes the claim that for over a century the Jehovah's Witnesses have "enjoyed spiritual enlightenment and direction."[37] But how can it be said that Jehovah's Witnesses have "enjoyed spiritual enlightenment and direction" by following the Society when it has consistently spewed forth false prophecies?

To illustrate the millennial madness of this devious cult, let us consider the teachings of the Watchtower Society on the "generation" mentioned in Matthew 24:34, a Scripture passage dealing with the end times. The Watchtower's *New World Translation* renders this verse, "Truly I say to you that *this generation* will by no means pass away until all these things occur" (emphasis added). The Watchtower Society teaches Jehovah's Witnesses that "this generation" is the 1914 generation (this is allegedly the year that the spiritual second coming of Christ occurred). It is this 1914 generation that will not pass away, they say, until all these things (prophecies, including Armageddon) will come to pass.

Now, it is an enlightening experience to study how the Watchtower Society has dealt with its commitment to the year 1914 throughout its history. Back in 1968, the Society was teaching its followers that Jehovah's Witnesses who were *15 years of age* in 1914 would be alive to see the consummation of all things. Indeed, a 1968 issue of *Awake!* magazine said of "this generation":

> Jesus was obviously speaking about those who were old enough to witness with understanding what took place when the "last days" began. . . . Even if we presume that *youngsters 15 years of age* would be perceptive enough to realize the import of what happened in 1914, it would still make the youngest of "this generation" nearly 70 years old today. . . . Jesus said that the end of this wicked world would come before that generation passed away in death (emphasis added).[38]

Some ten years later, a 1978 issue of *The Watchtower* magazine said, "Thus, when it comes to the application in our time, *the 'generation' logically would not apply to babies born during World War I*" (emphasis added).[39] It is clear that in 1978 the Watchtower Society was still holding out to the view that those who were teenagers during 1914 would see the culmination of all things.

However, as former Jehovah's Witness David Reed points out, "one need only calculate that someone fifteen years old in 1914 would be twenty-five years old in 1924, thirty-five years old in 1934—and eighty-five years old in 1984—to realize that the Watchtower's 'generation that will not pass away' was almost gone by the mid-1980s. The prophecy was about to fail. But, rather than change the prophecy, [Watchtower] leaders simply stretched the generation."[40]

A 1980 issue of *The Watchtower* magazine said of "this generation": "It is the generation of people who saw the catastrophic events that broke forth in connection with World War I from 1914 onward. . . . *If you assume that 10 is the age* at which an event creates a lasting impression. . . ." (emphasis added).[41] Watchtower leaders reduced the age from 15 to 10 in order to allow five more years for a "generation" that was quickly dying off.

The 1980 solution didn't alleviate the problem, though. Another step had to be taken. So, in a 1984 issue of *The Watchtower* magazine, we read,

"If Jesus used 'generation' in that sense and we apply it to 1914, then *the babies of that generation* are now 70 years old or older. . . . Some of them 'will by no means pass away until all things occur'" (emphasis added).[42]

Along these same lines, a 1985 issue of *The Watchtower* said, "Before the 1914 generation completely dies out, God's judgment must be executed."[43] More recently, a 1988 issue of *Awake!* magazine said, "Most of the generation of 1914 has passed away. However, there are still millions on earth who were born in that year or prior to it. . . . Jesus' words will come true, 'this generation will not pass away until all these things have happened.'"[44]

*Reasoning from the Scriptures* (1989) tells us that time is running short: "The 'generation' that was alive at the beginning of the fulfillment of the sign in 1914 is now well along in years. The time remaining must be very short. World conditions give every indication that this is the case."[45]

Oh, the madness!

## Millennial Madness and Christians

Millennial madness has certainly afflicted Christians who write about the Rapture and the second coming of Christ. In recent years it seems as if more and more date-setters are coming out of the woodwork making predictions about the exact timing of these events. Let's look at a few of the more notable examples.

### Edgar C. Whisenant and His "88 Reasons"

Edgar C. Whisenant wrote a book entitled *88 Reasons Why the Rapture Will Be in 1988*. This 58-page book sold a whopping 4.5 million copies and stirred no small controversy in the church. The Rapture, Whisenant said, would occur between September 11 and 13, 1988.

In his calculations, Whisenant relied on such unchristian sources as pyramidology, astrology, divination, and numerology.[46] For reasons 64 and 65 he relied on the testimony of astrologer-psychic Jeane Dixon.[47]

In his book *Soothsayers of the Second Advent*, William Alnor points out that Charles Taylor, founder of Today in Bible Prophecy, Inc., planned his 1988 tour of Israel to coincide with Whisenant's date. Taylor used the possibility of being raptured from the Holy Land as a sales incentive: "'Only $1,975 from Los Angeles or $1,805 from New York (and return if necessary),' said his *Bible Prophecy News*. In a later pitch for the tour, he stated:

'We stay at the Intercontinental Hotel right on the Mount of Olives where you can get the beautiful view of the Eastern Gate and the Temple Mount. And if this is the year of our Lord's return, as we anticipate, you may even ascend to Glory from within a few feet of His ascension.' "[48]

As one might expect, when Whisenant's date of the Rapture did not pan out, he adjusted his calculations and set forth other dates. First he settled on October 3, and when that date failed, he affirmed, "It is going to be in a few weeks anyway." Did Whisenant repent when that failed as well? No! Instead, he then claimed his calculations were off by a year and that Christ would return during Rosh Hashanah (September 30) in 1989, or perhaps at the end of the Feast of Tabernacles on October 14-20, 1989.[49]

### Predictions of the Rapture from Korea

A full-page ad that appeared in the October 20, 1991, issue of _USA Today_ said, "RAPTURE: OCTOBER 28, 1992—JESUS IS COMING IN THE AIR." Those who ran the ad also said that on October 28, "50 million people will die in earthquakes, 50 million in traffic accidents, 50 million from fire, 50 million from collapsed buildings, 1.4 billion from World War III, and 1.4 billion from a separate Armageddon."[50]

Who ran these apocalyptic messages? They are from the worldwide _Hyoo-go_ ("rapture") or _Jong Mal Ron_ ("end-time theory") movement—a "loose connection of Korean sects mixing fanaticism, mysticism, and apocalyptic zeal."[51] Various press estimates of the size of this movement range from 20,000 to 100,000 people.[52]

A special report on this movement in the _Christian Research Journal_ said that "as the predicted doomsday drew near, the Hyoo-go adherents provoked social upheaval in Korea." The report notes that "at least four suicides and several abortions were linked with the movement—the latter because some women were afraid of being 'too heavy' to be caught up to heaven. Numerous secondary and elementary school students abandoned classes. Parents and families of the movement's followers feared that if the Rapture did not take place as predicted there would be a mass suicide."[53]

Finally, the anticipated day arrived. Faithful believers gathered in the church in Seoul, Korea, to await the Rapture. "Some 1,500 police officers and 200 detectives were posted outside and inside the church in case anyone became violent or attempted suicide. Yet when the appointed hour passed uneventfully, many of the people simply wept. Said one devastated member: 'God lied to us.' "[54]

|| *This tragedy illustrates just how far* ||
|| *people can go in their apocalyptic zeal.* ||

Why mention this Korean tragedy in a book on the culting of America? First, this movement ran an ad in *USA Today*, trying to reach the American public with the message of the coming Rapture. No doubt some in America had a few preapocalyptic shivers as October 28 drew near. And second, this event illustrates just how far people can go in their apocalyptic zeal. Let this be a warning to all who have ears to hear!

## Harold Camping Predicts a 1994 Rapture

In his controversial book *1994?* Harold Camping of "Family Radio" predicts that Jesus Christ will return in September of 1994. "No book ever written is as audacious or bold as one that claims to predict the timing of the end of the world," he writes, "and that is precisely what this book presumes to do."[55]

"If I am correct in this," he says deliberately, "and there is every indication that I am, we have a very short time left to get right with God." In his book he warns that "when September 6, 1994 arrives, no one else can become saved. The end has come."[56] Camping says that the likelihood of him being wrong on his calculations is "very remote."[57] He affirms, "I would be very surprised if the world reaches the year 2000."[58]

## The Escalation of Millennial Madness

There are other millennially mad Christians we could point to. For example, prophecy teacher Mary Stewart Relfe says she received "divine revelations from the Lord" indicating that the second coming of Christ will occur in 1997.[59] Lester Sumrall said in his book, *I Predict 2000 A.D.*, "I predict the absolute fullness of man's operation on planet Earth by the year 2000 A.D. Then Jesus Christ shall reign from Jerusalem for 1,000 years."[60]

I suspect we have witnessed only the beginning of millennial madness for the coming decade. As one observer commented, the approach of the year 2000 will undoubtedly bring "a synergistic climb toward panic" that will produce social effects that are both "substantial" and "potentially dangerous."[61]

Now, having said all this, I need to clarify that I am a firm believer in the Rapture and the second coming of Christ. It is right and proper that Christians look forward to these glorious events with great anticipation. Christians _should_ be excited that our Lord is coming (I am!). However, we simply do not know the precise timing or dates of these events. And anyone who claims that he _does_ know the dates is not a trustworthy expositor of Scripture.

## Why Christians Should Not Succumb to Millennial Madness

I can think of at least ten good reasons why Christians should not succumb to millennial madness.

First, over the past 2,000 years, the track records of those who have predicted or expected "the end" have been _100 percent wrong_. The history of doomsday predictions is little more than a history of dashed expectations. Though it is _possible_ we are living in the last days, it is also possible that Christ's second coming is still a long way off.

Second, those who give in to millennial madness may end up making harmful decisions for their lives. Selling your possessions and heading for the mountains, going off to join survivalist sects and purchasing bomb shelters, removing family members from school, and leaving your family and friends are all destructive actions that can potentially _ruin_ your life.

Third, Christians who get caught up in millennial madness—by expecting the Rapture to occur by a specific date, for example—may end up damaging their faith when their expectations fail. These same Christians may also find their overall confidence in the Bible waning, all because of misplaced hopes.

Fourth, if believers lose their confidence in the prophetic portions of Scripture, then biblical prophecy will cease to be a motivation to purity and holiness in daily life (_see_ Titus 2:12-14; 2 Peter 3:11; 1 John 3:2,3).

Fifth, Christians who succumb to millennial madness may damage the faith of new or immature believers when predicted events fail to materialize.

Sixth, millennial madness may lead to an atmosphere of what we might call "prophetic agnosticism" in the church. With all of the failed predictions and dashed hopes, people may develop an attitude that "we can't be sure of what the future holds"—even with reference to _biblical_ prophecies.

Seventh, prophets and soothsayers of millennial madness tend to be sensationalistic, and sensationalism is unbefitting to a follower of the Lord Jesus Christ. Christ calls His followers to live _soberly_ and _alertly_ as they await His coming (_see_ Mark 13:32-37).

> **Plan** *your life as though Christ will not be coming in your lifetime;* **live** *your life as though He is coming today.*

Eighth, Christians who get caught up in millennial madness can potentially do damage to the cause of Christ. Humanists, skeptics, atheists, and secularists enjoy talking scornfully about Christians who have put stock in end-time predictions—especially when specific dates have been attached to specific events.[62] Why give more ammunition to those who are antagonistic toward Christianity?

Ninth, Christians who give in to millennial madness may get sidetracked from their first priority—living righteously and in holiness in daily fellowship with the Lord Jesus Christ.

And tenth, the *when* of end-time events is completely in God's hands (Acts 1:7), and we haven't been given the precise details. In view of that, perhaps the best policy is this: *Plan* your life as though Christ will not be coming in your lifetime; *live* your life as though He is coming today.

# Part 4

# *Redeeming America*

# 14

# Against the Darkness

*All that is necessary for the triumph of evil is that good men do nothing.*[1]

—Edmund Burke

*The Christians who have turned the world upside down have been men and women with a vision in their hearts and the Bible in their hands.*[2]

—T.B. Maston

IN THE INTRODUCTION OF this book we took an imaginary journey from the port of Boston to the Carolinas in 1725. We spoke of the rich religious diversity a person would encounter along the way. "America is a vast religious melting pot," it was concluded.

What would we encounter *today* on this same journey from Boston to the Carolinas? At the very least, I think we would witness the following:

- rapidly eroding spiritual foundations, with the majority of Americans rejecting any concept of absolute truth;

- a majority of people holding to moral relativism;

- a Christianity that is only one choice in a vast and ever-growing smorgasbord of religious options;

- a large number of impotent and lifeless Christian churches that have produced indifference, lack of commitment, spiritual dryness, doctrinal immaturity, and biblical illiteracy among members;

- a deluge of cultic and occultic groups vying for the American mainstream;

- an incredible increase in Eastern religions on American soil;

- a cultic and occultic penetration of America's businesses, health facilities, and public schools;

- a shifted family structure, with many children growing up in single-parent households—many of which provide little or no religious foundation for the children;

- a pervasive disillusionment and lack of direction among America's youth;

- a perverted emphasis and use of money, sex, and power in a number of religious groups and cults;

- a surprising number of people who believe that extraterrestrials are presently visiting planet earth and communicating religious messages to humankind;

- an ever-growing number of people who look to the year 2000 as a pivotal year for change—either doomsday or a coming utopia.

A journey from Boston to the Carolinas today might well lead us to conclude that we are living in the twilight of Western culture. The winds of change have swept across America's religious landscape with hurricane force, and the landscape has been ravaged. Is there any hope?

## A Call to Christian Involvement

It is truly unfortunate that many believers today seem to be secret-agent Christians who have never "blown their cover" before an unregenerate world. The fact is, many Christians have little or no impact on their world for Christ or for biblical values.

Many such Christians have a hideous disease that Dr. Walter Martin appropriately labeled *non-rock-a-boatus*. This disease has so effectively neutralized believers that the cancer of cultism has been free to spread at an incredible, unprecedented pace in America.

Christians are so fearful of rocking the boat that they clam up and keep their faith to themselves. They think that if they speak forth for Christ and for biblical values in this predominantly anti-Christian culture they may offend someone or perhaps be ridiculed and embarrassed.

If this disease continues unchecked, you can count on the continued deterioration of America as well as the continued *culting* of America. If Christians do not act, *the cults will*. The war is on—and you as a Christian will be either a soldier in the midst of the conflict or a casualty on the sidelines. Which will it be?

|| *The task begins with a* || *single person*—you. ||

The task cannot be shoved into the hands of the professional clergy. The challenge is just too massive for church leaders alone. Turning back the tide will require the involvement of every single Christian. As Blaise Pascal once put it, "The entire ocean is affected by a single pebble."

The task begins with a single person—*you*. A great thinker once said, "Let him that would move the world, first move himself."[3] If you really want to see the religious climate in America get better, why not take the first step—*you*, without waiting for others to act—and commit to being an agent of change?

## Flexing Apologetic Muscle

When we talk about Christian apologetics, we are not talking about apologizing for our faith, or feeling sorry about our beliefs. "Apologetics" comes from the Greek work *apologia*, which means "defense."

Apologetics—which focuses on the *defense* of Christianity—is seemingly a lost art in today's church. Today the prevailing emphasis could well be summed up this way: "God is a God of love. Let's just love everyone. We shouldn't challenge other people's beliefs because that is unloving." Well, Jesus Christ—*love incarnate*—constantly challenged the beliefs of those who adhered to false teaching (e.g., Matthew 23). We must follow His example.

In view of what we have learned about the culting of America, it is obvious that the need for apologetics today is absolutely critical. Believers must realize that we are living in a post-Christian era with a host of religions, cults, and occultic systems vying continuously for people's commitments and, indeed, for their very lives. We must face these challenges head-on.

The Bible provides us with role models when it comes to apologetics. The apostle Paul is an example. He acted as an apologist when he gave reasons for the faith to both the Jews and Greeks (Acts 17:16-34; 18:4). Apollos is another great example. In Achaia, he earnestly contended for the faith, refuting unbelievers in public debate and "proving from the Scriptures that Jesus was the Christ" (Acts 18:24-28).

Through the use of apologetics we can provide well-reasoned evidences to the nonbeliever as to why he ought to choose Christianity rather than any other religion. Apologetics can be used to show the unbeliever that all the other options in the smorgasbord of world religions *are not really options at all*, since they are false. Apologetics can remove the mental roadblocks that prevent a nonbeliever from responding to the gospel.

Apologetics provides not only a defense for the faith, it also provides security to Christians who seek assurance that their faith is not a blind leap into a dark chasm, but rather, that it is founded on fact. Apologetics demonstrates *why* we believe *what* we believe. It does not *replace* our faith, it *grounds* our faith.

## Contending for the Faith

With the above in mind, we must recognize that each and every Christian is called by God to "contend earnestly for the faith which was once for all delivered to the saints" (Jude 3 NASB). Because the original Greek text of this verse is so rich with meaning, I'd like to share a few observations with you.

To begin, the definite article ("the") preceding "faith" points to the *one and only* faith; there is no other faith. *"The* faith" refers to the body of truth God gave the church through divine revelation. References to this orthodox body of truth are sprinkled throughout the New Testament. Note the following (and pay special attention to the emphasized words):

- Acts 6:7 indicates that following Pentecost, "the word of God kept on spreading; and the number of the disciples continued to increase greatly in Jerusalem, and a great many of the priests were becoming obedient to *the faith*" (NASB).

- Later, after Paul had become a believer, Galatians 1:23 says of him that "he who once persecuted us [believers] is now preaching *the faith*" (NASB).

- Speaking prophetically, this same Paul writes that "in later times some will abandon *the faith*" (1 Timothy 4:1).

According to Jude 3, this body of truth was _"once for all_ delivered to the saints" (emphasis added). The Greek word translated "once for all" _(apax)_ refers to something that has been done for _all_ time, something that _never_ needs repeating. The revelatory process was _over and done with_ after this "faith" had "once for all" been delivered.

It is noteworthy that the word translated "delivered" in Jude 3 is what Greek grammarians call an aorist passive participle, which indicates an act that was _completed in the past_ with _no continuing element_. There would be no new "faith" or body of truth communicated through psychics or channelers or cultists!

Now, it is important to recognize that you and I as Christians are called to contend for this faith. What does it mean to _"contend_ earnestly for the faith"? The word translated "contend" was often used in New Testament times to refer to competition in athletic contests. The idea behind the word, then, is that of an intense and vigorous struggle to defeat the opposition.

The English word "agony" comes from the noun form of "contend" (Greek: _agonia)_. In ancient times, athletes would push themselves to the _point of agony_ in their struggle to win. Likewise, believers are to engage in _an intense and vigorous struggle_ to defend Christianity—"the faith"— against intrusive cultic challengers.

> _Unfortunately, many Christians today are running around waiting for a_ **convenient** **moment** _to contend for the faith—a moment that never comes._

As Christians, we are called to contend for the faith by "telling it like it is." Look at it this way: Would we have had a Reformation if Martin Luther hadn't told it like it was to the Roman Catholic church? No, we wouldn't. Luther saw a deviation from "the faith" and he accordingly contended for the faith. We must follow Luther's example.

Unfortunately, many Christians today are running around waiting for a _convenient moment_ to contend for the faith—a moment that never comes. Let's be clear on this: God doesn't care about convenience; _God cares about obedience_. We are called to contend for the faith, regardless of whether it is convenient or inconvenient. We must contend for the faith whenever and wherever the opportunity arises.

## Prepared to Give Answers

Scripture exhorts us to always be prepared to give people reasons why we believe the way we do. First Peter 3:15 says, *"Always* be prepared to give an answer to everyone who asks you to give the reason for the hope that you have. But do this with gentleness and respect" (emphasis added).

The only way to be always prepared to give an answer to everyone is to become equipped with apologetic answers. With the resources that are available today, this is not difficult to do. All it requires is a commitment of time.

As a start, there are many dozens of free apologetic items available from the Christian Research Institute, where I serve. Write me—I'll send you a list of free materials that will help you build up your apologetic muscle.[4] Also, see the appendix for a list of recommended books that will help ground you in the essentials of the Christian faith.

## Christians as Salt and Light

Most important of all, we who are Christians must commit to being salt and light in our society.

Jesus said, "You are the salt of the earth; but if the salt has become tasteless, how will it be made salty again? It is good for nothing any more, except to be thrown out and trampled under foot by men" (Matthew 5:13 NASB). Salt is known for its effectiveness as a preservative. We are to have a preserving effect on the world by influencing it for Christ.

In order to accomplish this, however, we must first make sure we are fully committed to the Savior and are preserved in purity as individuals. Then and only then can we act as a preserving agent in our society. As Bible teacher Alfred Plummer has put it, Christians "must beware lest, instead of preserving others, they themselves become tainted with rottenness. The salt must be in close contact with that which it preserves; and too often, while Christians raise the morality of the world, they allow their own morality to be lowered by the world."[5]

*The Christian should stand out like a sparkling diamond.*

Jesus also said, "You are the light of the world. A city set on a hill cannot be hidden" (Matthew 5:14 NASB). Jesus did not call us to be "secret agent"

Christians. We are not to cloak our lights. Someone once said, "No one is a light unto himself, not even the sun."[6] Because the darkness of the cults is hovering over Western culture as never before, there has never been a time when the light of each individual Christian has been more needed. As evangelist Billy Graham said, "The Christian should stand out like a sparkling diamond."[7]

In what specific ways can we as Christians be salt and light? Well, we can begin with where God has placed us right now—in our family, church, workplace, school, and so on. For example:

- As Christians we can be salt and light in our own churches by making sure a heavy emphasis is placed on learning and being grounded in basic Christian doctrine, and by equipping ourselves to defend, contend for, and give reasons for our faith.

- As Christian parents we can be salt and light in our own families by putting Christ first and setting a godly example for our children, providing them with biblical values and direction.

- As Christian parents we can be salt and light by uniting with other Christian parents to collectively influence state and district choices in school curriculum materials. We can also volunteer and become involved in our children's schools to ensure that New Age ideas are not being taught in the classroom.

- As Christian professionals we can be salt and light at the workplace by reflecting Christ in our actions and speech. We can also take a respectful but unbendingly firm stand against New Age human-potential seminars.

- As Christian citizens active in society, we can be salt and light by standing against societal intruders such as secular humanism and moral relativity whenever and wherever they surface.

By being salt and light in these and other areas, we can make a real difference in our world and go a long way toward the *un*culting of America. Also, in the appendixes I've listed a number of individuals and organizations that can help you be salt and light in various areas of American culture. It would be worth your while to check out what resources are available to you.

Will you be a part of the solution? Will you take a stand with me? If so, I'd like to hear from you. Write me:

**Ron Rhodes**
Christian Research Institute
P.O. Box 500
San Juan Capistrano, CA 92693

*Recommended Books*

*Recommended Organizations*

*Notes*

*Bibliography*

*Subject Index*

# Appendix A

## Recommended Books

The following books are highly recommended for helping to ground you in the essential doctrines of the Christian faith:

Enns, Paul. *Approaching God: Daily Readings in Systematic Theology*. Chicago: Moody Press, 1991.

Enns, Paul. *The Moody Handbook of Theology*. Chicago: Moody Press, 1989.

Hanegraaff, Hank. *Christianity in Crisis*. Eugene, OR: Harvest House Publishers, 1993.

Lightner, Robert P. *Evangelical Theology*. Grand Rapids: Baker Book House, 1986.

Packer, J.I. *Knowing God*. Downers Grove, IL: InterVarsity Press, 1979.

Rhodes, Ron. *Christ Before the Manger: The Life and Times of the Preincarnate Christ*. Grand Rapids: Baker Book House, 1992.

Rhodes, Ron. *Reasoning from the Scriptures with the Jehovah's Witnesses*. Eugene, OR: Harvest House Publishers, 1992.

Ryrie, Charles C. *Basic Theology*. Wheaton, IL: Victor Books, 1986.

Ryrie, Charles C. *What You Should Know About Social Responsibility*. Chicago: Moody Press, 1982.

Swindoll, Charles R. *Growing Deep in the Christian Life*. Portland, OR: Multnomah Press, 1986.

Thiessen, Henry C. *Lectures in Systematic Theology*. Grand Rapids: Eerdmans, 1981.

# Appendix B

## Recommended Organizations

The following ministries are recommended as resources that may be of help to you in your efforts to be salt and light in our society. You may wish to contact them and request that they add your name to their respective mailing lists.

(Please note that inclusion on this list does not imply a full endorsement of every aspect of these ministries.)

## General Countercult Ministries

*Christian Research Institute International*, P.O. Box 500, San Juan Capistrano, CA 92693; (714) 855-9926. This is the largest countercult ministry in the world. Produces many materials (some free) on the cults, the occult, the New Age movement, world religions, and apologetic issues. Write or call for a free *Resource Catalogue*. A subscription to the quarterly *Christian Research Journal* is available for $16.00/year.

*Christian Research Institute Canada*, John Tiebe, P.O. Box 3216, Station B, Calgary, Alberta, Canada, T2M 4L7; (403) 277-7702. Great materials on the cults, the occult, the New Age movement, and general apologetics.

*Cornerstone Apologetics Research Team*, Eric Pement, 920 W. Wilson Ave., Chicago, IL 60640-5718; (312) 989-2080. Focuses on the cults, the occult, and general apologetics. Contact this ministry for information on ordering *The Directory of Cult Research Organizations*.

*Personal Freedom Outreach*, P.O. Box 26062, St. Louis, MO 63136; (314) 388-2648. Focuses on the cults, the occult, and the New Age movement.

*Spiritual Counterfeits Project* (SCP), P.O. Box 4308, Berkeley, CA 94704; (510) 540-0300. This ministry produces good materials on the cults, the occult, and the New Age movement.

*Watchman Fellowship, Inc.*, Rick Branch, P.O. Box 13251, Arlington, TX 76094-0251; (817) 277-0023. Focuses on the cults and apologetics.

## Ministries to Jehovah's Witnesses

*Comments from the Friends*, David Reed, P.O. Box 840, Stoughton, MA 02072; (508) 584-4467. This is an ex-Jehovah's Witness support ministry. They send out an excellent newsletter. David Reed is a regular contributor to the *Christian Research Journal*.

*Witness, Inc.*, Duane Magnani, P.O. Box 597, Clayton, CA 94517; (510) 672-5979. This ministry publishes excellent materials on the Jehovah's Witnesses, and is the best resource for copies of old Watchtower publications.

## Ministries to Mormons

*Gospel Truths Ministries*, Luke Wilson, 1340 Monroe Ave., N.W., Grand Rapids, MI 49505; (616) 451-4562. This organization produces helpful materials on witnessing to Mormons.

*Utah Lighthouse Ministry*, Jerald and Sandra Tanner, P.O. Box 1884, Salt Lake City, UT 84110; (801) 485-8894. This ministry produces helpful materials on witnessing to Mormons. They are also a great resource for finding rare Mormon documents.

## Ministry to Hindus

*East-West Gospel Ministries*, Rabi Maharaj, 1605 E. Elizabeth St., Pasadena, CA 91104; (818) 398-2345. This ministry focuses on Hinduism, Eastern religion, and the New Age movement.

## Ministry to Buddhists

*Sonrise Center for Buddhist Studies*, James Stephens (Director), Box 4796, Panorama City, CA 91412; (818) 797-9008.

## Ministry to UFO Advocates

*Eastern Christian Outreach*, William Alnor, P.O. Box 11322, Philadelphia, PA 19137; (215) 289-7885.

## Cult Rehabilitation

*Wellspring Retreat and Resource Center*, Paul Martin, P.O. Box 67, Albany, OH 45710; (614) 698-6277. Wellspring is a residential facility for cult rehabilitation on 400 acres near Albany, Ohio. They provide professional counseling and therapy.

## Ministries to the Family

*FamilyLife Conferences*, P.O. Box 23840, Little Rock, AR 72221-3840; (800) 999-8663. I can tell you from firsthand experience that attending this conference is one of the best things you can do for your family. Chuck Swindoll says, "Looking for positive solutions based on biblical and workable principles that will strengthen your commitment to marriage and pull your family closer together? You've found it! The FamilyLife Conferences will make it happen."

*Focus on the Family*, 8605 Explorer Drive, Colorado Springs, CO 80920; (719) 531-3400. This organization offers numerous helpful books related to marriage, the family, and raising kids.

# Statistics

*Barna Research Group, Ltd.*, P.O. Box 4152, Glendale, CA 91222-0152. This group, headed by George Barna, is a full-service marketing research company that specializes in research for Christian churches and church-related groups, the media, advertising agencies, and nonprofit organizations. They regularly publish helpful books and reports relevant to religion in America.

# Notes

**The Approaching Darkness**
1. Sydney E. Ahlstrom, *A Religious History of the American People* (New York: Image Books, 1975), 31.
2. Ahlstrom, *Religious History*, 31.
3. Martin E. Marty, "Religious Pluralism," in *Dictionary of Christianity in America*, ed. Daniel G. Reid (Downers Grove, IL: InterVarsity Press, 1990), 912.
4. Ahlstrom, *Religious History*, 31.
5. *See* William W. Sweet, *The Story of Religion in America* (Grand Rapids: Baker Book House, 1979), 66.
6. J.E. Wood, "Separation of Church and State," in *Dictionary of Christianity in America*, 268.
7. James Madison; cited by Wood, 267.
8. The term "cult" is not intended as a pejorative, inflammatory, or injurious word. The term is used in this book simply as a means of categorizing certain religious or semireligious groups in modern America.

   A cult may be defined from both a sociological and a theological perspective. Sociologically speaking, a cult is a religious or semireligious sect or group whose members are controlled or dominated almost entirely by a single individual or organization. A sociological definition of a cult generally includes (but is not limited to) the authoritarian, manipulative, and sometimes communal features of cults.

   In this type of cult, converts are sometimes cut off from all former associations, including their own families. The Hare Krishnas, The Family ("Children of God"), and Sun Myung Moon's Unification Church are examples of this kind of cult.

   Theologically speaking, a cult is a religious group that claims to be Christian but in fact denies one or more of the essential doctrines of historic, orthodox Christianity (as defined in the major historic creeds of Christianity). Such groups deny or distort essential Christian doctrines such as the deity of Christ, the personality and deity of the Holy Spirit, the Trinity, and salvation by grace through faith alone. Cults that fall into this category include the Mormons and Jehovah's Witnesses.

**Chapter 1: Cult Explosion U.S.A.**
1. George Gallup; cited in Russell Chandler, "The Changing Church," *Moody Monthly*, January 1992, 13.
2. Walter Martin, *Martin Speaks Out on the Cults* (Ventura, CA: Regal Books, 1983), 91.
3. George Barna, *Absolute Confusion: How Our Moral and Spiritual Foundations Are Eroding in This Age of Change* (Ventura, CA: Regal Books, 1993), 15.
4. Chuck Colson, *Against the Night: Living in the New Dark Ages* (Ann Arbor, MI: Servant Publications, 1989), 22.
5. Ibid., 19.
6. Carl F. Henry, *Twilight of a Great Civilization* (Westchester, IL: Crossway Books, 1988).
7. Malcolm Muggeridge, *The End of Christendom* (Grand Rapids: Eerdmans, 1980).
8. These publications are cited by Colson, 10.
9. *See* Walter Martin, *The Kingdom of the Cults* (Minneapolis: Bethany House Publishers, 1985).
10. *Arizona Republic*; cited in *Christian Research Newsletter*, September/October 1991, 6.
11. Ibid.
12. Ibid.
13. Ibid.
14. Ibid.
15. Ibid.
16. "LDS Church Gains Converts Through Media Campaign," *The Salt Lake Tribune*, 6 December 1989, 16A.
17. Ibid.
18. Russell Chandler, *Racing Toward 2001* (Grand Rapids: Zondervan Publishing House, 1992), 188.
19. *Christian Research Newsletter*, November/December 1991; 6; cf. *Church News*, 5 October 1991.
20. George Barna, *The Barna Report 1992-93* (Ventura, CA: Regal Books, 1993), 201.
21. Ibid.
22. *The Watchtower*, 1 January 1993.
23. "The Growth of Jehovah's Witnesses," *Christian Research Newsletter*, January/February 1992, 2; cf. *The Watchtower*, 1 January 1993, 6.
24. *The Watchtower*, 1 January 1993, 15.
25. *See* the book *Reasoning from the Scriptures with the Jehovah's Witnesses* (Eugene, OR: Harvest House Publishers, 1993).
26. *The Christian Herald*, February 1988, 51.
27. Ron Rhodes, *The New Age Movement*, series ed. Alan Gomes (Grand Rapids: Zondervan Publishing House, 1994); cf. Elliot Miller, *A Crash Course on the New Age Movement* (Grand Rapids: Baker Book House, 1989), 16.
28. *See* Rhodes, *New Age Movement*, Part I.
29. Russell Chandler, *Understanding the New Age* (Dallas: Word Publishing, 1991), 8-9.
30. Ibid., 8.
31. "Current Research: Recent Findings on Religious Attitudes and Behavior," *Religion Watch*, February 1993, 3.
32. Ibid.
33. Gallup Poll; *Los Angeles Times*, 8 August 1993, E3.
34. Richard Morin, "A Revival of Faith in Religion," *The Sacramento Bee*, 4 July 1993, 1.
35. Chandler, *Understanding the New Age*, 8.

36. Morin, 1.
37. Ruth Tucker, *Another Gospel: Alternative Religions and the New Age Movement* (Grand Rapids: Zondervan Publishing House, 1989), 320.
38. Chandler, *Understanding the New Age*, 9.
39. Marilyn Ferguson, book review of *Heaven on Earth* by Michael D'Antonio, *Los Angeles Times*, 16 February 1993, 1.
40. Ibid.
41. Miller, 141.
42. Chandler, *Understanding the New Age*, 8.
43. Ibid.; cf. John Ankerberg and John Weldon, *Cult Watch: What You Need to Know About Spiritual Deception* (Eugene, OR: Harvest House Publishers, 1991), 141.
44. Barna, *The Barna Report 1992-93*, 74.
45. Ibid.
46. Ibid.
47. Ibid.
48. Ibid.
49. Miller, 22.
50. Ibid.
51. Cf. John Ankerberg and John Weldon, *The Facts on Hinduism in America* (Eugene, OR: Harvest House Publishers, 1991), 8.
52. Chandler, *Racing Toward 2001*, 189.
53. Ibid.
54. "New-Style Hindu Missionaries Coming to the West," *Religion Watch*, February 1991, 4.
55. Ibid.
56. *See* Robert Morey, *The Islamic Invasion* (Eugene, OR: Harvest House Publishers, 1992), 7.
57. Richard Bernstein, "A Growing Islamic Presence," *New York Times*, 2 May 1993, A14.
58. Morey, 6.
59. Colin Chapman, "The Riddle of Religions," *Christianity Today*, 14 May 1990, 16.
60. Morey, 6.
61. Chandler, *Racing Toward 2001*, 185.
62. Peter Steinfels, "Despite Role on World Stage, Muslims Turn to the Personal," *New York Times*, 7 May 1993, A1.
63. Bernstein, 1.
64. Chandler, *Racing Toward 2001*, 184.
65. Steinfels, A13.
66. Chandler, *Racing Toward 2001*, 184.
67. Bernstein, 14.
68. Ibid.
69. Ibid.
70. Ibid.
71. George Barna, *What Americans Believe* (Ventura, CA: Regal Books, 1991), 36.
72. Ibid., 175.
73. Ibid.
74. Barna, *The Barna Report 1992-93*, 169.
75. Wade Clark Roof, "The Four Spiritual Styles of Baby Boomers," *The Denver Post*, 21 March 1993, 4.
76. Ibid., 5.
77. Ibid.
78. Ibid.
79. Richard N. Ostling, "The Church Search," *Time*, 5 April 1993, 46.
80. Roof, 5.
81. Ostling, 46.
82. *Newsweek*, 17 December 1991; cited in *Christian Research Newsletter*, January/February 1991, 3.
83. Ostling, 45.
84. Ibid.

## Chapter 2: Christianity Astray

1. *Draper's Book of Quotations for the Christian World*, ed. Edythe Draper (Wheaton, IL: Tyndale House Publishers, 1992), 84.
2. Cited in Chuck Colson, *Against the Night: Living in the New Dark Ages* (Ann Arbor, MI: Servant Publications, 1989), 159-60.
3. *Spiritual Counterfeits Project Newsletter*; cited in Ronald Enroth, *The Lure of the Cults* (Downers Grove, IL: Inter-Varsity Press, 1987), 110.
4. John Blanchard, *More Gathered Gold* (Hertfordshire, England: Evangelical Press, 1986), 49.
5. George Barna, *What Americans Believe* (Ventura, CA: Regal Books, 1991), 167; cf. George Barna, *Absolute Confusion: How Our Moral and Spiritual Foundations Are Eroding in This Age of Change* (Ventura, CA: Regal Books, 1993), 59-60.
6. Ibid.
7. Barna, *What Americans Believe*, 29.
8. George Barna, *The Barna Report 1992-93* (Ventura, CA: Regal Books, 1993), 43.
9. Ibid., 54.

10. Ibid., 82.
11. Russell Chandler, *Racing Toward 2001* (Grand Rapids: Zondervan Publishing House, 1992), 112.
12. Chandler, 112.
13. John Wesley; cited in Blanchard, 43.
14. Draper, 83.
15. Ibid., 79-80.
16. *EP News Service*, 24 May 1991, 8.
17. Ibid., 8.
18. Barna, *The Barna Report 1992-93*, 21.
19. Chandler, 216.
20. Ibid., 216.
21. *See* Walter Martin, *The Kingdom of the Cults* (Minneapolis: Bethany House Publishers, 1985), 11-37; Walter Martin, *The New Cults* (Ventura, CA: Regal Books, 1980), 22; Enroth, 103-11.
22. Paul R. Martin, "Dispelling the Myths: The Psychological Consequences of Cultic Involvement," *Christian Research Journal*, Winter/Spring 1989, 11.
23. Josh McDowell and Don Stewart, *Understanding the Cults* (San Bernardino, CA: Here's Life Publishers, 1983), 20.
24. Ruth A. Tucker, *Another Gospel: Alternative Religions and the New Age Movement* (Grand Rapids: Zondervan Publishing House, 1989), 25.
25. J.K. Van Baalen; cited in Walter Martin, *The Kingdom of the Cults*, 14.
26. Paul R. Martin, 11.
27. *See* Harold Bussell, "Why Evangelicals Are Attracted to the Cults," *Moody Monthly*, March 1985, 111-13.
28. Paul R. Martin, 11.
29. Bussell, 111.
30. Chandler, 165.
31. Chuck Colson, interview published in the *Christian Research Newsletter*, March/April 1993, 1.
32. Ibid.
33. Chuck Colson, "Welcome to McChurch," *Christianity Today*, 23 November 1992, 30.
34. Dwight L. Moody; cited in Blanchard, 45.
35. J. Gordon Melton; cited in Tucker, 26.
36. Orville Swenson, *The Perilous Path of Cultism* (Caronport, Saskatchewan, Canada: Briercrest Books, 1987), 87.
37. Swenson, 14.
38. Barna, *The Barna Report 1992-93*, 59.
39. Barna, *What Americans Believe*, 173.
40. Barna, *The Barna Report 1992-93*, 67.
41. Ibid., 68.
42. Ibid.
43. Enroth, 49.
44. Robert and Gretchen Passantino; cited in Swenson, 96.
45. Enroth, 48.
46. Barna, *The Barna Report 1992-93*, 64.
47. Walter Martin, *The Rise of the Cults* (Ventura, CA: Regal Books, 1983), 24.
48. Kenneth Woodward; cited in Colson, "Welcome to McChurch," 31.
49. Barna, *The Barna Report 1992-93*, 50.
50. Karl Menninger, *What Ever Became of Sin?* (New York: Hawthorne Books, 1973).
51. Barna, *The Barna Report 1992-93*, 43, 50.
52. Ibid., 52.
53. Ibid.
54. Ibid., 41.
55. John MacArthur, "But What Does It Mean to Me?" *Masterpiece*, September/October 1989, 2.
56. Ibid., 3.
57. Colson, *Christian Research Newsletter*, 2.
58. Ibid.
59. Ibid.
60. Cited in Colson, *Against the Night*, 163.

## Chapter 3: Truth Decay

1. Chrysostom; cited in John Blanchard, *More Gathered Gold* (Hertfordshire, England: Evangelical Press, 1986), 31.
2. John Calvin; cited in Chuck Colson, *Against the Night: Living in the New Dark Ages* (Ann Arbor, MI: Servant Publications, 1989), 152.
3. George Barna, *What Americans Believe* (Ventura, CA: Regal Books, 1991), 289.
4. George Barna, *The Barna Report 1992-93* (Ventura, CA: Regal Books, 1993), 189.
5. Mortimer J. Adler; cited in *Illustrations for Biblical Preaching*, ed. Michael P. Green, © 1989. Electronic media, hypercard stack for Macintosh. (IBP-PC, P.O. Box 06746, Ft. Myers, FL 33906.)
6. The One-Minute Bible, ed. John. R. Kohlenberger III (Bloomington, MN: Garborgs, 1993); advertisement in *Christian Retailing*, June 1993, 41.
7. Ibid.
8. Kenneth Woodward et al., "A Time to Seek," *Newsweek*, 17 December 1990, 54.
9. Interview with R.C. Sproul; published in *Christian Research Newsletter*, November-December 1993, 1-3.

10. Barna, *What Americans Believe*, 217.
11. Ibid.
12. Lee Strobel, *Inside the Mind of Unchurched Harry & Mary* (Grand Rapids: Zondervan Publishing House, 1993), 51.
13. George Barna, *Absolute Confusion: How Our Moral and Spiritual Foundations Are Eroding in This Age of Change* (Ventura, CA: Regal Books, 1993), 139.
14. "U.S. Values on Zigzag Course, Polls Indicate," *Los Angeles Times*, 13 March 1993, B9.
15. Ibid.
16. Barna, *Absolute Confusion*, 74-75.
17. Ibid., 83.
18. *See* Harold Bussell, "Why Evangelicals Are Attracted to the Cults," *Moody Monthly*, March 1985, 111.
19. Walter Martin, *Martin Speaks Out on the Cults* (Ventura, CA: Regal Books, 1983), 23.
20. Walter Martin, *Kingdom of the Cults* (Minneapolis: Bethany House Publishers, 1985), 20.
21. Mary Baker Eddy; cited in James Sire, *Scripture Twisting: 20 Ways the Cults Misread the Bible* (Downers Grove, IL. InterVarsity Press, 1980), 107.
22. Cited in Sire, 108.
23. Mark and Elizabeth Clare Prophet; cited in Ron Rhodes, *The Counterfeit Christ of the New Age Movement* (Grand Rapids: Baker Book House, 1990), 83.
24. Ibid.
25. Ibid.
26. Ibid.
27. David Spangler; cited in Rhodes, 80.
28. John Boykin, "The Baha'i Faith," in Ronald Enroth, *A Guide to Cults and New Religions* (Downers Grove, IL: InterVarsity Press, 1983), 29.
29. Ibid., 34-35.
30. Ibid.
31. Ibid.
32. Hank Hanegraaff, *Christianity in Crisis* (Eugene, OR: Harvest House Publishers, 1993), 220.
33. Ibid., 91.
34. Ibid., 36, 52, 53.
35. Jerry Savelle, "The Authority of the Believer," *The Word Study Bible* (Tulsa, OK: Harrison House, 1990), 1141
36. Kenneth E. Hagin, *Zoe: The God-Kind of Life* (Tulsa, OK: Kenneth Hagin Ministries, Inc., 1989), 35-36, 41.
37. Robert A. Traina, *Methodical Bible Study* (Wilmore, KY: Asbury Theological Seminary, 1952), 5.
38. Norman L. Geisler, *Explaining Hermeneutics: A Commentary*, with Exposition by J.I. Packer (Oakland, CA: International Council on Biblical Inerrancy, 1983), 7.
39. Tal Brooke, *When the World Will Be as One* (Eugene, OR: Harvest House Publishers, 1989), 118.
40. Quoted by Russell H. Dilday, Jr., *The Doctrine of Biblical Authority* (Nashville, TN: Convention Press, 1982), 120.
41. Ibid.
42. Bernard Ramm, *Protestant Bible Interpretation* (Grand Rapids: Baker Book House, 1978), 105.
43. J.I. Packer, *"Fundamentalism" and the Word of God* (Grand Rapids: Eerdmans, 1958), 102.
44. *See* Rhodes, *The New Age Movement*.
45. E.g., Roy B. Zuck, *The Holy Spirit in Your Teaching* (Wheaton, IL: Victor Books, 1963), and "The Role of the Holy Spirit in Hermeneutics," *Bibliotheca Sacra* 141 (April-June 1984):120-30.
46. Sire, 17.
47. Zuck, 126.
48. Cited in Ramm, 14.
49. Ramm, 18.

### Chapter 4: Broken Children in Broken Families

1. *Draper's Book of Quotations for the Christian World*, ed. Edythe Draper (Wheaton, IL: Tyndale House Publishers, 1992), 460.
2. Armand Nicholi, "What Do We Know About Successful Families?" This monograph is available from Grad Resources, 13612 Midway Road, Suite 500, Dallas, TX 75244.
3. Ibid.
4. Ibid.
5. George Barna, *The Future of the American Family* (Chicago: Moody Press, 1993), 37.
6. Russell Chandler, *Racing Toward 2001* (Grand Rapids: Zondervan Publishing House, 1992), 91.
7. Ibid.
8. Ibid., 93.
9. Barna, 41.
10. Ibid.
11. Ibid., 106.
12. Ibid., 26.
13. Ibid., 35.
14. Ibid.
15. George Barna, *What Americans Believe* (Ventura, CA: Regal Books, 1991), 301.
16. Chandler, 93; Barna, *The Future of the American Family*, 106.
17. Cited by Barna, *The Future of the American Family*, 105.
18. Ibid.

19. Barna, *What Americans Believe*, 301.
20. Chandler, 94.
21. Philip Elmer-DeWitt; cited in Chandler, 92.
22. Barna, *The Future of the American Family*, 100.
23. Ibid., 172.
24. George Barna, *The Barna Report 1992-93* (Ventura, CA: Regal Books, 1993), 117.
25. Ibid.
26. Barna, *The Future of the Family*, 137.
27. Ibid., 53.
28. Chandler, 95-96.
29. Barna, *The Future of the American Family*, 131.
30. Ibid., 46.
31. Chandler, 91.
32. Martin Luther; cited in John Blanchard, *More Gathered Gold* (Hertfordshire, England: Evangelical Press, 1986), 102.
33. Walter Martin, *The New Cults* (Ventura, CA: Regal Books, 1980), 28.
34. Berit Kjos, *Your Child and the New Age* (Wheaton, IL: Victor Books, 1990), 39.
35. Ronald Enroth, *The Lure of the Cults* (Downers Grove, IL: InterVarsity Press, 1987), 48.
36. Ibid., 95.
37. Ibid.
38. Cited in Enroth, 51.
39. Enroth, 51.
40. *See* Ron Rhodes, *The Counterfeit Christ of the New Age Movement* (Grand Rapids: Baker Book House, 1990).
41. Enroth, 51.
42. Ibid.
43. Ibid., 52.
44. Paul Martin, *Cult-Proofing Your Kids* (Grand Rapids: Zondervan Publishing House, 1993), 48.
45. Enroth, 54.
46. Paul Martin, 48.
47. Ibid.
48. Ibid.
49. Ibid.
50. Cited in "Parent-Child Intimacy," unpublished essay by Ron Rhodes, on file with the author.
51. Paul Martin, 89.
52. Enroth, 102.
53. Ibid.
54. Ibid.
55. Perhaps the best place to start is to attend the "FamilyLife Conference." I can tell you from firsthand experience that attending this conference is one of the best things you can do for your family. Chuck Swindoll says, "Looking for positive solutions based on biblical and workable principles that will strengthen your commitment to marriage and pull your family closer together? You've found it! The FamilyLife Conferences will make it happen." For more information, you can write: FamilyLife Conferences, P.O. Box 23840, Little Rock, AR 72221-3840; or, call 1-800-999-8663.

   You may also want to get on the mailing list of Focus on the Family, 8605 Explorer Drive, Colorado Springs, CO 80920; or call 719-531-3400. This organization offers many helpful books related to marriage, the family, and raising kids.

   Finally, you can write me for a detailed bibliography of recommended books on marriage, the family, and parenting: Ron Rhodes, Christian Research Institute, P.O. Box 500, San Juan Capistrano, CA 92693.

## Chapter 5: America's Shifting Sands

1. Charles Colson, *Against the Night* (Ann Arbor, MI: Servant Publications, 1989), 19.
2. Norman Geisler and William Watkins, *Worlds Apart: A Handbook on World Views* (Grand Rapids: Baker Book House, 1989), 11.
3. Norman L. Geisler, *Is Man the Measure?* (Grand Rapids: Baker Book House, 1979).
4. *Humanist Manifesto II*, ed. Paul Kurtz (Buffalo, NY: Prometheus Books, 1973), n.p.
5. James Hitchcock, *What Is Secular Humanism?* (Ann Arbor, MI: Servant Books, 1982), vi.
6. Cited in *Christianity and Humanism*, 11, (n.p., n.d.); on file at CRI.
7. Carl Sagan, *Cosmos* (New York: Ballantine Books, 1985), 1.
8. Isaac Asimov, *Isaac Asimov's Book of Science and Nature Quotations* (New York: Weidenfeld & Nicolson, 1988), xvi.
9. Frederick Edwords, "The Humanist Philosophy in Perspective," *The Humanist*, January/February 1984 (n.p.).
10. *Christianity and Humanism*, 12.
11. Ibid.
12. Ibid.
13. *Humanist Manifesto II*, ed. Paul Kurtz.
14. Paul Kurtz, *Forbidden Fruit: The Ethics of Humanism* (Buffalo, NY: Prometheus Books, 1988), 243.
15. *Humanist Manifesto II*, ed. Paul Kurtz.
16. Douglas Groothuis, *Unmasking the New Age* (Downers Grove, IL: InterVarsity Press, 1986), 40.
17. Cited in Groothuis, 56.

18. Russell Chandler, *Understanding the New Age* (Dallas: Word Publishing, 1991), 268.
19. Charles Colson, *Kingdoms in Conflict* (New York: William Morrow, 1987), 78.
20. John Stott, lecture given at All Saints by the Sea Episcopal Church, Santa Barbara, CA, 14 November 1987; cited in Chandler, 268.
21. Groothuis, 41.
22. Orville Swenson, *The Perilous Path of Cultism* (Caronport, Saskatchewan, Canada: Briercrest Books, 1987), 13.
23. Ronald Enroth, *A Guide to Cults and New Religions* (Downers Grove, IL: InterVarsity Press, 1983), 7.
24. Groothuis, 52.
25. Ibid., 53.
26. Ibid.
27. Sydney E. Ahlstrom, *A Religious History of the American People* (New York: Image Books, 1975), 31.
28. Kenneth Boa, *Cults, World Religions, and You* (Wheaton, IL: Victor Books, 1979), 4.
29. Colin Chapman, "The Riddle of Religions," *Christianity Today*, 14 May 1990, 17.
30. Groothuis, 71.
31. George Barna, *Absolute Confusion: How Our Moral and Spiritual Foundations Are Eroding in This Age of Change* (Ventura, CA: Regal Books, 1993), 90.
32. Cited in Colson, *Against the Night*, 48.
33. Elliot Miller, "The 1993 Parliament of the World's Religions (Part One: Interreligious Dialogue or New Age Rally?)," *Christian Research Journal*, Fall 1993, 10.
34. Ibid.
35. Cited by Miller, 10.
36. Miller, 11.
37. Cited by Miller, 11.
38. Miller, 11.
39. Ibid.
40. Cited by Miller, 11.
41. For more details on Miller's message, *see* Miller, 11-13.
42. Cited by Miller, 12-13.
43. Miller, 11.
44. Julia Spangler, "Compass Points," *Lorian Journal* 1:2, 3.
45. David Spangler, *Emergence: The Rebirth of the Sacred* (New York: Dell, 1984), 41.
46. Levi Dowling, *The Aquarian Gospel of Jesus the Christ* (London: L.N. Fowler & Co., 1947), 56.
47. David Spangler, *Relationship & Identity* (Forres, Scotland: Findhorn Publications, 1978), 46-47.
48. George Barna, *What Americans Believe* (Ventura, CA: Regal Books, 1991), 175.
49. Ibid., emphasis added.
50. Barna, *Absolute Confusion*, 80.
51. Ron Rhodes, *The New Age Movement*, series ed. Alan Gomes (Grand Rapids: Zondervan Publishing House, 1994).
52. Os Guinness, *The Dust of Death* (Downers Grove, IL: InterVarsity Press, 1973), 195.
53. *See* Chandler, 11.
54. Cited in Ronald Enroth, *The Lure of the Cults* (Downers Grove, IL: InterVarsity Press, 1987), 42.
55. Ibid.
56. *The New Age Rage*, ed. Karen Hoyt (Old Tappan, NJ: Revell, 1987), 28.
57. James Sire, *The Universe Next Door* (Downers Grove, IL: InterVarsity Press, 1992), 138-39.
58. Ibid.
59. Ibid.
60. Ibid., 155.
61. Douglas Groothuis, *Confronting the New Age* (Downers Grove, IL: InterVarsity Press, 1988), 19.
62. Barna, *What Americans Believe*, 36.
63. Ibid., 83.
64. Elliot Miller, "Breaking Through the 'Relativity Barrier,'" *Christian Research Journal*, Winter/Spring 1988, 7.
65. Groothuis, *Confronting the New Age*, 114-15.
66. Quoted in Erwin W. Lutzer and John F. DeVries, *Satan's "Evangelistic" Strategy for This New Age* (Wheaton, IL: Victor Books, 1991), 91.
67. Shirley MacLaine, *Dancing in the Light* (New York: Bantam, 1985), 357.
68. Sidney B. Simon, Leland W. Howe, and Howard Kirschenbaum, *Values Clarification* (New York: Hart, 1978), back cover; cf. 18-22.
69. Carl F. Henry; cited in Chandler, 252.
70. Chandler, 258.
71. Ibid., 263.

## Chapter 6: Mainstreaming: Cultic Agenda for the 1990s

1. James M. Dunn, *New York Times*, 8 May 1993, A1.
2. Alexis de Tocqueville, *Democracy in America*, ed. J.P. Mayer and Max Lerner (New York: Harper & Row, 1966), 268, 271.
3. Russell Chandler, *Understanding the New Age* (Dallas: Word Publishing, 1991), 8-9.
4. Ibid., 8.
5. Ibid.
6. Ruth Tucker, *Another Gospel: Alternative Religions and the New Age Movement* (Grand Rapids: Zondervan Publishing House, 1989), 320.

7. "Right-Wing Purge Another Step to Mainstream Mormonism?" *Religion Watch*, ed. Richard P. Cimino, February 1993, 3.
8. John Ankerberg and John Weldon, *Cult Watch: What You Need to Know About Spiritual Deception* (Eugene, OR: Harvest House Publishers, 1991), ii.
9. Ron Rhodes, *The Counterfeit Christ of the New Age Movement* (Grand Rapids: Baker Book House, 1990), 243.
10. Chandler, 9.
11. Ankerberg and Weldon, 211.
12. Ibid., 210.
13. Ibid.
14. "U.S. Values on Zigzag Course, Polls Indicate," Associated Press report, *Los Angeles Times*, 13 March 1993, B9.
15. George Barna, *The Barna Report 1992-93* (Ventura, CA: Regal Books, 1993), 258.
16. Lloyd Shearer, "The Woman Behind the Woman Behind Ronald Reagan," *Parade*, 1 April 1990, 16.
17. Cited by Shearer, 16.
18. Cited by Shearer, 16.
19. Shearer, 16.
20. *See* Charles Strohmer, *What Your Horoscope Doesn't Tell You* (Wheaton, IL: Tyndale House Publishers, 1988).
21. Holly Selby, "Meditation Wins U.S. Converts," *Los Angeles Times*, 7 May 1990, E8.
22. Ibid.
23. Ibid.
24. Ibid.
25. Ibid.
26. Ibid.
27. Ibid.
28. Cited in Ronald Enroth, *The Lure of the Cults* (Downers Grove, IL: InterVarsity Press, 1987), 42.
29. Anita Manning, "Meditation on 30 Years of TM," *USA Today*, 17 August 1989, 1D.
30. Ibid.
31. Ibid.
32. *The Washington Times*, 13 May 1991; cited in *Christian Research Newsletter*, "What's New in the Headlines," May/June 1991, 3.
33. Ibid.
34. Ibid.
35. Ibid.
36. Manning, "Meditation on 30 Years of TM."
37. Ibid.
38. "Yoga," *Newsweek*, 2 February 1993, 9.
39. Ibid.
40. Ibid.
41. Douglas Groothuis, *Confronting the New Age* (Downers Grove, IL: InterVarsity Press, 1989), 135.
42. Miriam Starhawk, *Yoga Journal*, May/June 1986, 59.
43. Miriam Starhawk, *The Spiral Dance* (San Francisco: Harper & Row, 1979), 9.
44. Judith Weinraub, "Women of the Spiritual World," *The Washington Post*; reprinted in the *San Jose Mercury News*, 18 May 1991, 10C.
45. Richard N. Ostling, "When God Was a Woman," *Time*, 6 May 1991, 73.
46. Ibid.
47. Diana Hayes; cited in Weinraub, 10C.
48. "Horizon 2000," *Publisher's Weekly*, 7 December 1992; cited in *Christian Research Newsletter*, "What's New in the Headlines," January/February 1993, 3.
49. Tucker, 90.
50. Russell Chandler, *Racing Toward 2001* (Grand Rapids: Zondervan Publishing House, 1992), 188.
51. *Church News*, 5 October 1991; cited in *Christian Research Newsletter*, "What's New in the Headlines," November/December 1991, 6.
52. *Arizona Republic*, June 30-July 3, 1991; cited in *Christian Research Newsletter*, "What's New in the Headlines," September/October 1991, 6.
53. "LDS Church Gains Converts Through Media Campaign," *The Salt Lake Tribune*, 6 December 1989, 16A.
54. *New York Times*, 21 December 1992; cited in *Christian Research Newsletter*, "What's New in the Headlines," January/February 1993, 4.
55. Tucker, 91.
56. "Mormons Forge Links with Other Faiths," Associated Press report; on file at Christian Research Institute, P.O. Box 500, San Juan Capistrano, CA 92693.
57. Ibid.
58. Ibid.
59. Robert M. Bowman, "How Mormons Are Defending Mormon Doctrine," *Christian Research Journal*, Fall 1989, 26.
60. Ibid.
61. Joseph Smith—*History* 1:19; cited by Bowman, 26.
62. Cited by Bowman, 26.
63. Bowman, 26.
64. Stephen Robinson, *Are Mormons Christians?* vii; cited in Gordon R. Lewis, "A Summary Critique," *Are Mormons Christians?* by Stephen E. Robinson, *Christian Research Journal*, Fall 1992, 33.

65. Lewis, 33.
66. Cited in Lewis, 33.
67. Lewis, 33.
68. Robinson; cited in Lewis, 33.
69. Lewis, 34.
70. Ibid.
71. Ibid., 35.
72. "Moon Runs Fronts in U.S.," *Spotlight*, 18 February 1991, 12.
73. Orville Swenson, *The Perilous Path of Cultism* (Caronport, Saskatchewan, Canada: Briercrest Books, 1987), 85.
74. Ibid., 85-86.
75. *CARP: Collegiate Association for the Research of Principles*, promotional brochure of the Unification Church.
76. Ibid.
77. Ibid.
78. J. Isamu Yamamoto, "Unification Church (Moonies)," in *A Guide to Cults and New Religions*, ed. Ronald Enroth (Downers Grove, IL: InterVarsity Press, 1983), 156.
79. Ibid., 160.
80. Ibid., 159.
81. *The Divine Principle*; cited in Ronald Enroth, *The Lure of the Cults*, 79.
82. *CARP: Collegiate Association for the Research of Principles*.
83. Write to the Spiritual Counterfeits Project, P.O. Box 4308, Berkeley, CA 94704.
84. Write to the Christian Research Institute, P.O. Box 500, San Juan Capistrano, CA 92693; or call (714) 855-9926.
85. Dunn.

### Chapter 7: Media Savvy and the Culting of America

1. Sören Kierkegaard; in Chuck Colson, *Against the Night: Living in the New Dark Ages* (Ann Arbor, MI: Servant Publications, 1989), 41.
2. Russell Chandler, *Racing Toward 2001* (Grand Rapids: Zondervan Publishing House, 1992), 120.
3. George Barna, *Absolute Confusion: How Our Moral and Spiritual Foundations Are Eroding in This Age of Change* (Ventura, CA: Regal Books, 1993), 114.
4. Ibid.
5. Ibid., 105.
6. Ibid., 114.
7. George Barna, *The Future of the American Family* (Chicago: Moody Press, 1993), 99.
8. "Cults and the Media," *Cult Awareness Network News*, ed. Cynthia Kisser, December 1990, 6.
9. Ibid.
10. *Los Angeles Times*, 3 March 1991; cited in "What's New in the Headlines," *Christian Research Newsletter*, March/April 1991, 6.
11. Ibid.
12. Ibid.
13. Ibid.
14. Ibid.
15. Ibid.
16. Ibid., emphasis added.
17. Barna, *Absolute Confusion*, 74-75.
18. *Arizona Republic*, June 30-July 3, 1991; cited in "What's New in the Headlines," *Christian Research Newsletter*, September/October 1991, 6.
19. Andy Hall, Jerry Kammer, and Mark Trahant, "LDS Media Empire: A Voice for Mormon Values," *Las Vegas Review Journal*, 18 July 1991, 1D.
20. Ibid., 2D.
21. Ibid.
22. William Alnor, "Sects Increasingly Using Media to Bolster Ranks," *Christian Research Journal*, Winter 1991, 5.
23. "Media Messages Boost Missionary Work," *The Ensign*, May 1989, 106.
24. Ibid.
25. Ibid., 105, insert added.
26. Ibid., 105.
27. Ibid.
28. Ibid.
29. Ibid., insert added.
30. Ibid., 105.
31. Alnor, 5.
32. Ibid.
33. Ibid.
34. Hall, Kammer, and Trahant, 2D.
35. Alnor, 5.
36. Ibid.
37. Hall, Kammer, and Trahant, 1D.
38. Ibid.
39. "Media Messages Boost Missionary Work," 106.

40. Hilary Groutage, "Mormons Polish Message in Public-Service Ads," *The Salt Lake Tribune*, 12 June 1993, D-1.
41. Ibid.
42. Ibid.
43. Ibid.
44. Ibid.
45. Ibid.
46. Ibid., D-2.
47. "LDS Church Gains Converts Through Media Campaign," *The Salt Lake Tribune*, 6 December 1989, 16A.
48. Ibid.
49. Ibid.
50. Ibid.
51. Ibid.
52. Craig Branch, "The Media or the Medium?" from computer database of articles published by Watchman Fellowship, P.O. Box 13251, Arlington, TX 76094-0251.
53. Ibid.
54. Norman L. Geisler and Jeff Amano, *The Infiltration of the New Age* (Wheaton, IL: Tyndale House Publishers, 1990), 9.
55. *Body Mind & Spirit*, ed. Paul Zuromski, 1993 issues, cover flap containing advertisement.
56. Ibid.
57. Ibid.
58. Ibid.
59. Ibid.
60. Ibid.
61. Ibid.
62. Lou Mulkern, "Videos for a New Age," *Video Business*, 26 May 1989, 22.
63. Ibid.
64. Ibid.
65. Ron Rhodes, *The Counterfeit Christ of the New Age Movement* (Grand Rapids: Baker Book House, 1990), 132.
66. Ibid.
67. Ibid., 133.
68. Ibid., 135.
69. Ibid.
70. Ibid.
71. "TM's Deceptions," *The Cult Observer*, vol. 8, no. 10, 1991, 3.
72. Ibid.
73. Ibid.
74. Ibid.
75. Ruth Tucker, *Another Gospel: Alternative Religions and the New Age Movement* (Grand Rapids: Zondervan Publishing House, 1989), 22.
76. Ibid., 264.
77. Cited in Tucker, 264.
78. Unification Church letter, entitled "Interdenominational Conferences for Clergy. A project of the International Religious Foundation, Inc., for conferences to be held in Flagstaff, AZ; San Diego, CA; and Santa Cruz, CA.
79. Ibid.
80. *Orange County Register*; cited in Ron Rhodes, "What's New in the Headlines," *Christian Research Newsletter*, May/June 1991, 3.
81. Ibid.
82. Ibid.
83. Orville Swenson, *The Perilous Path of Cultism* (Caronport, Saskatchewan, Canada: Briercrest Books, 1987), 82.

**Chapter 8: The Hollywood Connection**

1. Paul Thigpen, "Cleaning up Hollywood," *Charisma*, December 1991, 39.
2. Jan Golab, "A Cruise in Outer Space," *California*, June 1991, 47.
3. Michael Hirsley, "A Gentle Reaction: Religious Beliefs Help Buddhists with Tragedy," *San Jose Mercury News*, 31 August 1991, 10C.
4. Andrew Kopkind, "C'est le Gere," *Premiere*, March 1993, 53f.
5. Andrew Maykuth, "Dalai Lama Talks About Everything, Nothing: Exiled Tibetan Leader Starts 3-Week U.S. Visit," *San Jose Mercury News*, 13 September 1990, 2A.
6. "Gere as Buddha?" Compiled from Mercury News wire services, *San Jose Mercury News*, 6 February 1990, 4A.
7. E.g., Joel Sappell and Robert W. Welkos, "The Courting of Celebrities," *Los Angeles Times*, 24 June 1990; John H. Richardson, "Catch a Rising Star," *Premiere*, September 1993; Richard Behar, "The Thriving Cult of Greed and Power," *Time*, 6 May 1991.
8. Cited in James Sire, *The Universe Next Door* (Downers Grove, IL: InterVarsity Press, 1992), 191.
9. Russell Chandler, *Understanding the New Age* (Dallas: Word Publishing, 1991), 117.
10. Douglas Groothuis, "A Summary Critique" of *It's All in the Playing*, *Christian Research Journal*, Fall 1987, 28, emphasis added.
11. Shirley MacLaine, *Out on a Limb* (New York: Bantam, 1983), 204.
12. Ibid., 209.

13. Shirley MacLaine, *Dancing in the Light* (New York: Bantam, 1985), 354.
14. Ibid., 358.
15. Ibid., 133.
16. MacLaine, *Out on a Limb*, 347.
17. MacLaine, *Dancing in the Light*, 412.
18. MacLaine, *Out on a Limb*, 233.
19. Ibid., 45.
20. George Barna, *The Barna Report 1992-93* (Ventura, CA: Regal Books, 1993), 86.
21. Jean-Noel Bassior, "Linda Evans and J.Z. Knight," *Body Mind & Spirit*, May/June 1992, 44.
22. Ibid., 45.
23. Ibid.
24. Ibid., 46.
25. Ibid.
26. Ibid.
27. Ibid.
28. Ibid.
29. Ibid.
30. Ibid., 47.
31. Martha Smilgis, "Mother Teresa for the '90s?" *Time*, 29 July 1991, 60.
32. "Guru of the Moment," *Between the Lines*, 5:10, 29 May 1992, 2.
33. *See* Ron Rhodes, *The Counterfeit Christ of the New Age Movement* (Grand Rapids: Baker Book House, 1991), 224.
34. Terry Pristin, "The Power, the Glory, the Glitz," *Los Angeles Times Calendar*, 16 February 1992, 75.
35. Ron Rhodes and Paul Carden, "What's New in the Headlines," *Christian Research Newsletter*, March/April 1992, 3.
36. "A Miracle on Your Doorstep," *Newsweek*, 23 March 1992, 65; cited in Rhodes and Carden, 3.
37. Dean C. Halverson, "A Summary Critique" of *A Return to Love*, *Christian Research Journal*, Summer 1992, 35.
38. Ibid.
39. Pristin, 6.
40. Smilgis, 60.
41. "A Miracle on Your Doorstep," *Newsweek;* cited in Rhodes and Carden, 3.
42. Mike Capuzzo, "The Divine Ms. Williamson," Knight-Ridder Newspapers, 5 February 1993, D3.
43. Isobel Bilden, "LeVar Burton," *Body Mind & Spirit*, November/December 1989, 20.
44. Ibid.
45. Ibid.
46. Ibid., 28.
47. Elliot Miller, *A Crash Course on the New Age Movement* (Grand Rapids: Baker Book House, 1989), 189.
48. Bilden, 28, inserts added.
49. After all, Burton was spotlighted on the cover of *Body Mind & Spirit* magazine with a feature interview inside (November/December 1989).
50. Isobel Bilden, "Stephanie Kramer," *Body Mind & Spirit*, August/September 1989, 12.
51. Ibid.
52. *1987 National New Age Yellow Pages*, 96..
53. Bilden, "Stephanie Kramer," 12.
54. Ibid.
55. Ibid., 14.
56. George Lucas; quoted by Edwin A. Roberts, Jr., in the *Tampa Tribune*, 5 April 1992; in *Classic and Contemporary Excerpts*," *Christianity Today*, 20 July 1992, 41.
57. John Styll, "The Gospel of Lucas," *Contemporary Christian Magazine*, August 1983, 36.
58. "Parade's Special Intelligence Report," *Parade*, 20 February 1994, 20.
59. Styll, "The Gospel of Lucas," 36.
60. Dale Pollock, *Skywalking: The Life and Films of George Lucas* (New York: Harmony Books, 1983); 139; Norman L. Geisler and J. Yutaka Amano, *Religion of the Force* (Dallas, TX: Quest Publications, 1983), 22.
61. Styll, 36.
62. Cited in Geisler, 34.
63. Gary DeMar, "The Devil in Hollywood," *The Biblical Worldview*, 5:1, January 1989, 2.
64. Ibid.
65. Ibid., 3.
66. Ibid., 4.
67. Joseph P. Gudel, "Religious Radicalism: Right or Wrong?" *Christian Research Journal*, Winter/Spring 1990, 17-18.
68. Ibid.
69. Ibid., 18.
70. Ibid.
71. Ibid.
72. *Body Mind & Spirit*; cited in "What's New in the Headlines," *Christian Research Newsletter*, January/February 1991, 3.
73. Ibid.
74. Ibid.
75. Ibid.
76. Ibid.

77. Ibid.
78. Thigpen, 40.
79. Ibid.
80. Ibid., 36.
81. Ibid.
82. Ibid.
83. Ibid., 39.
84. Ibid.
85. Ibid., 40.

## Chapter 9: Conquering America with 26 Letters

1. Ecclesiastes 12:12.
2. David A. Reed, *Jehovah's Witness Literature* (Grand Rapids: Baker Book House, 1993), 9.
3. Ibid.
4. *The Watchtower*, 1 January 1993, 19b; cf. *Jehovah's Witnesses: The Organization Behind the Name*, video produced by The Watch Tower Bible and Tract Society (Brooklyn, 1990).
5. *Jehovah's Witnesses: The Organization Behind the Name*.
6. Reed, 9.
7. Ibid.
8. *The Watchtower*, 15 January 1917, 6033.
9. *The Watchtower*, 1 April 1919, 6414.
10. *The Watchtower*, 1 May 1938, 169.
11. *The Watchtower*, 1 June 1985, 19.
12. *The Watchtower*, 1 July 1973, 402.
13. *The Watchtower*, 15 June 1957, 370.
14. *The Watchtower*, 1 March 1983, 25.
15. *The Watchtower*, 15 March 1969, 172.
16. *The Watchtower*, 1 May 1957, 274.
17. *The Watchtower*, 1 December 1981, 27.
18. *The Watchtower*, 1 May 1957, 274.
19. *The Watchtower*, 15 January 1983, 22.
20. Ibid., 27.
21. *The Watchtower*, 15 September 1911, 4885.
22. *The Watchtower*, 1 October 1967, 587.
23. *Qualified to Be Ministers* (Brooklyn: Watchtower Bible and Tract Society, 1955), 156.
24. *The Watchtower*, 1 July 1965, 391.
25. "The Growth of Jehovah's Witnesses," *Christian Research Newsletter*, January/February 1992, 2; cf. *The Watchtower*, 1 January 1993, 6.
26. Ruth Tucker, *Another Gospel* (Grand Rapids: Zondervan Publishing House, 1989), 142.
27. Robert H. Countess, *The Jehovah's Witnesses' New Testament* (Phillipsburg, NJ: Presbyterian and Reformed Publishing Co., 1982), 91.
28. Ibid.
29. Ibid.
30. Julius R. Mantey; cited in Erich and Jean Grieshaber, *Redi-Answers on Jehovah's Witnesses Doctrine* (Tyler, TX: n.p., 1979), 30.
31. Bruce Metzger; cited in Erich and Grieshaber, 30.
32. William Barclay; cited in Grieshaber, 31.
33. David Reed, *Jehovah's Witnesses Answered Verse by Verse* (Grand Rapids: Baker Book House, 1992), 71.
34. Erich and Jean Grieshaber, *Exposé of Jehovah's Witnesses* (Tyler, TX: Jean Books, 1982), 100.
35. Ibid.
36. Marilyn Ferguson, *The Aquarian Conspiracy* (Los Angeles: J.P. Tarcher, 1980), 151.
37. Nina Easton, "Shirley MacLaine's Mysticism for the Masses," *Los Angeles Times Magazine*, 6 September 1987, 33.
38. Stuart Applebaum; cited in Russell Chandler, *Understanding the New Age* (Dallas: Word Publishing, 1991), 116.
39. Kevin Ryerson and Stephanie Harolde, *Spirit Communication* (New York: Bantam, 1989); cited in Ron Rhodes, "What's New in New Age Books," *Christian Research Journal*, Winter/Spring 1990, 28.
40. Ibid.
41. Ibid.
42. Ibid.
43. Matthew Fox, *The Coming of the Cosmic Christ* (San Francisco: Harper & Row, 1989), 144-49.
44. Ibid., 13-17.
45. Ibid., 35-74.
46. Ibid., 133-35.
47. Ibid., 134.
48. Ibid., 228.
49. Ibid., 64.
50. Ibid., 57.
51. Ibid., 52.
52. William Bole, "Bill Moyers Chases the New Big Story—Faith," *San Jose Mercury News*, 29 April 1989, 10.

53. Ibid.
54. Joseph Campbell, *The Power of Myth* (New York: Doubleday, 1988), 69.
55. Ibid., 70.
56. Ibid., 56.
57. Ibid.
58. Ibid., 57.
59. Ibid., 56-57.
60. Ibid., 56.
61. Douglas Groothuis, "A Summary Critique" of *The Power of Myth*, *Christian Research Journal*, Fall 1989, 29.
62. Ibid., 30.
63. Al Gore, *Earth in the Balance: Ecology and the Human Spirit* (Houghton Mifflin, 1992), 193; cf. Dean Halverson, review of *Earth in the Balance: Ecology and the Human Spirit*, *Christian Research Journal*, Summer 1993, 41.
64. Gore, 12.
65. Ibid.
66. Halverson, 41.
67. Ibid.; cf. *Christianity Today*, 14 September 1992, 26.
68. Halverson, 41-42.
69. Ibid., 42-43.
70. Ibid., 43.
71. Berit Kjos, "Paganism on the Rise," *Christian Research Newsletter*, July/September 1992, 2.
72. Ibid.
73. "Horizon 2000," *Publishers Weekly*, 7 December 1992; cited in *Christian Research Newsletter*, January/February 1993, 4.

## Chapter 10: The Culting of American Education...

1. Berit Kjos, "Paganism on the Rise," *Christian Research Newsletter*, July/September 1992, 1.
2. *The Wall Street Journal*, 24 July 1987; quoted in *Spiritual Counterfeits Journal*, 9:1, 9-10.
3. Marilyn Ferguson, *The Aquarian Conspiracy* (Los Angeles: J.P. Tarcher, 1980), 242.
4. Cited in Berit Kjos, *Under the Spell of Mother Earth* (Wheaton, IL: Victor Books, 1992), 75, insert added.
5. Ibid.
6. Ibid., 75-76.
7. Kjos, "Paganism on the Rise," 1.
8. Berit Kjos, *Your Child and the New Age* (Wheaton, IL: Victor Books, 1990), 20; Douglas Groothuis, *Confronting the New Age* (Downers Grove, IL: InterVarsity Press, 1988), 131-32.
9. Kjos, *Your Child and the New Age*, 26.
10. Richard John Neuhaus, "Belief Is in the Eye of the Beholder," *Religion and Society Report*, August 1986, 2.
11. Mel and Norma Gabler, *What Are They Teaching Our Children?* (Wheaton, IL: Victor Books, 1985), 22; Groothuis, 130.
12. Ferguson, 315.
13. Ibid., 316.
14. Matthew Fox, *The Coming of the Cosmic Christ* (San Francisco: Harper & Row, 1989); cited in Ron Rhodes, *The Counterfeit Christ of the New Age Movement* (Grand Rapids: Baker Book House, 1990), 222.
15. Shirley MacLaine; cited in Russell Chandler, *Understanding the New Age* (Dallas: Word Publishing, 1991), 25.
16. Shirley Correll, "Quieting Reflex and Guided Imagery: Education for the New Age," *Pro-Family Forum Alert*, September 1985, 5.
17. Caryl Matrisciana, *Gods of the New Age* (Eugene, OR: Harvest House Publishers, 1985), 172-73.
18. Groothuis, 183.
19. *See* Kjos, *Your Child and the New Age*, 39.
20. Ibid., 38-50.
21. Cited in Kjos, *Your Child and the New Age*, 39.
22. Vander Velde and Hyuung-Chan, *Global Mandate*, 3, 17, 25, 26; quoted in Eric Buehner, "Terminal Vision," *Education Newsline*, February/March 1987, 1-3.
23. Groothuis, 136-40.
24. William Bennett; cited in Kjos, *Your Child and the New Age*, 65.
25. Robert Müller, *New Genesis: Shaping a Global Spirituality* (New York: Doubleday and Co., 1982), 49; cited in Kjos, *Your Child and the New Age*, 59.
26. These steps are adapted from Kjos, *Your Child and the New Age*, 28-37.
27. Peter Drucker, *The Wall Street Journal*, 9 February 1989; quoted in *Spiritual Counterfeits Journal*, 9:1, 8.
28. *The Wall Street Journal*, 24 July 1987; quoted in Tal Brooke, "Gates of Entry for the Occult," *Spiritual Counterfeits Journal*, 9:1 (1989):9-10.
29. Chandler, 130.
30. Ron Rhodes, *The New Age Movement*, series ed. Alan Gomes (Grand Rapids: Zondervan Publishing House, 1994), II.G.
31. Drucker, *Spiritual Counterfeits Journal*, 9.
32. *Fortune*, 23 November 1987; quoted in Tal Brooke, "Gates of Entry," 9:1 (1989):10.
33. *Los Angeles Times*, 25 March 1989; cited in Ron Rhodes, "Troubled Waters for New Age Seminars," *Christian Research Newsletter*, May/June 1989, 2:3, 2.
34. Ibid.

35. Ibid.
36. For more on this, *see* Rhodes, *The New Age Movement.*
37. Tal Brooke, "Gates of Entry for the Occult," 9:1 (1989):11.
38. Suzanne Perkins; quoted by John Bode, "The Forum: Repackaged Est?" *The Chicago Tribune*, 27 February 1985, section 5, 6.
39. Werner Erhard and Associates, *The Forum* (1986), n.p.
40. Brooke, 13.
41. Ibid.
42. Douglas Groothuis, *Unmasking the New Age* (Downers Grove, IL: InterVarsity Press, 1986), 79.
43. *The Lifespring Family News*, July 1978, 14; cited in "Lifespring: New-Age Danger?" Information sheet on file at CRI.
44. Ibid.
45. Ibid.
46. Groothuis, *Confronting the New Age*, 163-65.
47. Ibid., 246.
48. *1987 National New Age Yellow Pages*, 112.
49. John Ankerberg and John Weldon, *The Facts on Holistic Health and the New Medicine* (Eugene, OR: Harvest House Publishers, 1992), 5.
50. Sharon Begley, "Helping Docs Mind the Body," *Newsweek*, 8 March 1993, 61.
51. *Religious News Service*, 4 January 1992.
52. "Many Christians Found to Hold New Age Beliefs," *Los Angeles Times*, 4 January 1992, F23.
53. Thelma Moss, *The Probability of the Impossible: Scientific Discoveries and Explorations of the Psychic World* (New York: New American Library, 1974), 84, emphasis added.
54. Elliot Miller, *A Crash Course on the New Age Movement* (Grand Rapids: Baker Book House, 1989), 187.
55. Groothuis, *Unmasking the New Age*, 63.
56. Elliot Miller, "The Christian, Energetic Medicine, and 'New Age Paranoia,'" *Christian Research Journal*, Winter 1992, 26.
57. Ibid.
58. E.g., John Ankerberg and John Weldon, *The Facts on Holistic Health and the New Medicine* (Eugene, OR: Harvest House Publishers, 1992); Paul C. Reisser, Teri K. Reisser, and John Weldon, *New Age Medicine* (Chattanooga, TN: Global Publishers, 1988).
59. John Thie, *Touch for Health* (Marina del Rey, CA: DeVorss, 1973).
60. *See* the Christian Chiropractors Association's "Policy Statement on New Age Healing" (CCA, 3200 S. Lemay Ave., Fort Collins, CO 80525-3605).
61. Miller, "The Christian, Energetic Medicine, and 'New Age Paranoia,'" 27.
62. Ibid.

## Chapter 11: The Lure of Money, Sex, and Power

1. Frederick K.C. Price, "Ever Increasing Faith" program on TBN (9 December 1990). (Note: Many of the citations related to the Word-Faith movement in the endnotes are thoroughly documented by Hank Hanegraaff, *Christianity in Crisis* [Eugene, OR: Harvest House Publishers, 1993].)
2. David Berg, *Come On Ma!—Burn Your Bra!* (Children of God, 22 December 1973, GP No. 286), 2; cited in Walter Martin, *The New Cults* (Ventura, CA: Regal Books, 1980), 168.
3. David Gershon and Gail Straub, *Empowerment: The Art of Creating Your Life as You Want It* (New York: Delta, 1989), 36.
4. *See* Richard Foster, *Money, Sex, and Power* (San Francisco: Harper & Row, 1985), front flap.
5. See Hanegraaff, *Christianity in Crisis.*
6. *See* Hanegraaff, 29, 246.
7. Ron Rhodes, *The Counterfeit Christ of the New Age Movement* (Grand Rapids: Baker Book House, 1990), 149.
8. Kenneth Hagin; quoted in D.R. McConnell, *A Different Gospel* (Peabody, MA: Hendrickson Publishers, 1988), 175.
9. Frederick K.C. Price, *Faith, Foolishness, or Presumption?* (Tulsa, OK: Harrison House, 1979), 34.
10. Robert Tilton, "Success-N-Life" television program (27 December 1990).
11. Frederick Price; quoted in McConnell, 170.
12. Frederick K.C. Price, "Ever Increasing Faith" program on TBN (9 December 1990).
13. John Avanzini, "Was Jesus Poor?" videotape (Hurst, TX: His Image Ministries, n.d.).
14. John Avanzini, "Believer's Voice of Victory" program on TBN (20 January 1991).
15. Ibid.
16. John Avanzini, "Praise the Lord" program on TBN (15 September 1988).
17. Price, "Ever Increasing Faith" program on TBN (23 November 1990).
18. Kenneth Copeland; cited in McConnell, 171.
19. Marilyn Hickey; *see* Hanegraaff, 31, 36, 63, 79, 203, 207, 238, 249, 351-52, 417.
20. Kenneth Copeland; cited in McConnell, 173.
21. Ibid., 172.
22. Kenneth Copeland, *Laws of Prosperity* (Fort Worth, TX: Kenneth Copeland Publications, 1974), 67; cf. Bruce Barron, *The Health and Wealth Gospel* (Downers Grove, IL: InterVarsity Press, 1989), 89.
23. Copeland, *Laws of Prosperity*, 67.
24. Ibid.
25. Paul Crouch, "Praise the Lord" program on TBN (21 July 1992).

26. Kenneth E. Hagin, *Exceedingly Growing Faith*, 2d ed. (Tulsa, OK: Kenneth Hagin Ministries, 1988), 10; cited in Barron, 103.
27. *See* Barron and Hanegraaff.
28. Ron Enroth, *The Lure of the Cults* (Downers Grove, IL: InterVarsity Press, 1987), 85.
29. Moses David, "The Flirty Little Fishy!" (London: Children of God, 1974), 2340-43; cited in Ruth Tucker, *Another Gospel: Alternative Religions and the New Age Movement* (Grand Rapids: Zondervan Publishing House, 1989), 238.
30. Moses David, "The Flirty Little Fishy," in *The Basic Mo Letters* (Hong Kong: Children of God, 1976), 528; cited in Martin, 171.
31. Moses David, *FFer's Handbook!—Condensed Selected Quotes from More than 50 FF Letters!* ed. Justus Ashtree (Rome: Children of God, January 1977), 3; quoted in Martin, 172.
32. Deborah Davis, *The Children of God* (Grand Rapids: Zondervan Publishing House, 1984), 122-23; cited in Tucker, 238.
33. David Moses Berg, *Time*, 22 August 1977, 48; quoted in Ronald Enroth, *The Lure of the Cults* (Downers Grove, IL: InterVarsity Press, 1987), 87.
34. Berg, *Come On Ma!—Burn Your Bra!* 2; quoted in Martin, 168.
35. Berg; cited in Martin, 171.
36. Moses David, *God's Whores?* (Rome: Children of God, 26 April 1976, DO No. 560), 3; quoted in Martin, 171.
37. "The Children of God: Disciples of Deception," *Christianity Today*, 18 February 1977, 20; quoted in Enroth, 87.
38. *See* James Sire, *Scripture Twisting: Twenty Ways the Cults Misread the Bible* (Downers Grove, IL: InterVarsity Press, 1980).
39. Roy Rivenburg, "A True Conversion?" *Los Angeles Times*, 21 March 1993, E4.
40. Berg; *see* Martin, 168.
41. Berg; quoted in Martin, 175.
42. Dalva Lynch with Paul Carden, "Inside the 'Heavenly Elite': The Children of God Today," *Christian Research Journal*, Summer 1990, 16.
43. Ibid., 17.
44. Ibid.
45. Ibid.
46. Ibid.
47. Ibid., 18.
48. Ibid.
49. Ibid.
50. Ibid., 16.
51. Ibid., 18.
52. Ibid., 19.
53. Ibid.
54. Ron Rhodes, "What's New in the Headlines," *Christian Research Newsletter*, March/April 1993, 4.
55. Joe Maxwell, "Children of God Revamp Image, Face Renewed Opposition," *Christian Research Journal*, Fall 1993, 5.
56. Paul Carden, "Raids Rock COG," *Christian Research Newsletter*, September/October 1993, 11.
57. Ibid.
58. Gershon and Straub, 5.
59. Ibid., xii.
60. Ibid., 21.
61. Ibid., 35.
62. Ibid., 36.
63. Ibid., 23.
64. Ibid.
65. Ibid., 36.
66. Ibid., 200.
67. Ibid., 199.
68. Ibid.
69. Ibid., 200.
70. Ibid., 152.
71. Ibid., 36.
72. Ibid., 38.
73. Douglas Groothuis, A Summary Critique, *It's All in the Playing*, *Christian Research Journal*, Fall 1987, 28.
74. Ibid.

## Chapter 12: Extraterrestrials and the Culting of America

1. William M. Alnor, *UFOs in the New Age* (Grand Rapids: Baker Book House, 1992), 84.
2. Brad Steiger, *Gods of Aquarius* (New York: Berkley Books, 1976), 40.
3. James Oberg, "Space Encounters," *The Omni Book of the Paranormal & the Mind*, ed. Owen Davies (New York: Kensington, 1983), 107-13; cf. Alnor, 79.
4. Alnor, 35.
5. Ibid., 73.
6. I.D.E. Thomas, *The Omega Conspiracy* (Oklahoma City: Hearthstone Publishing Ltd., 1986), 37.
7. William M. Alnor, "The Alien Obsession . . . with Repudiating Christianity," *SCP Journal*, 17:1-2, 1992, 28.

8. Cited in Brooks Alexander, "Theology from the Twilight Zone," *Christianity Today*, 18 September 1987, 22.
9. Alexander, 22.
10. Philip J. Imbrogno, "Close Encounters of the Tristate Kind," *Spotlight*, February 1990, 39.
11. Russell Chandler, *Doomsday: The End of the World* (Ann Arbor, MI: Servant Publications, 1993), 187; cf. Hillel Schwartz, *Century's End* (New York: Doubleday, 1990), 260.
12. Randall N. Baer, *Inside the New Age Nightmare* (Lafayette, LA: Huntington House, 1989), 146.
13. Alnor, "The Alien Obsession... with Repudiating Christianity," 32.
14. John Wiley, "Phenomena: Comment and Notes," *The Smithsonian*, January 1983, 24.
15. Ibid.
16. Alnor, *UFOs in the New Age*, 199.
17. Vishal Mangalwadi, *When the New Age Gets Old* (Downers Grove, IL: InterVarsity Press, 1993), 103.
18. *See* Alnor, "The Alien Obsession... with Repudiating Christianity," 40; cf. von Daniken manuscript on file at the Christian Research Institute, P.O. Box 500, San Juan Capistrano, CA 92693.
19. Russell Chandler, *Understanding the New Age* (Dallas: Word, 1991), 75.
20. *See* Alnor, *UFOs in the New Age*, 106.
21. Cited in Antonio Huneeus, "Shirley MacLaine's Extraterrestrial Connection," *UFO Universe*, September 1988, 33.
22. Douglas Groothuis, *Unmasking the New Age* (Downers Grove, IL: InterVarsity Press, 1986), 24.
23. *See* Alnor, *UFOs in the New Age*, 106.
24. Huneeus, 32.
25. *See* Alnor, *UFOs in the New Age*, 100-01.
26. Philip J. Klass, "UFO-Abductions: Dangerous Games," in *Not Necessarily the New Age*, ed. Robert Basil (Buffalo, NY: Prometheus Books, 1988), 221.
27. *See* William Alnor, "UFO Cults Are Flourishing in New Age Circles," *Christian Research Journal*, Summer 1990, 5.
28. Whitley Strieber, *Communion* (New York: Beech Tree, 1987), 28-30.
29. *See* David Wimbish, *Something's Going On Out There* (Old Tappan, NJ: Revell, 1990), 16.
30. *See* Alnor, "UFO Cults Are Flourishing in New Age Circles," 5.
31. *See* Wimbish, 16.
32. Baer, 40-41.
33. Ibid., 146.
34. Ibid., 40-41.
35. Ibid.
36. Ibid.
37. Brooks Alexander, "Machines Made of Shadows," *SCP Journal*, 17:1-2, 1992, 9.
38. John Ankerberg and John Weldon, "UFO Encounters," *SCP Journal*, 17:1-2, 1992, 17.
39. Ibid.
40. *See* Alnor, *UFOs in the New Age*, 76.
41. Ankerberg and Weldon, 16.
42. Ralph Rath, *The New Age: A Christian Critique* (South Bend, IN: Greenlawn Press, 1990), 82.
43. David Icke; quoted in Mangalwadi, 98.
44. Brad Steiger, *The Fellowship* (New York: Ballantine, 1989), 67-68.
45. Baer, 29-30.
46. Alnor, *UFOs in the New Age*, 42.
47. Brad Steiger, *Gods of Aquarius* (New York: Berkley Books, 1976), 40.
48. Gabriel Green; quoted in Robb Fulcher, "Story of Spacemen Broadcast by Man," *The Oregonian*, 8 May 1984, B2.
49. *See* Alnor, *UFOs in the New Age*, 25.
50. Alnor, *UFOs in the New Age*, 43.
51. Alnor, "The Alien Obsession... with Repudiating Christianity," 29.
52. Whitley Strieber, *Transformation: The Breakthrough* (New York: Avon, 1989), 69.
53. Jacques Vallee, *Confrontations: A Scientist's Search for Alien Contact* (New York: Ballantine, 1990), 17.
54. Ibid.
55. *See* Alnor, *UFOs in the New Age*, 133.
56. Jacques Vallee, *Messengers of Deception: UFO Contacts and Cults* (Berkeley, CA: And Or Press, 1979), 19.
57. Jacques Vallee, *The Invisible College* (New York: Dutton, 1975), 3, 201, 204.
58. Strieber, *Communion*, 94-95.
59. Strieber; quoted in Wimbish, 48.
60. John Weldon; quoted in Rath, 86.
61. Alexander, "Machines Made of Shadows," 11.
62. John Weldon with Zola Levitt, *UFOs: What on Earth Is Happening?* (Irvine, CA: Harvest House Publishers, 1975), 101.
63. *See* Alnor, "UFO Cults Are Flourishing in New Age Circles," 5.
64. Strieber; quoted in Alnor, *UFOs in the New Age*, 105.
65. Wimbish, 158.
66. Ibid., 164.
67. Official policy statement found in *Flying Saucer Review* descriptive brochure, 1992 (FSR, P.O. Box 162, High Wycombe, Bucks, HP13 5D2 England); cited in Ankerberg and Weldon, 20.
68. Mark Albrecht; quoted in Rath, 83.
69. Ankerberg and Weldon, 21, emphasis added.
70. Ron Rhodes, *Christ Before the Manger: The Life and Times of the Preincarnate Christ* (Grand Rapids: Baker Book House, 1992), 55-56.

71. *See* Elliot Miller, "Questions and Answers," *Christian Research Newsletter*, July/September 1992, 4.
72. Ibid.
73. Rath, 84.
74. Wimbish, 46.
75. Ibid.
76. Weldon with Levitt, 101; Alnor, "UFO Cults Are Flourishing in New Age Circles," 5.
77. Brooks Alexander; quoted by Baer, 108.
78. John Keel, *UFOs: Operation Trojan Horse* (New York: G.P. Putnam's Sons, 1970), 215, 299.
79. Vallee, *Messengers of Deception: UFO Contacts and Cults*, 15.
80. Vallee, *Confrontations: A Scientist's Search for Alien Contact*, 160-61.
81. Lynn E. Catoe; cited in Thomas, 73.
82. Baer, 109.
83. Steiger, *Gods of Aquarius*, 6.
84. Keel, 143.

## Chapter 13: Millennial Madness and the Rise of Doomsday Shivers

1. Stanley Young, "End of the World or End of an Illusion?" *Utne Reader*, March/April 1990, 94.
2. Ted Daniels, press release, "Millennium News," Millennium Watch Institute, February 1993.
3. Paul Saffo, "Prepare for a 10-Year 'Silly Season,'" *Los Angeles Times*, 30 January 1991, D3.
4. Charles Berlitz, *Doomsday 1999 A.D.* (New York: Doubleday & Company, 1981), 9.
5. Based on Berlitz, and Frederick H. Marten, *The Story of Human Life*; cited in "Doomsday: 1999 A.D." *Critique*, vol. 31 (1989):65.
6. E.g., Bill Lawren, "Are You Ready for Millennial Fever?" *Utne Reader*, March/April 1990; Saffo, "Prepare for a 10-Year 'Silly Season'"; Stanley Young, "An Overview of the End," *Critique*, vol. 31, (1989):28-31; and Berlitz, *Doomsday 1999 A.D.*.
7. Note that most of the accounts of the turbulence and panic that accompanied the arrival of A.D. 1000 come indirectly from the *Histories* of Raoul Glaber, a Burgundian monk born in the late tenth century.
8. Russell Chandler, *Doomsday: The End of the World* (Ann Arbor, MI: Servant Publications, 1993), 54.
9. Chandler, 52.
10. Yuri Rubinsky and Ian Wiseman, *A History of the End of the World* (New York: William Morrow and Co., 1982), 66.
11. Chandler, 54.
12. Ibid.
13. Louis Berkhof, *The History of Christian Doctrines* (Grand Rapids: Baker Book House, 1981), 263.
14. Philip Schaff, *History of the Christian Church*, vol. 2 (New York: C. Scribner's, 1910), 348.
15. Stanley J. Grenz, *The Millennial Maze: Sorting Out Evangelical Options* (Downers Grove, IL: InterVarsity Press, 1992), 14.
16. Ibid., 44.
17. Henri Focillon, *The Year 1000* (New York: Frederick Ungar Publishing Co., n.d.), 59.
18. Ibid., 60.
19. R. Gustav Niebuhr, "Millennium Fever: Prophets Proliferate, The End Is Near," *The Wall Street Journal*, 5 December 1989, A5.
20. Grenz, 19.
21. Ibid., 22.
22. Chandler, 60.
23. Ibid., 67.
24. "S.W. Madhunad Interviews John Hogue, Author of *The Millennium: The Last Predictions—Nostradamus and Our Future*," *Critique*, vol. 31, (1989):43.
25. Chandler, 62.
26. Nostradamus, *Century X*, quatrain 72.
27. Lawren, 96.
28. David Spangler, *Emergence: The Rebirth of the Sacred* (New York: Dell, 1984), 19.
29. John Dart, "Sect Leader Continues to Spread Word Despite Uproar Over Forecasts," *Los Angeles Times*, 23 February 1991, F20.
30. *See* Ron Rhodes, "What's New in the Headlines," *Christian Research Newsletter*, 3:3 (May/June 1990):6.
31. Timothy Egan, "Guru's Bomb Shelter Hits Legal Snag," *New York Times*, 24 April 1990, A8.
32. "Horizon 2000," *Publishers Weekly*, December 1992; *Christian Research Newsletter*, 3.
33. Ibid.
34. Ibid.
35. Ibid.
36. *1980 Yearbook of Jehovah's Witnesses* (Brooklyn: Watchtower Bible and Tract Society, 1980), 30-31.
37. John Ankerberg and John Weldon, *The Facts on Jehovah's Witnesses* (Eugene, OR: Harvest House Publishers, 1988), 35.
38. *Awake!*, 8 October 1968, 13.
39. *The Watchtower*, 1 October 1978, 31.
40. David Reed, *Jehovah's Witnesses Answered Verse by Verse* (Grand Rapids: Baker Book House, 1992), 57.
41. *The Watchtower*, 15 October 1980, 31.
42. *The Watchtower*, 15 May 1984, 5.
43. *The Watchtower*, 1 May 1985, 4.

44. *Awake!* 8 April 1988, 14.
45. *Reasoning from the Scriptures* (Brooklyn: Watchtower Bible and Tract Society, 1989), 239.
46. William Alnor, *Soothsayers of the Second Advent* (Grand Rapids: Eerdmans, 1989), 31.
47. Alnor, 33.
48. Cited in Alnor, 29.
49. Alnor, 31.
50. Cited by B.J. Oropeza, "One More End-Time Scare Ends with a Whimper," *Christian Research Journal*, Winter 1993, 6, 43.
51. Oropeza, 43.
52. Ibid.
53. Ibid.
54. Ibid.
55. Perucci Ferraiuolo, "Could '1994' Be the End of Family Radio?" *Christian Research Journal*, Summer 1993, 5.
56. Ibid.
57. Harold Camping, "Open Forum" program, 4 September 1992.
58. Harold Camping, *1994?* (New York: Vantage Press, 1992), xvi.
59. Mary Stewart Relfe, *Economic Advisor*, 28 February 1983.
60. Lester Sumrall, *I Predict 2000 A.D.*, 74; cited in Ron Rhodes, "Millennial Madness," *Christian Research Journal*, Fall 1990, 39.
61. James Oberg; cited in Lawren, 97.
62. Gerald A. Larue, "Survival in the Apocalyptic Era: A Humanist Prescription for Countering Biblical Apocalypticism," *The Humanist*, September/October 1987, 11f.

## Chapter 14: Against the Darkness

1. Edmund Burke, *Correct Quotes*, WordStar International © 1993, electronic media, hypercard stack for Macintosh.
2. T.B. Maston; cited in John Blanchard, *More Gathered Gold* (Hertfordshire, England: Evangelical Press, 1986), 26-27.
3. Socrates, *Correct Quotes*.
4. Ron Rhodes, Christian Research Institute, P.O. Box 500, San Juan Capistrano, CA 92693.
5. Cited in Charles C. Ryrie, *What You Should Know About Social Responsibility* (Chicago: Moody Press, 1982), 62.
6. Antonio Porchia; cited in John Blanchard, *More Gathered Gold* (Hertfordshire, England: Evangelical Press, 1986), 168.
7. Billy Graham; cited in John Blanchard, *More Gathered Gold* (Hertfordshire, England: Evangelical Press, 1986), 38.

# Bibliography

Ahlstrom, Sydney E. *A Religious History of the American People*. New York: Image Books, 1975.

Alnor, William. *Soothsayers of the Second Advent*. Grand Rapids: Eerdmans, 1989.

Alnor, William. *UFOs in the New Age*. Grand Rapids: Baker Book House, 1992.

*The American Heritage Dictionary*. Ed. William Morris. Boston: Houghton Mifflin Company, 1978.

Ankerberg, John and John Weldon, *Cult Watch: What You Need to Know About Spiritual Deception*. Eugene, OR: Harvest House Publishers, 1991.

Ankerberg, John and John Weldon, *The Facts on Hinduism in America*. Eugene, OR: Harvest House Publishers, 1991.

Ankerberg, John and John Weldon, *The Facts on Holistic Health and the New Medicine*. Eugene, OR: Harvest House Publishers, 1992.

Ankerberg, John and John Weldon, *The Facts on Jehovah's Witnesses*. Eugene, OR: Harvest House Publishers, 1988.

Asimov, Isaac. *Isaac Asimov's Book of Science and Nature Quotations*. New York: Weidenfeld & Nicolson, 1988.

Baer, Randall N. *Inside the New Age Nightmare*. Lafayette, LA: Huntington House, 1989.

Barna, George. *Absolute Confusion: How Our Moral and Spiritual Foundations Are Eroding in This Age of Change*. Ventura, CA: Regal Books, 1993.

Barna, George. *The Barna Report 1992-93*. Ventura, CA: Regal Books, 1993.

Barna, George. *The Future of the American Family*. Chicago: Moody Press, 1993.

Barna, George. *What Americans Believe*. Ventura, CA: Regal Books, 1991.

Barron, Bruce. *The Health and Wealth Gospel*. Downers Grove, IL: InterVarsity Press, 1989.

Berg, Moses David. *FFer's Handbook!—Condensed Selected Quotes from More than 50 FF Letters!* Ed. Justus Ashtree. Rome: Children of God, January 1977.

Berkhof, Louis. *The History of Christian Doctrines*. Grand Rapids: Baker Book House, 1981.

Berlitz, Charles. *Doomsday 1999 A.D.* New York: Doubleday & Company, 1981.

Boa, Kenneth. *Cults, World Religions, and You*. Wheaton, IL: Victor Books, 1979.

Brooke, Tal. *When the World Will Be as One*. Eugene, OR: Harvest House Publishers, 1989.

Capra, Fritjof. *The Turning Point*. New York: Simon and Schuster, 1982.

Chandler, Russell. *Doomsday: The End of the World*. Ann Arbor, MI: Servant Publications, 1993.

Chandler, Russell. *Racing Toward 2001*. Grand Rapids: Zondervan Publishing House, 1992.

Chandler, Russell. *Understanding the New Age*. Dallas: Word Publishing, 1991.

Church of Scientology Information Service, Department of Archives. *Scientology: A World Religion Emerges in the Space Age* (1974).

Colson, Charles. *Kingdoms in Conflict*. New York: William Morrow, 1987.

Colson, Chuck. *Against the Night: Living in the New Dark Ages*. Ann Arbor, MI: Servant Publications, 1989.

Copeland, Kenneth. *Laws of Prosperity*. Fort Worth, TX: Kenneth Copeland Publications, 1974.

Corydon, Brent and L. Ron Hubbard, Jr. *L. Ron Hubbard: Messiah or Madman?* Secaucus, NJ: Lyle Stuart, 1987.

Davis, Deborah. *The Children of God*. Grand Rapids: Zondervan Publishing House, 1984.

*Dictionary of Christianity in America*. Ed. Daniel G. Reid. Downers Grove, IL: InterVarsity Press, 1990.

Dilday, Russell H. Jr. *The Doctrine of Biblical Authority*. Nashville, TN: Convention Press, 1982.

Enroth, Ronald. *A Guide to Cults and New Religions*. Downers Grove, IL: InterVarsity Press, 1983.

Enroth, Ronald. *The Lure of the Cults*. Downers Grove, IL: InterVarsity Press, 1987.

Ferguson, Marilyn. *The Aquarian Conspiracy*. Los Angeles: J.P. Tarcher, 1980.

Fields, Rick et al. *Chop Wood, Carry Water*. Los Angeles: J.P. Tarcher, 1984.

Focillon, Henri. *The Year 1000*. New York: Frederick Ungar Publishing Co., n.d.

Foster, Richard. *Money, Sex, and Power*. San Francisco: Harper & Row, 1985.

Fox, Matthew. *The Coming of the Cosmic Christ*. San Francisco: Harper & Row, 1989.

Gabler, Mel and Norma. *What Are They Teaching Our Children?* Wheaton, IL: Victor, 1985.

Geisler, Norman and William Watkins. *Worlds Apart: A Handbook on World Views*. Grand Rapids: Baker Book House, 1989.

Geisler, Norman L. and J. Yutaka Amano. *Religion of the Force*. Dallas, TX: Quest Publications, 1983.

Geisler, Norman L. and Jeff Amano. *The Infiltration of the New Age*. Wheaton, IL: Tyndale House Publishers, 1990.

Geisler, Norman L. *Explaining Hermeneutics: A Commentary*. With Exposition by J.I. Packer. Oakland, CA: International Council on Biblical Inerrancy, 1983.

Geisler, Norman L. *Is Man the Measure?* Grand Rapids: Baker Book House, 1979.

Gershon, David and Gail Straub. *Empowerment: The Art of Creating Your Life as You Want It*. New York: Delta, 1989.

Gore, Al. *Earth in the Balance: Ecology and the Human Spirit*. Houghton Mifflin, 1992.

Grenz, Stanley J. *The Millennial Maze: Sorting Out Evangelical Options*. Downers Grove, IL: InterVarsity Press, 1992.

Groothuis, Douglas. *Confronting the New Age*. Downers Grove, IL: InterVarsity Press, 1988.

Groothuis, Douglas. *Unmasking the New Age*. Downers Grove, IL: InterVarsity Press, 1986.

Guinness, Os. *The Dust of Death*. Downers Grove, IL: InterVarsity Press, 1973.

Hagin, Kenneth E. *Exceedingly Growing Faith*, 2d ed. Tulsa, OK: Kenneth Hagin Ministries, 1988.

Hanegraaff, Hank. *Christianity in Crisis*. Eugene, OR: Harvest House Publishers, 1993.

Henry, Carl F. *Twilight of a Great Civilization*. Westchester, IL: Crossway Books, 1988.

Hitchcock, James. *What Is Secular Humanism?* Ann Arbor, MI: Servant Books, 1982.

Hubbard, L. Ron. *The Creation of Human Ability*. Los Angeles: The Publications Organization Worldwide, 1968.

Keel, John. *UFOs: Operation Trojan Horse*. New York: G.P. Putnam's Sons, 1970.

Kjos, Berit. *Under the Spell of Mother Earth*. Wheaton, IL: Victor Books, 1992.

Kjos, Berit. *Your Child and the New Age*. Wheaton, IL: Victor Books, 1990.

Kurtz, Paul. *Forbidden Fruit: The Ethics of Humanism*. Buffalo, NY: Prometheus Books, 1988.

Levi, *The Aquarian Gospel of Jesus the Christ*. London: L.N. Fowler & Co., 1947.

Lutzer, Erwin W. and John F. DeVries. *Satan's "Evangelistic" Strategy for This New Age*. Wheaton, IL: Victor Books, 1991.

MacLaine, Shirley. *Dancing in the Light*. New York: Bantam Books, 1985.

MacLaine, Shirley. *It's All in the Playing*. New York: Bantam Books, 1987.

Mangalwadi, Vishal. *When the New Age Gets Old*. Downers Grove, IL: InterVarsity Press, 1993.

Martin, Paul. *Cult-Proofing Your Kids*. Grand Rapids: Zondervan Publishing House, 1993.

Martin, Walter. *Martin Speaks Out on the Cults*. Ventura, CA: Regal Books, 1983.

Martin, Walter. *The Kingdom of the Cults*. Minneapolis: Bethany House Publishers, 1985.

Martin, Walter. *The New Cults*. Ventura, CA: Regal Books, 1980.

Martin, Walter. *The Rise of the Cults*. Ventura, CA: Regal Books, 1983.

Matrisciana, Caryl. *Gods of the New Age*. Eugene, OR: Harvest House Publishers, 1985.

McConnell, D.R. *A Different Gospel*. Peabody, MA: Hendrickson Publishers, 1988.

McDowell, Josh and Don Stewart. *Understanding the Cults*. San Bernardino, CA: Here's Life Publishers, 1983.

Miller, Elliot. *A Crash Course on the New Age Movement*. Grand Rapids: Baker Book House, 1989.

Morey, Robert. *The Islamic Invasion*. Eugene, OR: Harvest House Publishers, 1992.

Muggeridge, Malcolm. *The End of Christendom*. Grand Rapids: Eerdmans, 1980.

Müller, Robert. *New Genesis: Shaping a Global Spirituality*. New York: Doubleday and Co., 1982.

*The New Age Rage*. Ed. Karen Hoyt. Old Tappan, NJ: Revell, 1987.

*1980 Yearbook of Jehovah's Witnesses*. Brooklyn: Watchtower Bible and Tract Society, 1980.

*Not Necessarily the New Age*. Ed. Robert Basil. Buffalo, NY: Prometheus Books, 1988.

Packer, J.I. *"Fundamentalism" and the Word of God*. Grand Rapids: Eerdmans, 1958.

Pollock, Dale. *Skywalking: The Life and Films of George Lucas*. New York: Harmony Books, 1983.

Price, Frederick K.C. *Faith, Foolishness, or Presumption?* Tulsa, OK: Harrison House, 1979.

*Qualified to Be Ministers*. Brooklyn: Watchtower Bible and Tract Society, 1955.

Ramm, Bernard. *Protestant Bible Interpretation*. Grand Rapids: Baker Book House, 1978.

*Reasoning from the Scriptures*. Brooklyn: Watchtower Bible and Tract Society, 1989.

Reed, David. *Jehovah's Witness Literature*. Grand Rapids: Baker Book House, 1993.

Reed, David. *Jehovah's Witnesses Answered Verse by Verse*. Grand Rapids: Baker Book House, 1992.

Reisser, Paul C., Reisser, Teri K. and John Weldon, *New Age Medicine*. Chattanooga, TN: Global Publishers, 1988.

Rhodes, Ron. *Christ Before the Manger: The Life and Times of the Preincarnate Christ*. Grand Rapids: Baker Book House, 1992.

Rhodes, Ron. *Reasoning from the Scriptures with the Jehovah's Witnesses*. Eugene, OR: Harvest House Publishers, 1993.

Rhodes, Ron. *The Counterfeit Christ of the New Age Movement*. Grand Rapids: Baker Book House, 1990.

Rozman, Deborah. *Meditating with Children*. Boulder Creek, CA: University of the Trees Press, 1975.

Rubinsky, Yuri and Ian Wiseman. *A History of the End of the World*. New York: William Morrow and Co., 1982.

Ryerson, Kevin and Stephanie Harolde. *Spirit Communication*. New York: Bantam, 1989.

Ryrie, Charles C. *What You Should Know About Social Responsibility*. Chicago: Moody Press, 1982.

Sagan, Carl. *Cosmos*. New York: Ballantine Books, 1985.

Schwartz, Hillel. *Century's End*. New York: Doubleday, 1990.

Simon, Sidney B., Howe, Leland W. and Howard Kirschenbaum. *Values Clarification*. New York: Hart, 1978.

Sire, James. *Scripture Twisting: Twenty Ways the Cults Misread the Bible*. Downers Grove, IL: InterVarsity Press, 1980.

Sire, James. *The Universe Next Door*. Downers Grove, IL: InterVarsity Press, 1992.

Spangler, David. *Emergence: The Rebirth of the Sacred*. New York: Dell, 1984.

Spangler, David. *Relationship & Identity*. Forres, Scotland: Findhorn Publications, 1978.

Starhawk, Miriam. *The Spiral Dance*. San Francisco: Harper & Row, 1979.

Steiger, Brad. *Gods of Aquarius*. New York: Berkley Books, 1976.

Steiger, Brad. *The Fellowship*. New York: Ballantine, 1989.

Strieber, Whitley. *Communion*. New York: Beech Tree, 1987.

Strieber, Whitley. *Transformation: The Breakthrough*. New York: Avon, 1989.

Strobel, Lee. *Inside the Mind of Unchurched Harry & Mary*. Grand Rapids: Zondervan Publishing House, 1993.

Sweet, William W. *The Story of Religion in America*. Grand Rapids: Baker Book House, 1979.

Swenson, Orville. *The Perilous Path of Cultism*. Caronport, Saskatchewan, Canada: Briercrest Books, 1987.

Thie, John. *Touch for Health*. Marina del Rey, CA: DeVorss, 1973.

Thomas, I.D.E. *The Omega Conspiracy*. Oklahoma City: Hearthstone Publishing Ltd., 1986.

Tocqueville, Alexis de. *Democracy in America*. Eds. J.P. Mayer and Max Lerner. New York: Harper & Row, 1966.

Traina, Robert A. *Methodical Bible Study*. Wilmore, KY: Asbury Theological Seminary, 1952.

Tucker, Ruth. *Another Gospel: Alternative Religions and the New Age Movement*. Grand Rapids: Zondervan Publishing House, 1989.

Vallee, Jacques. *Confrontations: A Scientist's Search for Alien Contact*. New York: Ballantine, 1990.

Vallee, Jacques. *Messengers of Deception: UFO Contacts and Cults*. Berkeley, CA: And Or Press, 1979.

Vallee, Jacques. *The Invisible College*. New York: Dutton, 1975.

Weldon, John with Zola Levitt. *UFOs: What On Earth Is Happening?* Irvine, CA: Harvest House Publishers, 1975.

*What Is Scientology?* Ed. LRH Personal Secretary Office. Los Angeles: Church of Scientology of California, 1978.

Wimbish, David. *Something's Going On Out There*. Old Tappan, NJ: Revell, 1990.

# Subject Index

# Other Good
# Harvest House Reading

**REASONING FROM THE SCRIPTURES**
by *Ron Rhodes*

Ron Rhodes offers this complete hands-on guide to help you effectively respond to Jehovah's Witnesses and share the truth of God's Word in a loving, gracious way. *Reasoning from the Scriptures* provides: side-by-side comparisons of the Jehovah's Witnesses' Bible with the New American Standard and New International Version Bibles; tactics and arguments used by the Witnesses and the biblical responses to each one; penetrating questions you can ask to challenge the Jehovah's Witnesses' confidence in the Watchtower Society.

**CHRISTIANITY IN CRISIS**
by *Hank Hanegraaff*

*Christianity in Crisis* confronts head-on a cancer that is ravaging the body of Christ. Influencial teachers are utilizing the power of the airwaves as well as scores of books, tapes, and magazines to distort the biblical concept of the Creator and promote antibiblical doctrines that boggle the mind. The result is nothing less than a systematic subversion of the historic Christian faith. In addition to exposing darkness to light, *Christianity in Crisis* provides solutions for averting this crisis and restoring a Christianity centered in Christ.

**CONVERSATIONS WITH THE CULTS**

The popular "Conversations with the Cults" series gives unique insights into cults as they are experienced in everyday encounters. The creative story format presents the most pertinent information in dialogue readers can use in actual conversations. This series includes:

> *What You Need to Know About the New Age Movement*, Smith
> *What You Need to Know About Masons*, Decker
> *What You Need to Know About Mormons*, Decker
> *What You Need to Know About Jehovah's Witnesses*, MacGregor

**FAST FACTS ON FALSE TEACHINGS**
by *Ron Carlson* and *Ed Decker*

The answers to the basic questions regarding cults and false teachings are found in this all-in-one resource. *Fast Facts on False Teachings* offers quick and clear discussions of many major cult organizations, including Mormonism, Jehovah's Witnesses, Islam, and Satanism. As the false teachings are examined and refuted, you will find helpful, biblical insight for sharing the truth of the gospel with cult members.

Dear Reader:

We would appreciate hearing from you regarding this Harvest House nonfiction book. It will enable us to continue to give you the best in Christian publishing.

1. What most influenced you to purchase *The Culting of America*?
   - ☐ Author
   - ☐ Subject matter
   - ☐ Backcover copy
   - ☐ Recommendations
   - ☐ Cover/Title
   - ☐ _____

2. Where did you purchase this book?
   - ☐ Christian bookstore
   - ☐ General bookstore
   - ☐ Department store
   - ☐ Grocery store
   - ☐ Other

3. Your overall rating of this book:
   ☐ Excellent   ☐ Very good   ☐ Good   ☐ Fair   ☐ Poor

4. How likely would you be to purchase other books by this author?
   - ☐ Very likely
   - ☐ Somewhat likely
   - ☐ Not very likely
   - ☐ Not at all

5. What types of books most interest you? (check all that apply)
   - ☐ Women's Books
   - ☐ Marriage Books
   - ☐ Current Issues
   - ☐ Christian Living
   - ☐ Bible Studies
   - ☐ Fiction
   - ☐ Biographies
   - ☐ Children's Books
   - ☐ Youth Books
   - ☐ Other _____

6. Please check the box next to your age group.
   - ☐ Under 18
   - ☐ 18-24
   - ☐ 25-34
   - ☐ 35-44
   - ☐ 45-54
   - ☐ 55 and over

**Mail to:** Editorial Director
Harvest House Publishers
1075 Arrowsmith
Eugene, OR 97402

Name _____

Address _____

City _____ State _____ Zip _____

**Thank you for helping us to help you
in future publications!**